EREWHONS OF THE EYE

Erewhons of the Eye

Samuel Butler
as painter, photographer
and art critic

ELINOR SHAFFER

REAKTION BOOKS

Published by Reaktion Books
1–5 Midford Place, Tottenham Court Road
London W1P 9HH, UK

First published 1988

Photoset by
Rowland Phototypesetting Ltd, Bury St Edmunds, Suffolk

Colour printed in Great Britain by
Balding and Mansell Ltd, Wisbech, Cambs

Printed and bound in Great Britain
by Butler and Tanner Ltd, Frome, Somerset

British Library Cataloguing in Publication Data
Shaffer, Elinor
Erewhons of the eye: Samuel Butler as
painter, photographer & art critic.
1. English visual arts. Butler, Samuel
1835–1902
I. Title
709.2′4
ISBN 0-948462-01-9

Contents

ACKNOWLEDGEMENTS

The publishers would like to thank the Masters and Fellows of St John's College, Cambridge, for permission to reproduce works in the Butler Collection.

PHOTOGRAPHIC ACKNOWLEDGEMENTS

Photographs courtesy of: Chomon-Perino, Turin, 86; J.-P. Debon, Saint-Lô, 97; Alfredo Fusetti, Saronno, 89, 90; Marlborough Fine Art, London, 105; Phaidon, Oxford, 92; Amilcare Pizzi, s.p.a., Milan, 58, 85, 87, 88; Christopher Wood Gallery, London, 96; Bibliotheca Civica Farinone-Centa, Varallo, 55, 60.

Preface

I owe grateful thanks to many people and institutions who have helped to make this book possible, more than I can name. It is only right first to thank the Victorian Studies Association of Ontario, who in inviting me to give a plenary lecture at their Conference at the University of Toronto in 1979 first set me to work in earnest on Samuel Butler. That lecture, 'The Ironic Mode in Biblical Criticism: Samuel Butler's *The Fair Haven*', an abstract of which was published in the *Victorian Studies Newsletter* in that year, represents a further phase in the studies that began in '*Kubla Khan*' and *The Fall of Jerusalem: the Mythological School in Biblical Criticism and Secular Literature 1770–1880* (Cambridge University Press, 1975) and underlies the argument of this book. A Colloquium, 'Vom Fin-de-siècle zur Moderne', held at Bonn University in 1981, gave me my first opportunity to discuss the work of Butler as a painter and art critic; I should like to thank Professor L. Hönnighausen of the Englisches Seminar at Bonn in particular for his part in the organization of the Colloquium and for the stimulus of his own contributions to the study of late Victorian art.

I should also like to thank colleagues and students who have received lectures on various aspects of Samuel Butler with hospitality and constructive criticism in the Universities of Cambridge, Sheffield, Indiana at Bloomington, California at Los Angeles, Brown, and, in Australia, the University of Adelaide and the National University at Canberra, as well as at the IXth International Comparative Literature Congress held at Innsbruck in 1979. A Fellowship at the Humanities Research Centre at the Australian National University, Canberra in 1982 made it possible for me to examine manuscript and picture collections in Australia and New Zealand, and I wish to thank the Librarian, J. C. Eade, in particular for his help and advice. In New Zealand I received much invaluable help from the Alexander Turnbull Library in Wellington, the Canterbury Library and Museum, and the

Director of the Robert McDougall Gallery, Christchurch. I should also like to thank members of the English Department of the University of Wellington, in particular Professor Roger Robinson and Dr Jeremy Commons, for their enthusiasm and practical aid. I should also like to record a special debt of gratitude for his kind hospitality to Dr Peter Maling, who has done so much to keep Butler's memory fresh.

During the time I was Visiting Professor in English and Comparative Literature at Brown University in the United States in 1983 and 1984 I was able to consult the materials at the Chapin Library of Williams College, Williamstown, Massachusetts, and I should like especially to thank Mr Wayne G. Hammond, Assistant Librarian, and Editor of *The Samuel Butler Newsletter*, for his help, both in person and by correspondence.

In Italy too I have many debts. I shall always remember the kindness of Signora Fusetti, who showed me the beautiful photographs by Alfredo Fusetti of Gaudenzio Ferrari's cupola at Saronno, of which we are privileged to publish two here. I should also like to thank especially warmly Michela Cometti Valle, the Librarian of the Biblioteca Civica 'M. Farinone-Centa' in Varallo, who organized the exhibition on *Samuele Butler e la Valle Sesia* in 1986 for the 500th anniversary of the founding of the Sacro Monte of Varallo, and went so far out of her way to give help and advice with the documentation of Butler's Italian connections and the iconography of the Sacro Monte.

Nearer home, I should like to thank the British Library, the Students Room of the British Museum, the Tate Gallery and Library, the National Portrait Gallery, the Victoria and Albert Museum, the National Library of Art and Design, the Courtauld Institute, the Royal Photographic Society, the Library of the Royal Academy of Arts, and the Warburg Institute, for their courteous and efficient service. Many thanks are owing to Mr James Lawson, Librarian, The Schools, Shrewsbury, whose cordiality at Shrewsbury and his very extensive and fruitful replies to a number of further inquiries have added a great deal to our knowledge of Butler's early training. I am particularly indebted to Mr Mark Haworth-Booth of the Victoria and Albert Museum for valuable advice regarding the history of photography. Michael Bott of the Library of the University of Reading, and Terence Pepper of the National Portrait Gallery, were enlightening on the connection between Butler and Emery Walker. My greatest debt is certainly to St John's College, Cambridge, to the Master and Fellows for their permission to consult and to reproduce materials from the Samuel Butler Collection, and to the Sub-Librarian Mr M. B. Pratt and his staff, who have given me inestimable help in so many ways during my research on the Samuel Butler Collection. Mr Pratt in particular shared my labours over many months with unfailing courtesy, patience, and resourcefulness. I should also like to thank the Photographic Services of the University Library, Cambridge, in particular Mr G. D. Bye, for their painstaking care in the reproduction of materials from the Butler Collection.

I should also like to record my gratitude to Professor J. B. Trapp of the Warburg Institute for his immense learning and unobtrusive but indispensable aid, and most of all for being a fellow Butler lover who frequents the North Italian sites with *Alps and Sanctuaries* in hand. I also owe a great debt to Professor Michael Podro for his invaluable advice and enthusiasm at an early stage and for his astute reading of a draft of Chapter 2; to Dr John Gage for his helpful comments on a draft of Chapter 1; to Professor Hugh Lloyd-Jones for his critical reading of a draft of Chapter 3; and to Dr Stephen Bann for his constructive reading of the whole. To my colleagues Stephen Bann and John Gage go my thanks for many conversations and perhaps most of all for their example over the course of a number of years. Warm thanks are also owing to my research assistant, Richard Stemp, who helped greatly with the search for picture sources in the final stages of the work. Milo Shaffer was an ideal companion, unfailingly cheerful, keen, and inventive, throughout the long voyages to and from Erewhon. Nor can I omit to mention my late father, Vernon C. Stoneman, whose work on *John and Thomas Seymour: Cabinetmakers in Boston 1796–1816* was the companion of much of my own childhood. Finally, this book could scarcely have seen the light of day without the intense interest and unremitting attention of its publishers.

Cambridge, 1987   E. S. Shaffer

1. *Church Porch at Rossura, 1879*

Introduction

'The true writer will stop everywhere and anywhere to put down his notes, as the true painter will stop everywhere and anywhere to sketch', noted Butler.[1] He carried both sides of his analogy into vigorous practice. Yet Butler's primary career as a visual artist, and his contributions to art history and criticism, have been almost wholly neglected; and the assessment of his literary work has been impoverished as a consequence. It follows that the interactions between the verbal and visual that characterize both have barely been remarked.

Pen, paints, paper, pencils and brushes, camera, the 'top of my tin case for holding pencils'[2] – all these were his 'tools' in his own special sense of the word: parts and extensions of the body, as an Englishman's pipe and carriage were additional limbs. The full range of his extensions of the body must be attended to, for he went on to say: 'Surely the work done by the body is, in one way, more its true life than its limbs and organization are.'[3] All accounts so far given of Samuel Butler are truncated: they are savage amputations of the limbs of his life.

This book will be an offering of 'amputations', in that Butler's work in painting, drawing, photography, and art criticism demands to be reintegrated into a full account of his multifarious activity as writer, painter, and author of pungent and far-reaching critiques of literature, art, religion and science. While some have received notice in limited and dated contexts, there is no account of them as a whole. This larger work, doing justice to one of our major late Victorian and early Modern figures, is badly overdue. But it cannot be carried out until the lost limbs are recovered. Even in this more limited salvage operation a great deal remains to be done.

Why has Butler received so much less attention than his contemporaries, who have benefited from the outpouring of serious criticism on the Victorian and Modernist writers and their milieux? His status as a 'classic' has scarcely been in question; both *Erewhon* and *The Way of All*

Flesh are still very much in print in readable and inexpensive editions, and both have been re-edited. The Notebooks, among the most engaging and influential of his writings, are being re-edited and will at last be published in their entirety in chronological order, while the earliest, highly readable selection by his friend and biographer Henry Festing Jones has been reissued in an easily accessible form. A small quantity of the correspondence, the family letters and the exchange between Butler and Miss Savage, one of the most amusing and touching in the English language, has been published. Reprint houses have kept his scientific books available in libraries. Yet this very short list demonstrates the precariousness of his presence; more is submerged than is visible. Through the sheer lack of adequate comment on any aspect of his work, the almost complete lack of comment on some parts of it, and the absence of any adequate account of his achievement as a whole, his reputation is beginning to ebb away.

Where comment exists, the special note of hostility which characterizes the attitude of some critics towards him is partly accounted for by his own satiric sharpness, and still more by the irritation that critics in his own time felt after being caught out misconstruing the aim of his irony, as in their response to the novel, *The Fair Haven*, since then studiously neglected. Readers, cheated of the sentimental novel of religious conversion they had been led to expect, stayed away in droves. The very title of *The Authoress of the Odyssey* was enough to draw barbed comment and barrack-room humour, which kept serious comment at bay. The 'hypocrite lecteur' refused to call to recognize his kin and rested in his received ideas. As for Butler's art work, it is dismissed unseen.

To put the question in this form – why has he received less attention than his contemporaries? – is to find a partial answer: for who were Butler's contemporaries? He has fallen between two stools: his greatest influence was exerted in the first twenty years of the present century by his posthumously published novel, *The Way of All Flesh* (1903). This makes him a Modern, and the early discussions of his impact were in these terms, as a hero of the anti-Victorian reaction. Yet the novel was laid aside in 1886, unfinished, as Butler thought. It belongs then to the heyday of the later Victorian novel, to the period of Hardy and Meredith, while suggesting in part the Naturalism of Zola and Gissing. Specialists in the Victorian era tend to consider him a Modern; specialists in the Modern era consider him a Victorian. Both therefore ignore him. As a book on Victorian fiction that reached a wide readership put it:

The absence of Samuel Butler is to be attributed not only to the limited extent of his work in fiction but also to the fact that his only novel was not published until after the close of the Victorian period, and exerted its effects in the twentieth century.[4]

The absence of three other novels (or certainly 'fictions') by Butler, *Erewhon, Erewhon Revisited*, and *The Fair Haven*, from the mind of the learned editor is in itself remarkable, and shows the dwindling of his oeuvre. The effect of having no period, or being always out of his period, is exacerbated if we consider that he was born in 1835, was at Cambridge in the mid-Fifties, and in the early 1860s began to publish his responses to scientific and religious issues of the day. His last published work was *Erewhon Revisited* (1901). Thus his formative years fall remarkably early for a man whose voice spoke most powerfully to the writers of the early twentieth century, to Shaw, Graves, Forster, Lawrence, Strachey, Wyndham Lewis, and Joyce, and to critics like William Empson, heir to his provocative, ingenious and witty criticism, as well as to men of letters abroad, especially in France. There his reception, not merely as a writer but as an intellectual force, was prepared by the high quality of the translations and commentaries carried out by the writer Valery Larbaud (also the translator of *Ulysses*). Larbaud is especially important in our present context as one who followed in Butler's footsteps in Italy, and understood him as a model of the foreign sojourner in an adopted homeland of the imagination. If Butler in some moods posed as a curmudgeonly English philistine, he was in fact a well-travelled and well-read cosmopolitan who read, spoke and wrote French and Italian, taught himself German well enough to engage in learned controversy, translated from the classics (and, one might add, from Erewhonian), and who felt more at home in Italy than in England. His relation to Continental movements and his reception abroad is yet another topic of great interest that has been largely ignored.

Critics since 1935 have tended to register this interesting fact – the twentieth-century impact of the work of a mid-Victorian born and bred – in the unworthy form of a knowing sneer: Butler was, after all, a 'Victorian' of the kind he himself was among the first to attack, a Victorian in the pejorative sense he himself did so much to establish. He fell victim to the counter-revolution, the anti-anti-Victorian reaction. Yet the counter-revolution in favour of the eminent Victorians failed to operate in his favour; the upsurge of interest in the 'prophets' and 'sages' did not extend to the *enfant terrible* who had bashed their pretensions. He was dubbed 'Victorian' only to dim his lustre as a rebel and disqualify him from consideration among his coevals and peers, just as 'bourgeois' is used to disqualify Marxists of middle-class origin. He was cast aside as a Victorian prophet *manqué*. One of the very few critics worth hearing on Butler since then, P. N. Furbank, has noted this in no uncertain terms:

the last word upon Butler is at present a wholesale slaughter of his reputation as a character and writer, and . . . the only sympathetic yet intelligent criticism of him before the date of this total attack is of a kind that rather opens the way for such an attack than defends him from it.[5]

What is needed, then, is to take full account of both aspects of Butler, his mid-Victorian origins, and his capacity to operate a critique of them from within. Just as now we can see Hopkins both as an authentic early voice of Modernist poetry and as a Victorian Jesuit, so we must, without condemnation of either, see the sources of Butler's satiric and affective power not in one collision with his family origins but in the perpetual contradiction between his early environment and his long view. As a Lamarckist he did not turn from his origins but accorded them full weight in order to locate and relocate the growth point of consciousness, the seed of the new, at the point where habit and rote learning give way to the suffering of fresh evolution.

If general criticism of Butler's literary work (as opposed to profess-ional editing) has faltered and ground to a halt on account of the difficulty of 'placing' him, and a lingering fear of his barbed tongue and his shifting irony, the criticism of his art encounters similar but even more exacerbated difficulties. At the same time, to look at Butler from this fresh perspective throws light on the incomprehension with which his work has been greeted, and opens a path to revaluation. The story of his rebellion against Victorian forms of religion is familiar in outline at least; the story of his critique of the secular substitutes for religion, art and culture, is scarcely known. The history of art criticism in this country is itself scanty; and the history of the relations between literature and art is only beginning to be adequately explored. There is virtually no public comment on his own art, even on his exhibited paintings and, beyond its initial reception, virtually no comment on his quite substan-tial body of art criticism. His photographic plates, which have survived a hundred years, are now in a state of progressive deterioration. Even those who appear to approach his art merely evade it, as Furbank writing on 'The Samuel Butler Collection' used the occasion to pen a genial rumination on the lornness of bachelor relics. The question, Who were his contemporaries? is a still more awkward one for his art than for his literary output, for the alterations in style and taste which his life spans seem even greater and less reconcilable, and his opposition to the leading tendencies even more implacable. His art training began during the period of the triumph of English landscape painting and, under its auspices, bore through his art school days the strong imprint of the Pre-Raphaelite movement of the 1850s and early '60s which he nevertheless came to reject as offering no viable path for contemporary painters; it proceeded in the period dominated by the Victorian classicism that he came so bitterly to reject as the last stage of the decline of art, and ended in the embracing of the new medium of photography in the late '80s and '90s which he was pleased to greet as anti-aesthetic, technological, and 'non-art', and thus the commencement of a new age. His refusal of the road to Modernism that passed for many of his contemporaries through aestheticism and decadence isolates him still more, and makes him appear at once more traditional and more uncompromisingly modern than they. It is hardly surprising that his work bears the marks of these diverse and often conflicting frames of reference, and of his struggles to escape from the impasse. These conflicts, his lack of recognition, his turning from the English scene to Italy in the last two decades of his life, his disappointment in his art towards the end of his life, and the virtual disappearance of his work from public view (even the Tate's single painting by him, *Mr Heatherley's Holiday*, was taken down in 1972), have conduced to the assumption that his art was of no consequence. Without making any exaggerated claims for the quality of his artistic output, it would not be too much to say that if its value can best be seen in relation to his literary prose, as with other artists gifted in both the word and the image, like Victor Hugo, D. H. Lawrence, and Emile Zola (a fellow photographer), it is of no less independent interest than theirs. His photography, moreover, hitherto unknown except in a few items of biographical interest, compares well with that of his contemporaries (and here he does have contemporaries) and provided a liberation from and a resolution of his most painful dilemmas as an artist.

The study of an artist who failed in the terms of his time (and whose achievement still in the longer run looks modest) may, at the very least, tell us a great deal about those terms, and the mode of emergence of a new set. The application in retrospect of a rigid linear model on the development of art has the effect of suppressing the multiple possibilities of the time, as Foucault has taught us; a conscious and articulate artist like Butler opens them to view.

Moreover – and here we might find a still more compelling reason for the failure to attempt to comprehend his work – he attempted a critique from within of the kind he conducted in his literary output. Such a critique is intrinsically more difficult in artistic terms than in literary ones; the resources of visual irony are more limited and far less well understood than those of literature. If his subtle mastery of the literary techniques of the ironists of classical and English tradition, not only of Lucian, Swift, and the author of *Hudibras*, but of the Romantic ironists, has not been fully explicated, his attempts in and relative to the visual medium have attracted no comment whatever. This line of inquiry is of great continuing interest and has much to tell us about twentieth-century art.

His art criticism – the use of the literary medium to explicate visual ideas and images – goes far to illuminate all these matters. *Alps and Sanctuaries*, *Ex Voto*, and his series of articles in *The Universal Review* were well enough received in his day in the periodical press, though never profitable. Some portions of it survived in later publications of his more popular essays and the 'Art Notes' that formed part of the Notebooks, but truncated and severed from its context, and above all without the illustrations of his own and others' work which it required to be fully comprehensible. Most damagingly, it was left on one side by his early champions, who suspected without exploring an incipient conflict between Butler's passionate concern with the religious art of the 'Pre-Raphaelite' and early Renaissance and their portrait of him as a rebel against his religious training; at another level, his argument was too uncompromising: without the literalism of faith – to which it is impossible to return – Romantic and Victorian apologetics in the form of aesthetic culture and imaginative reconstructions of the lost past was mere hypocrisy giving rise to sham art. Hostile critics had no need to bestir themselves. The silence was broken only by an occasional dismissive gibe. Literary art critics such as Ruskin and more recently Pater have begun to receive the attention they deserve; Butler deserves no less. Indeed, much that he wrote on art may be read as a dialogue with them. If Butler missed his turn among the 'sages' and 'prophets', a criticism now grown more sceptical of such claims and such terms may feel more at home with the iconoclastic Butler – in his own sense of how prickly a place 'home' is. In the terms of our time, he is not a sage but a 'cultural critic'. It may now be possible to see his true originality in his aesthetics of the disabused eye, an eye disabused by his own relentless critiques of religion, science, art and culture.

The course of art and of art history and criticism since his time now combine to make Butler's contributions of considerably more than historical interest. Indeed, their neglect of him begins to appear an extraordinary lacuna in our knowledge. From the standpoint of the anti-Victorian reaction Butler's negative responses to much of the art around him seem largely justified, and at the very least prescient. His scathing and often hilarious critique of the institutions of art – the Academy and the schools; the 'authorities' in the university, the museums and galleries, and the press; the connoisseurs and the manipulators of the market; and not least the self-appointed sages and guardians of public morals such as Ruskin – carries on in the main tradition of English satire on public and state-sanctioned art which includes Swift, Dr Johnson, Hogarth, Blake, Lamb, and Hazlitt, among other ringing voices, and seems even apter now, when the scale of the transactions has grown so enormous, than in his day. If there is a trace of 'sour grapes' in Butler's attacks, that only gives greater zest and tang to his wit. The characteristic combination in prosperous artists of his time of late Romantic posturing with rising professionalism was a subject worthy of his satirical talents. Current interest in the economic and social relations of patron and artist will doubtless approve his recommendation of the study of what he ironically called 'the commercial history of art', and critics concerned with 'reception history' or the operations of making and breaking reputations will find congenial and instructive Butler's keen ear for the rhetoric of inflation and deflation of 'values'.

Moreover, Butler's critique took place at a time when what we now know as 'scientific' art history was taking definitive shape, and his positive contributions to it on the one hand and his scepticism about its basic assumptions on the other constitute an important and wholly unwritten chapter in the history of art criticism in the late nineteenth century. Both his contribution and his scepticism are of particular interest at present when the self-styled 'new' art history is challenging the 'old' monolith of 'scientific' art history.[6] This confrontation is in many respects artificial, and Butler's story helps to display the complexity of the issues at the point of their emergence.

His positive contribution in one of its aspects belongs to the art history whose tasks were seen as the discovery and enumeration of artists and the facts of their lives, authentication, attribution and dating of works, the definition of schools and 'isms, and their linear organization into a continuous story of art. His positive contribution is his enrichment of the canon of early Renaissance artists with the work of Gaudenzio Ferrari and the lesser artists Tabachetti and the brothers D'Enrico. He thus contributed to the 'Lives of the Artists' in the tradition of Vasari, much expanded and extended in his time through the rediscovery of the Italian Pre-Raphaelites and the early Flemish and German artists. He also forwarded the study in England of the 'poor relation' of Italian art, the schools of the North, of Lombardy, the Piedmont and the Ticino, usually ignored in favour of Tuscany and Venice. Although Gaudenzio was not unknown, Butler drew attention to unfamiliar ranges of his work and defended its integrity. In particular, he focused attention on the Sacro Monte, or 'Holy Mountain', a complex of architecture, fresco, and sculpture requiring modes of seeing only now beginning to be ad-equately explicated. Here again his contribution seems remarkably in advance of his day, and has been confirmed and extended by Italian art criticism of the last thirty years. Yet in English there has been only one full-length work on Gaudenzio, and none since 1904; nor have the Italian critics been translated. Looking again at Butler's criticism and not least at his fine photographs of these sites and sanctuaries will, I hope, draw attention once more to this artist, whose versatility, grace, fluency and dramatic verve are irresistible.

Butler's contribution to art history in the sense of the rediscovery of forgotten artists, the attribution of their works on the basis of dating and stylistic considerations, and their assignment to a particular phase in the linear development of European art, was thus considerable; and he also entered into discussions in this framework of the work of Holbein the Younger, the Bellini brothers and Cariani which stand up well to renewed scrutiny. But his scepticism about the kind of art history that was emerging, and thus his interest for the 'new' art history, is equally great. Again we see his capacity for exercising a critique from within. Butler's choice of artists, epochs, regions and styles was itself a deliberate provocation: he chose not the 'great' individual genius but the remote and despised or neglected craftsman, not the 'grand style' but the grotesque or the verist, not the centre but the periphery, not the capital but the province. While his treatment of Gaudenzio can be viewed as another addition to the canon of Renaissance artists, like Pater's of Botticelli or Giorgione, the addition of new artists and works – especially of a sort that do not fit easily into the established framework – undermines the canon and the process of canonization. He set his face against the aggrandizement of the individual artist, but he set it equally against the description of the individual artist's works in terms of the succession of 'isms and periods which distorted and splintered his experience and his *oeuvre*. In this Butler speaks as an art historian who is also a practitioner, and one who had himself suffered from the imposition of readily available yet inadequate and sometimes contradictory categories. The single line of epochs and styles gave a false image of 'progress' in art. Synchronic variations must be taken into account as much as diachronic 'advance'. The communal element in the experience of the Sacro Monte, for example, held steady throughout the play of styles of the Renaissance. The work of an artist like Gaudenzio took place inside a specific community whose values it expressed; but equally those values were filtered through the talent of the artist. The institutionalization, the centralization, and the jargonifying of art in the academy and in art history itself was an aspect of decline. The 'naive' artist ploughing his furrow in obscurity might nevertheless plant the seeds of the future. The evolutionary process depended on chance and locality in a way alien to the juggernaut of art-historical formulation.

Butler stood at a crucial crossroads in the development of art history: the German Romantic revaluation of the 'Pre-Raphaelite' painters at the expense of all that followed (including, in some hands, Raphael); the grounding of the notion of the Renaissance as an epoch in a progressive art history; and the formulation of national art histories. 'Scientific' art history itself was hardly monolithic: it was born of organic historicism, for which positivism was often an uneasy bedfellow; nor did its interpretative richness follow from its scientific apparatus, but from the practice of imaginative criticism. Scepticism about *Stilgeschichte* is as old as the history of styles itself, as Burckhardt himself shows. He used them against one another: against connoisseurship and aestheticism he used the formidable weapons of scientific art history; against 'scientific' art history he used the 'spiritual' values rediscovered in the Pre-Raphaelite painters of Europe; against all of them he used the weapons of irony and satire to question, as he always did, the claims of academic cant and convention and to make a little space for unblinkered perception. The complex situation was ideal for the operation of his method of shifting irony.

Butler was, finally, concerned to ground an art and a conception of art which would permit the growth of an English art history, and here again he speaks as a practitioner casting about for viable subjects, genres, and techniques. He grasped clearly the development of art history as a discipline in his day, and was able when it suited him to adopt its methods; but because he was unable to accept the art of his day, English art remained for him, unlike for some of his more confident fellow artists, in abeyance, hypothetical. Its way had still to be found. If it had been generally agreed that English art began with Hogarth, it sometimes seemed to Butler that it had ended with him. He thus associated his own methods of irony and satire with English art history. Butler's search for the materials of an English art history and above all an English art for the present and the future led him by curious and circuitous paths, and sometimes by leaps of intuition, to a number of the forms that Modernism took. One of the most compelling interests of Butler's life in art is the sense it conveys of how tortuous and unexpected the route may be to the styles of the next generation. The retraining of a sensibility shows more intimately than do his intellectual battles what and how much was at stake; finally, his more familiar religious and scientific dogfights may be best understood as expressions of his struggle to emerge as an artist, to see with his own eyes. To put it another way, modes of representation may epitomize and give a heightened account of ideological conflicts and historical conditions. The paths he found were more fully explored and embraced by Continental and international Modernism than by English art, a further reason for his neglect, both by those who forged ahead and by those who lagged behind. The primitive and the naive, children's painting, 'art brut', the fantastic map, the cartoon and the caricature, ironization of styles, verist sculpture, the photograph, and the literary text linked to the visual illustration in such a way as to lift and lighten the authority of the text alone – all these were explored, promoted, collected or practised by Butler. Diverse as they may seem when simply enumerated, they are held together by his own incisive temperament and talent, supported and confirmed by his historical and critical analysis, and represent a national and Northern European style that held an opportunity still not recognized or realized in his country's art. The wit of the naive – at first sight a paradox – brought him into the twentieth century.

Those tendencies in the present which are bringing to the fore the exploration of the relations of literature and art make Butler of special interest. He not only practised both, but combined them in a variety of ways. If writers made notes as painters made sketches, he went on to suggest that notes and other literary productions 'could be framed and glazed in small compass', exhibited and sold to the public. The interaction between verbal and visual, the transformation of one into the other, and in particular the setting of one within the frame of the other, is a vital and pervasive aspect of Butler's work. His literary work is full of description, allusion, and metaphor taken from the visual arts. He carried out paintings with narrative reference to his own literary works; literary works that form an extended ekphrasis on the compact insight of his own sketch or photograph; criticism of paintings past and present in a variety of genres – the anecdote or sketch, the aphorism, the quip, the 'life' or portrait, the travel account or voyage (real and fantastic), the word painting, the discourse on the nature of perception, and the comic essay. He set works – paintings, sketches and photographs – of his own and others within his art criticism in descriptive and narrative forms and in contrapuntal or ironic ones. The interplay of verbal and visual ironies creates an especially dazzling variety of shifting irony.

This book begins, then, with an account of Butler's career as a painter, up to the time of his increasing preoccupation with Italy. It proceeds in the second chapter to his art criticism including the two books *Alps and Sanctuaries* (1881), illustrated with his own paintings of Italian sites, and *Ex Voto* (1890), illustrated with the photographs which represent his rediscovery of early Renaissance artists in the Sacri Monti of Northern Italy. Chapter 3 looks at his views of Victorian Hellenism through one of his most characteristically bold, ingenious, and least appreciated full-scale critical works, *The Authoress of the Odyssey* (1897), which engages with the classical scholarship and archaeology of his day to suggest a new homeric and odyssean iconography and a new comic art for the future. Finally, the last chapter looks at his photography as a culmination of his artistic achievement, bringing together many of his themes, and underlining the radical and provocative quality of his art criticism for the training of eye and mind.

One of the main aims of the book is to provide substantial illustration of his works of art, which have hitherto been seen by very few. Landscapes and townscapes, portraits, genre pictures, and Pre-Raphaelite evocations are represented, in oil paintings, watercolours, drawings and sketches, a few etchings, and a large quantity of photographs. Many of the works have been scattered, first through his own habit of giving them away, and then through his executors' laudable wish to place them in appreciative hands in venues associated with Butler. Some are lost; even when within institutions they are not always catalogued. Although there have been some exhibitions of a handful of his paintings and drawings, almost always in company with other painters (a list of exhibitions is appended), his photographs are virtually unknown, except for a very few of biographical interest. Yet now that a serious evaluation of Victorian photography has been undertaken and an increasing number of exhibitions of nineteenth-century photographers provide a context, his work takes on added interest and significance.

Illustrations of the artists he wrote about, where these are difficult of access, are a second main concern. A third aim of the illustrations is to suggest by example some of the complexities of the interplay of visual and verbal in his texts, illustrated books, and art works.

'It is not the custom of modern writers to refer to the works to which they are most deeply indebted', as Butler remarked.[7] Frost's *Lives of Eminent Christians* was the book Butler most used – to prop up other books he was reading in the British Museum; the books I am indebted to are far from being mere bookrests, though they differ widely among themselves, and often make no reference to Butler. Everywhere we turn the work on Butler has not yet been done. Finally, I can only apologize for the interim nature of this book, whose first essays and assays must be carried on, extended, and amended by many others if Butler is to receive his due, criticism is to be enriched, and the public is to receive its full meed of pleasure.

Erewhons of the Eye

3. *Portrait of Samuel Butler*, 1890

2. *Soazza Church* (previous page)

CHAPTER ONE

'Wild and Tame Eyesight': Samuel Butler's Career as a Painter

———

Butler's career as a painter, for him his primary career, and one he actively pursued until nearly the end of his life, has been almost wholly overlooked. He has had his 'good average three-score years and ten of immortality', as he called it, but mainly as the author of the satiric utopia *Erewhon* (1872) and the novel *The Way of All Flesh* (1903).[1] Yet his will to become a painter set his course decisively and is ingrained in his subsequent experience and his writing. Born in 1835 at Langar Rectory near Nottingham, the son of the Revd Thomas Butler, Canon of Lincoln, and the grandson of Dr Samuel Butler, headmaster of Shrewsbury School and afterwards Bishop of Lichfield, he gradually came to set his face against his own impeccable Victorian credentials. Like Matthew Arnold 'a Philistine and the son of a Philistine', he sought a place to stand of his own making. The life of the artist became that place, though in the event far from the stereotypes that clung round that notion.

'Training on false principles'

He had begun in a small way, already painting quite accomplished watercolours, mainly landscapes, while still at school at Shrewsbury, under the tutelage of Philip Vandyck Browne (1801–68), a local artist, who exhibited regularly at the Royal Academy between 1824 and 1861, and had a considerable reputation. Butler found him congenial.[2] Browne belonged to the mainstream of English watercolourists, and was closely associated in the 1820s with David Cox, with whom he travelled and painted in Wales, the Rhine Valley, and the Netherlands. His works were almost entirely in watercolour, sepia and pencil, and consisted mainly of views of towns, picturesque scenes, and old buildings. From 1835 he taught drawing in Shrewsbury and at the School, and executed a series of local churches for Butler's grandfather, the headmaster, with whom he was on good terms. Butler became his pupil only well after this,

3

4. *Butler family*

when, from about 1850, he had turned from landscape to still life; yet the boy's essential training was undoubtedly in this school.[3] A set of early watercolours of Shrewsbury shows a predominance of landscapes (illus. 7–10) over school interiors (illus. 5, 6).[4] In later years, after his father's retirement and return to Shrewsbury, he often visited his family and the School, and took the occasion to spend a day or two painting in the countryside.

A second master at Shrewsbury, A. J. Paget, the mathematics master, played a role in the development of Butler's interest in comic illustration; a 'Paget Scrapbook' survives, with sketches by Paget and pupils (including one of Paget signed by Butler and dated 1852), and annotations by Butler, made in the 1890s. Paget's 'dry humour and clever caricatures' were much appreciated by the boys, and the caricatures – rapid line drawings hitting off character, often with comic titles – are still amusing.[5]

As an undergraduate at Cambridge he continued in his serious vein to

4

5. *An Interior*, 1854
6. *An Interior*, 1854

7. *Smite Bridge, Langar*, 1854

8. *Gateway and Tree*, 1854

9. *Shrewsbury from above the bathing-place*, 1854

10. *Belvoir Castle, nr Langar* 1854

execute sketches, watercolours and oils (illus. 12). In his set at St John's College he painted the view from his window, a familiar vantage point, which has been seen as Romantic,[6] but which Butler was to elaborate rather into a characteristic complex of enclosures of space suggesting a Dutch interior within nature. His small sketchbooks even of a much later date show him drawing in pencil and ink and wash in a variety of sites along the route of his travels, including studies of rocks, architectural features, and landscapes (illus. 13). Sometimes these were worked up on a larger scale (illus. 14). Similar subjects appear in his later etchings and drawings (illus. 16).

After acquitting himself well in the classical tripos he remained at Cambridge and continued to take drawing lessons. He wrote home: 'There is a Cambridge school of art established here and I have joined it and am receiving first rate drawing lessons which I enjoy exceedingly.'[7] In open combat with his family, he rejected their wishes, refused to be ordained, and declared for the career of an artist. His father was prepared to canvass a number of professions, but that of the artist was beyond the pale: 'The artist scheme I utterly disapprove. It will throw you into very dangerous society.'[8] After a painful dispute – for example, his first plan, to go to Liberia as a cotton-planter, his father had rejected out of hand as 'the wildest conceivable vision' – he struck a bargain with his father: to test his determination, his father would give him a 'stake' with which he might set out for New Zealand and set up as a sheep farmer; this was an occupation lucrative enough, if he made good, to earn him a profit on which he could live in whatever way he chose on his return to England. This fantastic and exotic detour presented itself as unassailable Victorian patriarchal logic: in order to earn the right to indulge in the irresponsible life of the artist, one had first to prove one's ability to deal with 'real' life at sea and on the frontier. The experience was formative, leaving deep traces on his writing and his painting. Like Baudelaire, subject to an autocratic step-father whose therapy for a young man with 'aesthetic' fancies was to send him on an ocean voyage to India, Butler was the permanent gainer. Whereas Baudelaire went only as far as Mauritius and turned back, though with a stock of images of the sea and exotic landscapes that served his poetry and paved the way for his later espousal of Delacroix as the leading Romantic painter, Butler went through with the passage to New Zealand. For four years Butler was an English colonist. He found and laid claim to land for his sheep farm in explorations of virgin territory that are recorded in his

11. *Langar Rectory,* 1854

12. *Beach Scene, England, c.* 1866

13. *Boulogne, 1868*

book *A First Year in Canterbury Settlement* (1863) – his letters home edited without his permission by his father – and in the vivid opening pages of *Erewhon* which conjure up the rugged landscape of New Zealand (illus. 17). His explorations, including his near discovery of the main pass through the mountains, are now firmly ensconced in the annals of the early explorers of New Zealand (illus. 18).[9] His account of the race to the land claim in *A First Year* is a short story reminiscent of Mark Twain or Bret Harte: a vigorous, humorous depiction of a frontier competition in which he came first by nerve and, ultimately, wit.

Landscape did not exist merely to be studied, contemplated, or as a backdrop to the Grand Tour. Butler's sensations of the negative, monotonous and harsh aspects of the new landscape reinforce those of many European travellers to Australia and New Zealand from Captain Cook onwards:

I soon found myself in the middle of the plains, with nothing but brown tussocks of grass before me and behind me, and on either side. The day was rather dark, and the mountains were obliterated by a haze. 'Oh the pleasure of the plains,' I thought to myself; but upon my word, I think old Handel would find but little pleasure in these. They are in clear weather, monotonous and dazzling; in cloudy weather monotonous and sad; and they have little to recommend them but the facility they afford for travelling, and the grass which grows upon them.[10]

The D. George Inn Edgeware.   Oct. 2. 1880.

14. *The Old George Inn, Edgeware*, 1880

The deprivation by contrast with the landscapes of Italy and Switzerland, with Handel's 'Verdi Prati' – 'How one does long to see some signs of human care in the midst of the loneliness! How one would like, too, to come occasionally across some little auberge, with its vin ordinaire and refreshing fruit!'[11] – contributes to the intensity of his later reunions with those European landscapes first experienced on a trip with his family when he was nine. These interweavings of exotic with familiar landscapes are matched in English only by such syncretic triumphs as Sir William Jones's letters from India to his former pupil, who made the Grand Tour in Italy in the late 1780s, which suggested to Jones a rich tapestry of classical allusions and reminiscences interwoven with fresh impressions of the strikingly exotic landscape around him in Bengal. Yet Jones's landscapes remain poetic and philological. A brief example of Butler's cross-referencing shows how he rapidly conjures up by a similitude the contrast to the known vista within the description firmly establishing the novel landscape:

We started from the bottom of this valley on a clear frosty morning – so frosty that the tea-leaves in our pannikins were frozen, and our outer blanket crisped with frozen dew. We went up a little gorge, as narrow as a street in Genoa, with huge black and dripping precipices overhanging it, so as almost to shut out the light of heaven.[12]

Dinant on the Meuse
by S. Butler

15. *Dinant on the Meuse, c.* 1866

16. *Houses, c.* 1881

This, like many of the descriptions in *A First Year*, is reworked in *Erewhon*, but with the Italian references excised, as inappropriate to the narrator. The sublime tone is deliberately lowered for the sake of realism, a technique of which he was master, and often used for satiric deflation:

Next morning we found our last night's tea-leaves frozen at the bottom of the pannikins, though it was not nearly the beginning of autumn; we breakfasted as we had supped, and were on our way by six o'clock. In half an hour we had entered the gorge, and turning round a corner we bade farewell to the last sight of my master's country.[13]

Although there is no overt reference to Italy, the view of the plain of Erewhon and the descent into it are drawn from Italian landscapes;[14] the landscape is still composite. This 'mapping' of one landscape onto another to create a fictional world we shall find a recurrent characteristic of Butler's imagination.

Butler played a role in the formation of the cultural life of the colony which is well known in New Zealand but scarcely mentioned in English critical writings on him. Once his sheep farm was established he spent a good deal of his time in town, at the Christchurch Club, and was instrumental in encouraging the first art exhibitions there. He seems also

17. Rakaia River Valley, Headwaters, 1960

to have done some sketching, but few traces have remained. His account in a letter to his aunt is mainly negative:

I don't draw at all. For one reason there is nothing to draw and, for another, I find very little time – for another, it is almost always blowing from some quarter or another, and there is no shade or shelter.[15]

Yet both his literary and his artistic achievements were moulded by his experience in the colonies. His first publications (apart from a few slight pieces in the St John's College magazine 'The Eagle') were in New Zealand, his first book was constructed of his racy letters from there, and his first major book on his return was set in the frame of the New Zealand landscape. It was more than an exotic décor to him: his Erewhon, his imaginary country, was carved out of the frontier.

New Zealand, moreover, played an important subsequent role in his

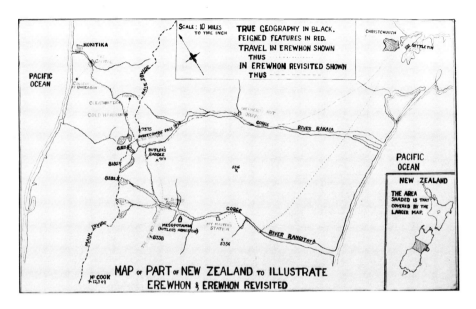

18. *Map of Erewhon and Erewhon Revisited*

career as an artist; a number of his sitters came from New Zealand; many of his works found their way there and are still in public and private collections; and only there has he received any recognition as a painter. As we shall see, he was caught in the pincer grip of High Victorian philistinism on the one side and the new Aesthetic Movement on the other, both of which he heartily disliked. The forerunners of each, Ruskin's lifetime crusade for morality in nature and the Pre-Raphaelite movement of the 1850s, were still intricately involved with the scene of art and largely governed the choices open to him. He had read Ruskin's *The Seven Lamps of Architecture* (1849) at Cambridge, a book that conveyed most of Ruskin's key ideas, and had been moved to enthusiasm; later he felt 'decided dislike' for him.[16] As Ruskin himself said, on publishing a revised edition in 1880, its partisanship for Protestantism had been too evident, and its style was 'overlaid with gilding, and overshot, too splashily and cascade-fashion, with gushing of words'.[17] But the movement from enthusiasm to dislike called out Butler's best efforts in art criticism and practice over a quarter of a century. His critique of the styles he came to abominate and his attempts to find a path of his own are illuminating, both of those styles and of the solitary way of the individual who glimpses, fitfully and painfully, but at times with a powerful lucidity, superior alternatives in the past and the future. His growing conviction of the decline of art in his own day trapped him in his own logic and demanded self-condemnation. His savage irony is often turned not only on his roots but on himself.

On his return to England in 1865, however, having realized a tidy profit, he set about his career as an artist in high hope. His father rejected the logic of the bargain and remained adamantly opposed to his son's course, but could no longer stand in his way. Butler first attended the Bloomsbury art school of Francis Stephen Cary, a painter of domestic interiors, with whom D. G. Rossetti had also studied for a time, and also attended the College of Art in South Kensington. He soon moved to the well-known art school, Heatherley's, at that time in Newman Street, off Oxford Street near Tottenham Court Road. After a group of students rebelling against academic restrictions had been expelled from the Government School of Design in Somerset House, a new school had been founded in 1845 and called after its first principal, J. M. Leigh (Etty's only pupil). Thackeray, who had worked there, had depicted 'Dagger' Leigh, trained in Paris and famous for his sharp criticism and his smart dinner parties, as Barker in *The Newcomes*. Well-known painters had worked there in considerable numbers and continued to do so.[18] It was now directed by Thomas J. Heatherley (1826–1914; principal 1860–87). Butler liked the restrained bohemianism of the School, and grew to have confidence in Heatherley as a man, if not as a painter, remaining on good terms with him long after he ceased to be an art student. Among his fellow apprentices he found his cousin Reginald Worsley, whose frank and pungent conversation was after his own heart; John Butler Yeats, the father of W. B. Yeats, who had abandoned the law in 1867 and was a passionate Pre-Raphaelite ('It enchanted me . . . to find in any stray model either the red hair or the columnar throat of the Rossetti woman'), later a competent portrait painter; the very young Johnston Forbes-Robertson, whom he befriended, afterwards the Shakespearean actor; Eliza Mary Ann Savage, who became a close comrade and friend, his literary confidante and his wittiest correspondent, until her early death in 1886; Frank Huddlestone Potter, whose work, based on strong observation of commonplace scenes (for example, his *Girl resting at the piano*) Butler always supported and some of whose paintings he bought at a memorial exhibition after the artist's early death in 1887;[19] and Charles Gogin, who became and remained one of his best friends, later collaborated with him on the illustrations to

Alps and Sanctuaries, and painted the portrait of Butler now in the National Portrait Gallery in London, perhaps his most familiar likeness. The School had from the beginning accepted women, whereas at the Royal Academy all life classes (even clothed) were segregated; Kate Greenaway was one of Heatherley's later pupils. Leighton and Millais lectured at the School. These encounters were immensely stimulating for Butler, to an extent underplayed by Henry Festing Jones, his close friend and biographer, who met him only later, in 1876.

The School was well-known for its informality. A twentieth-century principal, calling attention to the unbroken tradition from Heatherley's time, noted in 1954: 'It is, we believe, the only school in England where a student can enter and work without any formality, save that of paying fees; a practice common in the Paris schools. As a result of this freedom, the School always has a large number of part-time students in its studios.'[20]

If the School was informal, Butler sometimes seemed less so. Already aged twenty-nine, he was intent on making up for lost time. He wrote to Darwin: 'My *study* is art and anything else I may indulge in is only by-play.'[21] He worked seven hours a day, and continued to be addressed as 'Mr Butler'.

His friends and acquaintances at Heatherley's described him in their memoirs. Forbes-Robertson later recalled him with affection, admiration, and a touch of the ardent name-dropping that became him so well, as 'my special friend, a strange and most original character', with whom he had 'happy daily hobnobs' over lunch at The Horse Shoe pub:

He always wore rough homespun and thick boots, and his hair and beard were cut quite close, the face was short and the complexion ruddy. The eyes could snap and sparkle and they could beam with sympathy. His voice was sweet and low, his laugh quite infectious, and those few who knew him loved the man.[22]

Forbes-Robertson tells us that Butler 'was very anxious to become an Academy student. He sent in his drawings several times, but they were never passed', whereas Forbes-Robertson, advised by Rossetti to prepare at Heatherley's 'to draw from the Antique, to the end that I might compete for a studentship at the Royal Academy', had his drawings accepted 'in the course of about a year', and 'I became a student at the R A and had the advantage of the best training in art that England could afford'.[23] He left Butler behind, or so it seemed to him then.

J. B. Yeats, at the school in 1867–8, wrote a more penetrating account, which met Butler's wit on its own ground. He tells us that Butler was attempting at this time to paint in the manner of Giovanni Bellini:

To be a painter after the manner of John Bellini was for years the passion of his life. . . . He always occupied one place in the school chosen so that he could be as close as possible to the model and might paint with small brushes his kind of John Bellini art. . . .[24]

Despite his shrewd appreciation of Butler, whose 'emancipated intellect had won for his soul and senses a freedom which he wished to share with others', Yeats had scant respect for his attempts.

Butler's attempts to paint in the manner of Bellini convey the strength of Ruskin's influence at this stage, for Bellini, in Ruskin's hierarchy, was the epitome of the virtues of the Quattrocentro as yet uncorrupted by the Renaissance. Butler's striking early painting, *Two Heads after Bellini* (1866), represents one of his attempts at Pre-Raphaelite reanimation of the painting of the past (illus. 25). Although Butler grew rapidly disillusioned with the Pre-Raphaelite style in contemporary painting, his admiration for Bellini always remained with him.

This did not exhaust his experiments with Pre-Raphaelite styles, however, and some of his most successful paintings show the marks of an interest in the Nazarenes, which he most probably acquired through his acquaintance with Ford Madox Brown. Madox Brown had brought the news of the Nazarenes to England, after a study-tour on the Continent carried him to Rome, where in 1845 he made the acquaintance of the German 'Nazarene' painters still based there. As Holman Hunt put it in *Pre-Raphaelitism and the Pre-Raphaelite Brotherhood* (1905), he 'faced about to the opposite of his Antwerpian mode, to the new school under Overbeck and others, who set themselves to imitate all the child-like immaturities and limitations of the German and Italian Quattrocentists'. Brown, who remained outside the English Pre-Raphaelite Brotherhood, always referred to the Nazarene style as 'the early Christian style'. It was the case with Butler too that only in the Italian setting did he approach the still translucency and soft brilliance of the early masters, as in his unfinished watercolour (intended, Jones tells us, for the Academy) of *The Christening at Fobello* (1871; illus. 30), and in one of the most attractive of his paintings, the larger, finished oil study of the same subject (illus. 31). Although the painting was completed in London, Fobello itself was very close to the centre of his later art-historical interest, the Sacro Monte of Varallo. It uses the 'processional' motif prominent in the work of Franz Pforr and Friedrich Overbeck, but in the more intimate mood of J. Schnorr von Carolsfeld's *St Roch distributing Alms*. Butler's *Christening* resembles its combination of a group of people approaching the saint and their placement in relation to simple architectural elements within a predominantly natural setting, to produce an atmosphere of still, shared reverence. The church porch forming an architectural enclave in and open to nature remained one of his favourite subjects, as in the *Church Porch at Rossura* used in *Alps and Sanctuaries*, and in his later photographs. Madox Brown's encounter with the Nazarenes left a lasting mark on Butler; yet the direct or indirect imitation of a past master or historical style in a period antithetical to it could only be a *cul-de-sac*.

The Critique of the Academy: *Mr Heatherley's Holiday*

During the first phases of his art training we have only a few hints of the settled antagonism and hostility Butler was later to express against the whole manner of beaux-arts training of painting that formed and, he felt, deformed the painting of his half-century. As the few exercises that have survived from his art school days testify, he went through the prescribed motions like the well-behaved, assiduous pupil that he had always been, Headmaster Butler's grandson, and a classicist of no mean achievement at university. But his account of his training in drawing at the Cambridge School of Art had already contained a germ of satire:

I am getting on very nicely with my drawing; I go twice a week from eleven till one to the art school. I commenced with curved symmetrical lines very difficult indeed to copy accurately. I then went through a course of hands and am now going through a course of feet [illus. 19]; I have just blocked out the Venus de Medici's toes.[25]

Yet all told, he was in earnest:

There comes a man down from London to examine the drawings of the pupils now and then; and if they are not accurate he sits on the master here; so you may depend upon it that we have to be uncommonly exact, but as Harrie [Butler's sister Harriet, who was taught with him the rudiments of drawing by a governess] knows I always was an advocate for that; but this fellow makes us far more exact than I should have been. I am next to draw a figure or two from the flat and then from the plaster; the more accurately we draw the faster he lets us proceed.[26]

The accounts of charming informality at Heatherley's should not distract attention from the School's participation in the accepted

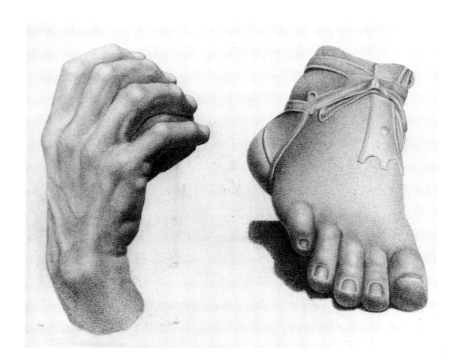

19. *Hand and Foot*, 1868

academic styles of teaching art, the programme of copying: from engravings, prints, and drawings; from casts; and finally from the live model. The Paris schools, though 'informal' in the sense described, were often a grueling training-ground.[27] We have one of his careful drawings of a classical cast, *Antinous as Hermes* (illus. 20), submitted to the Academy in the hope of gaining a place there.

The official view to this day, expressed in the Tate Gallery's catalogue entry on the one painting of his in its possession, is that Butler, though untalented, was pushed forward and propped up by training: 'With the help of various art schools, Heatherley's in particular, he did improve his technique considerably, and no. 2761 [*Mr Heatherley's Holiday*] can be considered one of his best works' (illus. 32).[28] It is hardly accidental that it is this painting which was exhibited in 1874 at the Royal Academy during his most 'successful' period, that it was after his death acquired by the Tate, and that it is the single one of his works to have been included in a major national exhibition in the twentieth century, touring the Empire in 1936 in an impressive array of British prowess in painting.

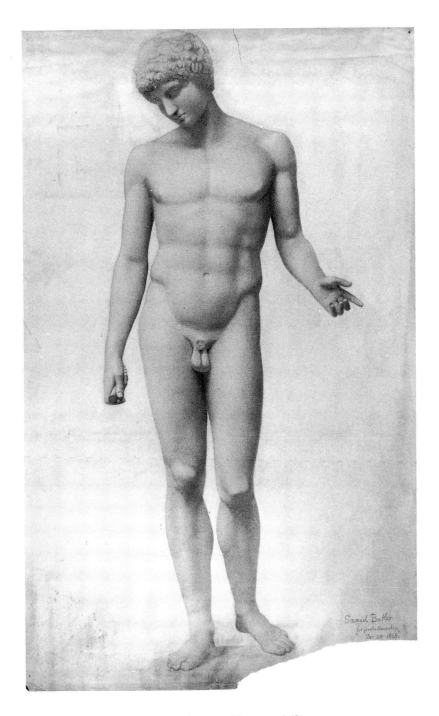

20. *Antinous as Hermes*, 1868

Beside this official view one may set the judgement of Graham Reynolds, virtually the only historian of Victorian art to discuss Butler's work, that *Mr Heatherley's Holiday* is 'an example of Butler's academic manner and the dryness which overcame him when painting to a formula'.[29] Butler's own later view was that what little talent he had had was misdirected and spoilt by a training on false principles. As he noted on a letter to Miss Savage in 1901 while preparing their correspondence for the press:

I did some water colours in 1871 which were just on the right track – but then on returning to England came autumn – *Erewhon* – and I drifted back to Heatherley's – so fatally facile. In 1876, at Fusio I did as I said I would and did some very decent water colours, two of which I still have. If I had found indoor subjects on my return, and stuck to water colour I believe I could have sold them and kept my head above water – but then came autumn – *Life and Habit* . . . and I drifted back to the fatal self deception of going to Heatherley's.[30]

This note was written at Wassen, Switzerland, where he did considerable painting; as we shall see, it was his trips to the Alpine regions of Switzerland and Northern Italy that again gave him a sense of what he could do, or could have done. The note of nostalgia for watercolour, his 'primal scene of painting', is a measure of his growing distrust of 'academicism':

As it is I have been all wrong, and it was South Kensington and Heatherley's that set me wrong. I listened to the nonsense about how I ought to study before beginning to paint, and the result was that I learned to study but not to paint.[31]

In the autumn of 1877 he did not return to Heatherley's: 'Here my art-student life may be said to end (for I never was more).'[32]

It was, nevertheless, during his days at Heatherley's that he began to formulate in his painting one aspect of his rebellion, using a style that was already available. His major painting, *Mr Heatherley's Holiday* (1873), sums up what the School meant to him at that time and the mode of his rebellion as far as he was able to carry it within the School's terms. The painting is neither an accolade to his drawing masters nor 'dry classicism'.

It is of great importance for the understanding of Butler's critique of classicism that Heatherley's also championed the new technique of photography. A splendid series of portrait heads by D. W. Wynfield, who strongly influenced Julia Cameron, began to be taken in 1862.[33] Julia Cameron was to say: 'To his beautiful photography I owe all my attempts, and indeed consequently all my success.' Butler's photograph of Forbes-Robertson, the extraordinarily attractive Pre-Raphaelite young man (who also sat for Rossetti as the young Eros), wearing a suit of burnished armour, is also clearly in this mode (illus. 106). Butler's nostalgic (and deliberately 'shocking') letter to his aunt from New Zealand prepares us for this, as for the homo-erotic streak in Butler that lay behind his misadventures with Pauli. The difficulty of drawing on his sheep farm in 'Mesopotamia' had led him to write:

If I had three or four thousand a year I should much like to buy a young conscientious artist with a dash of pre-raphaelitism in him, and keep him for my edification and instruction. . . . Colour is very scarce here.[34]

Even more tellingly for Butler, the practice of humorous photographic poses carried on the satiric tradition in painting and especially graphics, for example, Rowlandson's The 'Life-Class' at the Royal Academy, with its nude model posed as a Greek statue at the centre and its alternating tiers of real artists and studio busts equally remote from life; or the series of engravings by Daumier, The Connoisseur, which undermined both the pompous art collector and the objects of virtù that he fancied. This was an important line in the critique of classicism.[35] It expressed the insight already conveyed in Fuseli's grotesque of the modern man dwarfed by the enormous fragmented foot of the Capitoline Colossus.[36] It was often combined with the long established subject of the artist's studio, as in Butler's painting. If Butler's photograph of Forbes-Robertson has a worthy place in the gallery of 'beautiful photography', it has this other, ironic sense as well. The tradition of humorous poses, often in costume, continued in the School, with the principals posing with busts, the amusing Mrs Crompton, wife of Heatherley's successor, with Venus de Milo, about 1900, and Henry Massey, principal 1907–34, with the self-same suit of armour.[37] These student high-jinks – and there was an element in Butler that never ceased to savour a jape – form part of the style of flamboyant self-deprecation internalized in the history of photography.

Behind Mr Heatherley's Holiday lay a good deal of folklore and anecdote; and this 'literary' aspect of the painting chimes both with one major line of Victorian genre painting and with Butler's own talent, as well as with the one branch of art he thought was not degraded in his own time: book and periodical illustration. The school prospectus for 1956 describes Heatherley as follows: 'Robed in a crimson velvet dressing gown with long white hair and flowing beard and looking like a medieval alchemist, he ran the school for thirty years without break or holiday.'[38] This could not have characterized him when Butler met him, as Heatherley was only ten years his senior; but the legend that he 'never took a holiday' clearly plays a role in the busman's holiday he is seen enjoying in the painting. Heatherley was often used as a subject; as a young man he had been painted as *The Good Shepherd* by W. C. T. Dobson.[39] Jones adds a good deal to the background: Heatherley's was 'a wilderness of Flemish tapestry, Venetian mirrors, armour, tortoiseshell cabinets from Spain, pictures in gilded frames and chairs upholstered in tattered brocade'. On one occasion 'Butler played a minuet of his own composition, while Heatherley in his loose black velvet coat with his pale face and his straggling beard, stood over us like a medieval necromancer.'[40] Jones also supplies the anecdotal background to the painting. The picture, he tells us, shows the head of the school mending the school skeleton, and was originally called 'Tinkering a Skeleton'. It is called *Mr Heatherley's Holiday* because in fact Heatherley should have been on holiday in the country; but the students kept on breaking the skeleton's bones by dressing it up in bizarre costumes and dancing it through the studios. Once again, behind the clear compositional framework of the picture is a far more animated scene, a *danse macabre* which we know only from Butler's written description of it. It has been remarked that the skeleton is a female one. This grotesquerie is capped by a quotation from Mr Heatherley himself that exhibits his character to perfection. Jones refers back to one of Butler's own pungent stories about the school:

Mr Heatherley disliked the country; he much preferred London. Once when he had to go into the country on business he was obliged to sleep out of town; on his return one of the students asked him how he had liked it, saying that no doubt he felt refreshed by sleeping in country air. 'No,' said old Heatherley, 'country air has no *body* in it.'[41]

Like a good Londoner, Mr Heatherley enjoyed the thick, dusty, densely crowded space of street and studio.

Although the painting displays the classical casts, the props of art, so prominently, its central 'prop' is thus associated not with the classical anatomy lesson but with the Germanic and 'gothic' skeleton. There is a macabre life here that reminds us of Butler's admiration for Holbein's *Dance of Death*, interpreted rather in the ligher vein of Burns's poem 'Tam O'Shanter' in which the drunk man leaving the pub encounters in the middle of the rural night landscape a grotesque Black Mass in which the Devil himself plays the drum. A skeleton hanging on the gibbet plays a prominent role in the poem, and the encounter with it was also adapted and 'elevated' by Wordsworth in *Salisbury Plain* and *The Prelude*.[42] The rude or 'unlyrical ballad' in a sub-Burnsian manner, 'Wednesbury Cocking', probably Butler's own, points to his pleasure in burrowing beneath all 'sublime' styles; satire on Wordsworth was one of his prime sports.[43] The classical and the popular-gothic are in dialogue in this painting. At the same time, they are maintained effectively in the suspense of the 'absorption' in the act.

Not only the skeleton, but the Discobolus figures in Butler's literary oeuvre. 'A Psalm of Montreal', his poem on the 'Discobolus', features a similar scene of the modern misuse of the classics. He described the scene in a prefatory note:

In the Montreal Museum of Natural History I came upon two plaster casts, one of the Antinous and the other of the Discobolus . . . banished from public view to a room where all manner of skins, plants, snakes, insects, etc., and, in the middle of these, an old man stuffing an owl.

His dialogue with the repetitive old man forms all but the first stanza of the poem, surely a parody of Wordsworth's 'The Leech-Gatherer, or, Resolution and Independence' (also famously parodied by Lewis Carroll), and at the same time a travesty of a Horatian ode:

Stowed away in a Montreal lumber room
The Discobolus standeth and turneth his face to the wall;
Dusty, cobweb-covered, maimed and set at naught,
Beauty crieth in an attic and no man regardeth:
                O God! O Montreal! . . .

'The Discobolus is put here because he is vulgar –
He has neither vest nor pants with which to cover his limbs;
I, Sir, am a person of most respectable connections –
My brother-in-law is haberdasher to Mr Spurgeon.'
                O God! O Montreal! . . .

'Preferrest thou the gospel of Montreal to the gospel of Hellas,
The gospel of thy connection with Mr Spurgeon's haberdasher to the gospel of the
    Discobolus?
Yet none the less blasphemed he beauty saying, 'The Discobolus hath no gospel,
But my brother-in-law is haberdasher to Mr Spurgeon.'
                O God! O Montreal!

Butler's description of his composition of *Mr Heatherley's Holiday* throws unexpected light on the painting. A letter to Miss Savage in 1873 shows how he carried on all of the arts at once, even while painting it (and his fellow student was the sympathetic but incisive critic of his painterly as well as of his literary efforts):

I sent you the first 15pp. of my novel [*Ernest Pontifex*, or *The Way of All Flesh*], and will send as many more in a week. I have given up my music and write an hour in the evenings instead. I am painting an 'important' picture.[44]

In the complete description (cut in the version of the letters prepared in 1901) he continued:

A man mending old Heatherley's skeleton and a child looking on – background, all the pots and pans and knickknacks in the corner opposite the washing-stand, with the Discobolus and half the Ilyssus. I think it will come very well, but I am only just beginning it.[45]

The 'child looking on' is not in the finished painting. More significantly, the letter alerts us to the fact that the man in the painting was not intended to be a likeness of Thomas Heatherley. Jones indicates that a number of changes were made in the painting before it was exhibited at the Royal Academy; crucially, it may have become a portrait of Heatherley himself only over time.

We may conclude that part of the irony here is that the man mending the skeleton was not Mr Heatherley. On this one occasion, at least, when Butler conceived and began the painting, Mr Heatherley did take a holiday. Art is out to lunch. Butler made use of the folklore in order to undermine it. Not only is the studio full of the mere stage-props of art, as in the paintings of the immensely successful eighteenth-century portrait painter Pompeo Batoni, who painted members of the English upper classes making the Grand Tour against a backdrop of the Colosseum, a map of Rome, and a much-used bust of Minerva, but the man carefully keeping the props in repair for yet another generation is only an 'extra' standing in for the star.[46] He is the equivalent of the owl-stuffer. This gleeful satire on grandeur is a comic *mise-en-abîme* in which self-reflection renders the figure of man ever smaller. At the same time, the studio handyman (like the Ilyssus and the Discobolus) has a genuine practical function in the business of 'High Art'.

The Pre-Raphaelite Brotherhood ironized

Butler's ironic critique of the academic style from within is matched by his practice elsewhere in his painting. His dislike of the contemporary

Pre-Raphaelite painters (as opposed to the genuine Pre-Raphaelites of the past, such as Bellini) became as intense as his dislike of the academic, and he began to express it on canvas.

His unpleasant encounters with the Rossettis he described vividly, more than once. To Miss Savage he wrote:

> You ask me about Rossetti. I dislike his face, and his manner, and his work, and I hate his poetry, and his friends. He is wrapped up in self-conceit and lives upon adulation. I spent a whole evening in his company at H. Wallis's, W. B. Scott being the only other except Wallis, Rossetti and myself. I was oppressed by the sultry reticence of Rossetti's manner which seemed to me assumed in order to conceal the fact that he had nothing worth saying to say.[47]

Later he underlined his equal dislike of Rossetti's painting, entering in his notebook after attending a Rossetti exhibition in 1883: 'I have been to see it and am pleased to find it more odious than I had even dared to hope.'[48]

In 1884 he was invited to an 'at home' by Mrs William Rossetti and wrote to Miss Savage: 'I don't think I ought to go, for they are not a lot I like, but I don't quite know.'[49] In the event, he went, tempted by the idea that the invitation meant 'I am looking up' and still more by Mrs Rossetti's reminder that she was a daughter of Madox Brown, with whom he had once been on good terms, and who would 'much like to see' him. He had also been on good terms with Oliver Madox Brown, of whom his father had had high hopes, and who had just died, tragically young. He felt he ought to go. He had a disastrous evening, recorded at some length in his Notebooks. Old Madox Brown snubbed him, and 'would not know who I was'. His conversation with William Rossetti was scarcely better:

> I had a few words with William Rossetti. I said how beautiful his pictures were; in reality I hated them, but I did all as I should, and it was accepted as about what I ought to have said.[50]

Elsewhere in his Notebooks he tells an ironic anecdote about Holman Hunt setting up as interpreter of *The Light of the World* for art-loving ladies.[51] In short, he liked neither the Rossetti family, nor the Brotherhood, nor their works.

Yet his complex relationship with Pre-Raphaelitism, beginning with early attraction followed by disillusion fed by personal dislike, affected his painting in another way. If Butler's photograph of Forbes-Robertson shows he could muster the Pre-Raphaelite style when he chose, and

Yeats's testimony and that of several of his most interesting early paintings shows that for a time he took seriously the recommendation to adopt painters before Raphael as sources for contemporary works, his *Portrait of an Unidentified Woman* (1873; illus. 24) shows him deliberately undercutting one its most popular local manifestations.

The model might be described as a Pre-Raphaelite type: she sports a mane of wavy red hair parted in the centre, a somewhat jutting chin, full lips, an electric blue costume, and a brilliant terracotta background. These colours are quite unusual in Butler's palette. What Butler does is to render her as plain as plain can be: he turns 'The Lady of the Lake', as he put it, into 'The Woman of the Pond'. The spurious glamour and mystery of Rossetti's *Beata Beatrix*, or *Monna Vanna* (whom she particularly resembles), or the later *Astarte Syriaca*, is stripped off. Another target of 'The Woman of the Pond' (apart from Tennyson) is *The Virgin of the Rocks*, his least favourite Leonardo. His preference for the plain and unvarnished over the 'fine', the tarted up, and the pseudo-symbolic was inveterate. He warred against pretence by every means at his command. The acid power of his comment in paint stems from the Pre-Raphaelites' own oft-repeated claim, from *The Germ* (1850) onward, to be acolytes of nature, intent only on humbly revealing her every detail, as Ruskin recommended, without judgement or improvement. His attack is deliberately aimed at Rossetti in particular, who seemed to flout the stated principle of faithfulness to nature at every turn. Butler's painting antedates Beardsley's better-known visual mockeries of Rossetti, an important phase in the development of his style; 'it is in both sorrow and scorn that Beardsley revisits the ideal Pre-Raphaelite beauty', as John Dixon Hunt has phrased it.[52] Butler visited them more in scorn than in sorrow. His unidentified subject, unadorned by mythological reference or symbolic impedimenta, stood on her own, unavailable for service as the vainglorious painter's 'anima'.

In the light of this we must look again at his *Two Heads after Bellini* (illus. 25). The head of the woman bears a close resemblance to the same 'Pre-Raphaelite' model – Jones identified the sitters as two artists' models, Maria and Calarossi – and their stark contemporaneity against the Italianized landscape 'in the manner of Bellini' becomes itself an ironic comment on the wrong-headedness of attempting directly to ape the Quattrocento. For Butler, 'imitation' is always ironic, because of the unavoidable disparity between the original and the imitation; by emphasizing it he attacks not only the specific forms of Pre-Raphaelite imitation but the academic tradition in general (which the Pre-Raphaelites imagined themselves to be avoiding). The conscious, ironic disparity gives his painting a modern presence.

His dislike of the aesthetic style in literature, for example, Pater's, was equally deep-rooted:

Mr Walter Pater's style is, to me, like the face of some old woman who has been to Madame Rachel and had herself enamelled. The bloom is nothing but powder and paint and the odour is cherry-blossom.[53]

As Max Beerbohm, who also had a mordant eye for stylistic affectation, put it, Pater writes English as 'a dead language', in a 'sedulous ritual wherewith he laid out every sentence as in a shroud'.[54]

Arnold came off scarcely better in Butler's opinion: 'Mr Matthew Arnold's odour is as the faint sickliness of hawthorn.'[55] Butler in later years, as we shall see, assiduously sawed away at the great tree of 'the grand style' advocated by Arnold.

Thus in his painting of the brass-tacks Pre-Raphaelite woman Butler alludes to the idiom of the style he opposes in order to display its falsehood. A visual image grasps and sums up the antagonism afterwards spelled out discursively. In the Bellini in the style of the Pre-Raphaelites the effect is more complex: there is a double quotation, and each is a misquotation; the game of 'Familiar Misquotations' was one Butler often played with Miss Savage: 'The better part of valour is indiscretion';[56] or 'There is more truth in honest lies / Believe me, than in half the truths'.[57] He often used Biblical quotations, even whole narratives, in this way: 'Isaac offering up Abraham'.[58] The pictorial irony is analogous to the literary irony: the quotations must be recognized, and recognized to be wrong. Yet the 'wrongness' contains a grain of truth that casts doubt on the ease with which one repeats the familiar. The ironic use of style was one of Butler's hallmarks. In his painting, as in his novel *The Fair Haven* (reviewed as a serious 'conversion' story instead of the ironic portrayal of Victorian religion Butler revealed it to have been), it went largely unnoticed.

Portraits real and imaginary

The question of the identity of portrait subjects for Butler is an interesting one throughout his work, and links with the broader one of the relation of titles to depicted subjects generally, of special importance in the work of a literary artist – especially an ironist – in the pictorial medium. Further, it sheds light on the Victorian literary genre of 'the imaginary portrait'. Often the subjects were named (*Miss Atcheson*), but equally often they were simply identified generally, as in *Head of a Young Girl*. Two of the female portraits now in New Zealand have not been firmly identified, and their identity has given rise to considerable speculation. Often the paintings were given literary identifications (*Don Quixote*), while clearly being the portrait of a particular model; he did not, however, employ the familiar nineteenth-century device of citing a line or several lines from a poem as a title or tag. Nor for the most part did he give explanatory and dramatic narrative titles of the kind that were in vogue at the time (Collinson's *Answering the Emigrant's Letter*, O'Neil's *Eastward Ho! August 1857*, or the immensely popular *Chelsea Pensioners reading the Gazette of the Battle of Waterloo*, by Wilkie); *Mr Heatherley's Holiday* is the closest he came to a story title. Of the still more common descriptive titles for the popular genre painting of modern life, Butler's *Family Prayers* is in line with common practice, as in Dobson's *A Scottish Sacrament*, or Goodall's *Head of the House at Prayer*, which Miss Savage saw at an exhibition in 1877, commenting: 'The Head of the House is looking so cross and bored at having to pray, while the rest of the family are looking so pleased at not having to do so, that I am sure Goodall meant to convey a moral lesson.'[59] One of Butler's major subjects, of course, was himself; his self-portraits are perhaps his most familiar work, simply because they have been used to adorn editions of his books as frontispieces, biographical illustration, and more recently as covers for paperback editions. Doubtless it was convenient to sit for oneself; but we may also suspect the influence of his great admiration for Rembrandt. But these clear identifications of the familiar face of the author himself may obscure the more complex nature of the identifications, that is, the relations between the person depicted and the narrative material that lies behind it. In *Mr Heatherley's Holiday* the central figure came 'over time' to resemble Mr Heatherley; often, especially on his travels, Butler identified a person seen momentarily with a historical or more usually a literary figure and 'painted' his portrait in words. A striking example occurs in a Notebook entry that was to be included in a third volume of art-critical travels. While staying in the Ticino, he met a number of people in the village:

And presently the Devil came up to me. He was a nice, clean old man, but he dropped his h's, and that was where he spoiled himself – or perhaps it was just this that threw me off my guard, for I had always heard that the Prince of Darkness was a perfect gentleman. He whispered to me that in the winter the monks of St. Bernard sometimes say matins overnight.[60]

It is noticeable that no visual resemblance is explicitly set up, while the recognition is powerfully and instantly asserted (as in Blake's 'The Prophets Isaiah and Ezekiel dined with me', in *The Marriage of Heaven and Hell*), only to be undermined by a series of ironic doubts that make the visionary assertion risible.

A more complex example embedded in a narrative of a chance meeting in Switzerland is that of 'the two Beethovens', where the visual resemblance is itself made the source of a mischief directed at a composer Butler did not like. The first 'Beethoven' was 'a rather fine-looking young German with wild ginger hair that rang out to the wild sky like the bells in *In Memoriam*, and a strong Edmund Gurney cut'.[61] To tease the young man, who was clearly aware of the resemblance, Butler remarked that 'a little insignificant-looking engineer, the most commonplace mortal imaginable, who was sitting at the head of the table, was like Beethoven'. A few days later, the commonplace Beethoven was leaving, and the ginger-haired Beethoven pointed out to Butler an enormous cube of a trunk coming down the stairs: 'That's Beethoven's box.' Butler replied: 'And is he inside it?' 'It seemed to fit him and to correspond so perfectly with him in every way that one felt as though if he were not inside it he ought to be.' Thus the Beethoven he disliked was done away with, and the Romantic external appearance of Beethoven as the inspired musician is contrasted to his true, inward character visualized in the ponderous box. In a very brief paragraph Butler sketches a series of appearances, identifications, and re-identifications that carry a freight of analysis and emotion, as well as suggesting the opening passages of a story. As he saw neither Beethoven again as far as we are told, the story is also finished off with the burial in the box. Butler's sense of an ending, as well as a beginning, is strikingly visual.

This technique of momentary identification, often as a form of witty epiphany, he used to best effect in his photography, where the ephemeral identification is matched by the instantaneity of the snapshot. The joke often depends on the insubstantiality, changeability, or unlikeliness of the identification. In either case, whether as in *Mr Heatherley* through gradual alteration by overpainting, or whether as in 'Beethoven' or 'the Devil' through fleeting identification only, the link between the form and the name is a soluble one. 'Identity' itself is called in question by the rapidity with which it is created and uncreated. Identity is more often mistaken identity. It is a negative epiphany, like Stephen Hero's 'epiphany in the lavatory'. Butler's native wit was at home with speed, impermanence; Victorian aesthetics called for permanence, monumentality. The major portrait painter of the day was the highly successful G. F. Watts, whose work Butler regarded with a more fixed and principled dislike than that of any of his other *bêtes noires*. Watts was a reluctant portrait painter, and did his utmost to turn what he regarded as journeyman's work into essays in allegory. As Chesterton sneered, 'He is allegorical when he is painting an old alderman.'[62] A portrait, Watts said, must be a revelation of the sitter's greatness; 'it should have in it something of the monumental.' According to Chesterton, 'He scarcely ever paints a man without making him five times as magnificent as he really looks. The real men appear, if they present themselves afterwards, like mean and unsympathetic sketches from the Watts original.'[63] Butler's portraits deliberately undercut this style of 'noble' portrait, and sought to paint an alderman without badges of office or allegorical props, as in his portraits of Thomas Cass (illus. 26), John Marshman (illus. 27), and Alfred Cathie (illus. 28), and in his series of self-portraits (illus. 21, 22, 23). While propless and unadorned, these portraits preserve the integrity, even the dignity of the sitter. Replaced in this gallery the de-glamourized Pre-Raphaelite women reassume human presence. The artist, instead of painting himself as Titian (as Watts did), joined his sitters. They are deliberate exercises in the 'plain style'. In his photography there is a further step down from the pedestal, for the same subjects appear 'in shirtsleeves' and amid a rogues' gallery of other 'instantaneous' identities. Alfred in particular (Butler's manservant who, with his mother, figures in a number of humorous entries in the Notebooks) appears in a variety of gamin-like and puckish poses. Thus the tension was resolved for Butler as an artist only by the technology of the 'snap-shot' towards the end of the century.

At the same time these momentary portraits are closely allied with the technique of the literary 'imaginary portrait' often associated with Walter Pater, and with the mode of art criticism he developed. This is another instance of Butler's sharing of and absorption of elements from the work of those he claimed he couldn't abide. We must look further back for its source, both in Butler and in Pater. The hope of an English art (however inferior) to set beside the Italian had led Horace Walpole to write the *Anecdotes of Painting in England* (1762) to set beside Vasari's *Lives*. The genre of the 'Life of the Artist' was carried out brilliantly in

William Beckford's satiric portraits, *Biographical Memoirs of Extra-ordinary Painters* (1780), in which the dramatic encounter of Northern with Southern art is replayed in a series of imaginary lives; but it is notable that no English artist plays a title role. The major examples of the genre are German, for example, in Tieck. The 'Life of the Artist' was to be one of Butler's major genres; but the elusiveness of the English example continued. If the germ of the 'imaginary portrait' is in his Notebook entries, it was only in his Italian art criticism that Butler fully developed his own version of the technique, elaborating the portraits (including their visual analogues) of individual artists within a community into a 'Life'; later he was able to apply this as a method of literary and art criticism in his *Authoress of the Odyssey*. His critique of Romantic and Victorian styles, moreover, and the elusiveness of the English artist, which he came to identify also with his own status as artist *manqué*, led him to the comic imaginary portrait as the native English form. This is, then, one of the most significant aspects of his creative process.

During the time he was at Heatherley's Butler crowned his work of copying the masters in the accepted fashion by submitting his work to the Royal Academy, to be considered for hanging in the summer exhibition. A number of his paintings were hung during the decade of his attendance at Heatherley's. The Royal Academy itself lists:[64]

1869	(279)	*Miss Atcheson*
1871	(514)	*A Reverie*
1874	(134)	*A Child's Head*
	(959)	*Mr Heatherley's Holiday: an incident in studio life*
1876	(363)	*Don Quixote*

Jones lists in addition:[65]

| 1876 | | *A Girl's Head* |

Jones sheds some further light on these paintings, or at least on their titles (and so perhaps on *Mr Heatherley*). He viewed the *Don Quixote* and *A Girl's Head*:

The more important one was in oils; he called it 'Don Quixote', but admitted that it was only a study from a costume model at Heatherley's, and no more like one's notion of Don Quixote than it was like any other man in armour; but he was obliged to give it a title, otherwise, he said, the Academy would not look at it. He probably said much the same to Miss Savage, for when she went to the exhibition and saw the second picture, which was a watercolour of a girl's head, she wrote that, if it did not sell, he must call it 'Mignon' and send it to a provincial show.[66]

Butler himself seemed to be in some uncertainty about the dates, but he was at all events certain that after 1879 he submitted nothing more to the Royal Academy. This was not quite the case, however, for in 1883 he wrote to his sister May, 'I am sending in four pictures to the Academy'; but he went on, 'I am too old now to be sanguine about getting them in or to be much disappointed if I am turned out, though of course I should like to be in.'[67] Butler's letters often refer to his preparation of the paintings to be sent off, the rush to send them (sometimes from as far away as Italy), his dissatisfaction with them, the suspense of waiting to see whether or not they were accepted. There can be no doubt of the pleasure he took in being 'hung'. As he wrote to Miss Savage in 1871:

They have hung one picture for me at the Academy; it does not look well but that is not their fault. I was there all yesterday; it is a capital exhibition.[68]

He sold paintings from time to time; a typical price was £15.15 for the *Don Quixote*. His best year seems to have been 1874, when J. Pettie's *Juliet and Friar Lawrence*, Millais' *The Picture of Health*, and Alma-Tadema's *The Picture Gallery* were also hung; after that he experienced greater difficulty in having his pictures accepted. In 1878 he wrote to his sister May:

I sent in four things to the Academy – two portraits, an oil landscape, and a watercolour landscape, but I am not very sanguine – indeed I am distinctly depressed about my work at present and wonder whether I ever shall paint; on the other hand, I have had these depressions very often, and know that they come more from being able to see what I could not see before than from anything else.[69]

In the years after Butler ceased to submit his work the Academy flourished under the presidency of Frederic Leighton, and held very popular exhibitions of Watts, Alma-Tadema, and Leighton himself. The more it flourished the less was it a source of or venue for good art, in Butler's view. Its heyday was the high point of Victorian Hellenism, genre painting both of the sentimental and the melodramatic strain, and of the new social realism. Butler's dislike of Watts's work in particular is forcefully expressed in his Notebooks.[70] After seeing an exhibition of his at Christie's he recorded:

I never saw a more feeble, contemptible lot of pictures got together. You could see weak brag – such weakness, and such brag – in every picture, that it is difficult to understand how even in this press-ridden age Watts could have attained his reputation. Certainly he never could have attained it in an age in which men and women looked at pictures with their own eyes and not with those of other people.[71]

His instinct for sweeping away the overfurnished Victoriana expressed itself in a back-handed 'appreciation' of one of Watts's canvases:

The 'Return of the Dove to the Ark' was the best picture because there was least in it; flat sky, flat sea, a great deal of both, and both as near empty as they could be, a tiny, little ark, as cheap as cheap could be, and then one very poorly painted bird which I suppose may pass for a dove. It sold for about £700.[72]

The selection at the Royal Academy at the beginning of the 1870s was a mixed bag representing artists of different tendencies. But during precisely the period of Butler's withdrawal a number of other artists separated themselves from the Academy. In particular, of course, the Aesthetic movement began to gain ground and to find its own venues: the presence of many French artists in London (on account of the War of 1871) led to exhibitions of their works in French-run galleries, especially Monet and Pissarro, with those colleagues who in Paris in 1874 became known as 'Impressionists'; the opening of the Grosvenor Gallery in 1877, where Ruskin saw the paintings of Whistler that led to his condemnation in *Fors Clavigera* of the 'coxcomb' who dared ask two hundred guineas 'for flinging a pot of paint in the public's face', leading to the trial that brought so much publicity to the opposition between the two; the refounding of the alternative Society of British Artists under the leadership of Whistler in 1877. The strengthening of the Academy classicism through the demand for 'finish' produced by Ruskin's attack on Whistler, and the force of the counter-claims of the Aesthetic school, left Butler, who neither supported nor represented either, stranded. If Watts's work, with its feeble, forced classicism, was anathema to him, the Aesthetic school fared little better at his hands. He wrote to Miss Savage in 1871:

Nettleship brought an unpleasant picture of a black beast against a tapestry background (he said it was moonlight, but that was absurd) and two skins of snakes hard by, and wanted us to admire it, the other day; I disliked it very much. . . .[73]

J. T. Nettleship belonged to the circle of young painters and poets who professed the doctrine of 'Art for Art's Sake', which included the painter Simeon Solomon, the poet John Payne (devoté of Gautier), Swinburne, and Pater. The vogue – which lasted from Rossetti and Whistler through Art Nouveau – for peacocks and their feathers, all manner of serpentine creatures and devices, 'tapestry' backgrounds and black gloss, Butler summed up and dismissed in advance. The school is characterized through the *saignant* description of one painting taken as a type. Butler's 'word painting', like Ruskin's, creates a painting in words; but in its pungent satiric brevity it is a critique of Ruskin's verbose hosannahs (as, for example, to Turner's *Slave Ship*).[74] Butler was perfectly conscious of the word painting as genre: 'A new profession – Portrait painting in words which people should pay for as they pay for their pictures.'[75]

He was able to conjure up paintings and word paintings of his own which outdo the Aesthetes at their own game. In one of his fine flights of irony, he wrote to his sister:

I am painting a lovely charnel house. Also you know the aesthetic school have run sunflowers lately: for the last few years they have been all the rage, and I have been trying to think of something to cut them out. In the monk's garden I have found I think a combination that will do. It consists of chickory, French marigolds and seed onions. I am persuaded that as fine a melancholy may be seen among these as any other vegetables . . . in the world; no one hitherto has *felt* the poetry of seed onions.[76]

Butler took a satiric view not only of individual painters, paintings, and styles, but also of the art establishment and its 'hoodwinking' of the public. He fused his attack on art school training with his attack on the fleecing of the public in a note of an idea for *Erewhon Revisited*:

An art-class in which the first thing insisted on is that the pupils should know the price of all the leading modern pictures that have been sold during the last twenty years at Christie's, and the fluctuations in their values. Give an examination paper on this subject. The artist being a picture-dealer, the first thing he must do is to know how to sell his pictures, and therefore how to adapt them to the market. What is the use of being able to paint a picture unless one can sell it when one has painted it?[77]

The public might be fleeced intellectually as well as financially by the pastors and masters of art:

Jones knew an old lady who said she had been to Venice and seen St. Mark's. It was so beautiful. 'It is made of all the different kinds of architecture; there's Bissentine, and Elizabethan and Gothic, and perpendicular, and all the different kinds and Mr. Ruskin says it's lovely.'[78]

The art establishment, moreover, went in for what Butler called 'art-bullying' in order to buoy up the value of contemporary art. He drew attention to a specimen of it: a letter to the *Pall Mall Gazette* from three Slade professors exerting their combined authority to belabour the magazine for its criticism of Burne-Jones, in particular his

Annunciation, exhibited that year at the Grosvenor Gallery, and pronouncing the works, especially the *Annunciation*, 'of the very highest order both of imaginative and technical power, and such as not only do honour to the English school of painting, but would have done honour to any school at any period of history.'[79] Elsewhere he denounced 'the aesthetic reign of terror' that prevented one having or voicing unconventional views.

His attacks were not confined to passing savageries on topical matters, but took a profounder form in *Erewhon*, where the function of art in society is given extended discussion, especially in the chapter 'Views concerning Death'. Like the rest of his writings on art, it has received less comment than his insights into religion and technology, or his ingenious reversal of sin and disease. The grotesque statues which guard the borders of Erewhon and represent the early myths had given way to the self-regarding public statuary or 'stuffed men and women' that became a glut on the market and an obstruction to traffic, and were done away with (like machines) in two waves of iconoclasm. The present system was the enlightened one of breaking up all statues of public persons after fifty years, unless a jury of twenty-four citizens taken at random from the streets were to pronounce it worthy of a second fifty.

Perhaps a simpler plan would have been to forbid the erection of a statue to any public man or woman till he or she had been dead at least one hundred years, and even then to insist on reconsideration of the merit of the statue every fifty years . . .[80]

But in fact the system works well because knowing that the statues will be destroyed discourages people from ordering them, and the custom arises of paying the sculptor to desist from making them: thus 'the tribute of respect is paid to the dead, the public sculptors are not mulcted, and the rest of the public suffered no inconvenience.' His point is again a plea for the sweeping away of the mediocre public patronage of the past to make space for innovation and a new birth of art. There are deeper-lying concerns as well, about the nature of representation, posthumous reputation, and life after death.

Butler's satiric attack on the institutions of the art world was the latest in a long tradition of English attacks on 'academies', from Swift, Addison, and Dr Johnson and which, more recently, in the hands of the Romantics, had focused on the Royal Academy and its first president, Sir Joshua Reynolds. Whereas Walpole's *Anecdotes* had been animated by the hope that Hogarth could be seen not only as the first English painter but as founder of a line of succession leading to Reynolds and the Academy, the later eighteenth century distinguished Hogarth from Reynolds to the latter's disadvantage (as Hogarth himself disavowed the Academy when it ceased to be an association of equals). If Blake's 'Marginalia on Reynolds's *Discourses*' is now the best known of these attacks, in Butler's time the major essays were Lamb's 'On the Genius and Character of Hogarth', Hazlitt's 'On the works of Hogarth – On the Grand and Familiar Style of Painting' in his *Lectures on the English Comic Writers* (1819), and Hazlitt's extensive *Encyclopedia Britannica* article on 'The Fine Arts' (1824). Lamb, bracketing Hogarth with Shakespeare, saw Hogarth as the major English artist, the comic artist of real life, to be set against the imported neo-classic 'High Art' of the Academy. Lamb made an extended comparison, important also in the development of the art of description of paintings, of Poussin's *Plague at Athens* and Hogarth's *Gin Lane*, giving the preference to the latter, and pointing out that 'the great Historical School' of Reynolds 'exclude Hogarth . . . as an artist of an inferior and vulgar class. Those persons seem to me to confound the painting of subjects in common or vulgar life with the being a vulgar artist.'[81] Hazlitt, entirely in accord with Lamb's championship of Hogarth (though not with his view of Poussin), amplified the attack on Reynolds's own painting, and eloquently depicted the decline of art brought about by the Italian and then by the French and English academies. If Italian art declined from the time of Domenichino and the Carracci brothers, the founders of the Bologna Academy (a theme echoed by Butler), it 'expired with Guido Reni'. Hazlitt continued:

There is not a single name to redeem its faded glory from utter oblivion. Yet this has not been owing to any want of Dilettanti and Della Cruscan Societies, of Academies of Florence, of Bologna, of Parma, and Pisa, of honorary members, and foreign correspondents, of pupils and teachers, professors and patrons, and the whole busy tribe of critics and connoisseurs. Art will not be constrained by mastery, but at sight of the formidable array proposed to receive it,
  'Spreads its light wings, and in a moment flies.'[82]

The view that the decline of art dated from the Carracci gave new satiric force to Hogarth's use of the baroque models of the Carracci for his low-life scenes, for example, in his use of Annibale Carracci's *Marriage of Bacchus and Ariadne* for his *Hudibras meets the Skimmington*.[83] The theme of the decline of art through the academies was taken up by Ruskin (in conjunction with the Pre-Raphaelite periodization which saw the Italian 'primitives' as the high point), and was given a new turn by Butler who, as we shall see, developed the case for the comic tradition through Hogarth in his own way.

The 'naive' style: *Family Prayers*

Butler's own view of how disastrous his academic training had been is borne out by the fact that one of his first paintings on his return from New Zealand in 1864 was *Family Prayers* (illus. 29). This painting is in an entirely different style from *Mr Heatherley's Holiday*, and forms the basis for his own sense that his true direction as a painter lay quite elsewhere, in a naive or 'primitive' style. Inscribed at the top in pencil by Butler is the telling statement: 'I did this in 1864 and if I had gone on doing things out of my own head instead of making studies, I should have been all right.' This direction was confirmed in a few other works, and recognized in the exhibition of his work held in New Zealand in 1972 in which his work was linked with 'New Zealand Primitivism'. It was also confirmed in important ways that have never been pointed out by his gradually developing view of the nature of the superiority of the 'primitives' of the early Italian Renaissance, by the terms of his con-demnation of the decadence of art in his own time, and by his attempts to foster 'natural' artists and to forward the reform of art training from childhood, a reform which took place on the Continent in his own lifetime but in England only in the 1920s.

Family Prayers strikingly represents that major motif of Butler's art and experience, the grim tensions of family devotions. Behind this depicted scene again lies a narrative, this time a literary narrative from *The Way of All Flesh* itself. In Chapter 22 of the novel young Ernest Pontifex is beaten by his father, Theobald, Canon Pontifex – a scene that immediately precedes family prayers. The passage that bears on the painting deserves quotation in full. One should note that it is the children's artistic inclinations in particular which are being stifled in this scene, first their wish to use their paintbox and then their love of music. The narrator is visiting the Pontifex family:

I was there on a Sunday, and observed the rigour with which the young people were taught to observe the Sabbath; they might not cut out things, nor use their paint-box on a Sunday, and this they thought rather hard, because their cousins the John Pontifexes might do these things. Their cousins might play with their toy train on a Sunday, but though they had promised they would run none but Sunday trains, all traffic had been prohibited. One treat only was allowed them – on Sunday evenings they might choose their own hymns.

In the course of the evening they came into the drawing-room, and, as an especial treat, were to sing some of their hymns to me, instead of saying them, so that I might hear how nicely they sang. Ernest was to choose the first hymn, and he chose one about some people who were to come to the sunset tree. I am no botanist, and do now know what kind of tree a sunset tree is, but the words began, 'Come, come, come; come to the sunset tree for the day is past and gone.' The tune was rather pretty and had taken Ernest's fancy, for he was unusually fond of music and had a sweet little child's voice which he liked using.

He was, however, very late in being able to sound a hard 'c' or 'k', and, instead of saying 'Come,' he said 'Tum, tum, tum.'

'Ernest,' said Theobald, from the arm-chair in front of the fire where he was sitting with his hands folded before him, 'don't you think it would be nice if you were to say "come" like other people, instead of "tum"?'

'I do say tum,' replied Ernest, meaning that he had said 'come'.

Theobald was always in a bad temper on Sunday evening. Whether it is that they are as much bored with the day as their neighbours, or whether they are tired, or whatever the cause may be, clergymen are seldom at their best on Sunday evening; I had already seen signs that evening that my host was cross, and was a little nervous at hearing Ernest say so promptly 'I do say tum,' when his papa had said he did not say it as he should.

Theobald noticed the fact that he was being contradicted in a moment. He got up from his arm-chair and went to the piano.

'No, Ernest, you don't,' he said, 'you say nothing of the kind, you say "tum," not "come." Now say "come" after me, as I do.'

'Tum,' said Ernest, at once, 'Is that better?' I have no doubt he thought it was, but it was not.

'Now, Ernest, you are not taking pains: you are not trying as you ought to do. It is high time you learned to say "come," why, Joey can say "come," can't you, Joey?'

'Yeth, I can,' replied Joey, and he said something which was not far off 'come.'

'There, Ernest, do you hear that? There's no difficulty about it, nor shadow of difficulty. Now, take your own time, think about it, and say "come" after me.'

The boy remained silent for a few seconds and then said 'tum' again.

I laughed, but Theobald turned to me impatiently and said, 'Please do not laugh, Overton; it will make the boy think it does not matter, and it matters a great deal;' and then turning to Ernest, he said, 'Now, Ernest. I will give you one more chance, and if you don't say "come," I shall know that you are self-willed and naughty.'

He looked very angry, and a shade came over Ernest's face, like that which comes upon the face of a puppy when it is being scolded without understanding why. The child saw well what was coming now, was frightened, and, of course, said 'tum' once more.

'Very well, Ernest,' said his father, catching him angrily by the shoulder, 'I have done my best to save you, but if you will have it so, you will,' and he lugged the little wretch, crying by anticipation, out of the room. A few minutes more and we could hear screams coming from the dining-room, across the hall which separated the drawing-room from the dining-room, and knew that poor Ernest was being beaten.

'I have sent him to bed,' said Theobald, as he returned to the drawing-room, 'and now, Christina, I think we will have the servants in to prayers,' and he rang the bell for them, red-handed as he was.[84]

The painting, then, shows the scene immediately following the above passage: the family prayers described in Chapter 23. In the novel eight people are present: father, mother, narrator (Overton), and five servants (mother's maid, the cook, the housemaid, the man-servant William, and the coachman). The order of their entrance is described but not the seating arrangements. In the painting there are nine people, the father reading at one end of the table, then a row of figures corresponding to the three female servants (in caps) and the two male servants, and in the left-hand corner the mother, bolt upright in a stiff-backed chair. Behind the father is a figure looking ill at ease, staring straight forward out of the picture, who might correspond to the narrator. To the far right, also a little out of the family circle, is another female figure in a more comfortable chair.

In the novel, the narrator watches the faces of the servants as a chapter of the Bible is read out: 'They were nice people, but more absolute vacancy I never saw upon the countenances of human beings.'[85] In the painting he is not in a position to see their faces. The father reads from the fifteenth chapter of Numbers, which Butler gives in full: it is the passage where Jehovah calls on the people of Israel to keep the Sabbath, and a man caught gathering sticks is stoned to death. The narrator comments that 'the spirit that breathed throughout the whole seemed to me to be so like that of Theobald himself that I could understand better after hearing it, how he came to think as he thought, and act as he acted'. The sentence after this in Butler's manuscript was cut by the first editor, as too strong: 'How is it, I wonder, that all religious officials from God the Father to the parish beadle shall be so arbitrary and exacting?'[86]

In the painting, then, the patriarchal rule, the silent terror, the hypocritical primness, and the necessary stoicism which these methods were aimed at producing are depicted. It is the 'spirit that breathed through the whole', the punishing, blighting spirit of narrowness that is shown in the act of transfixing the figures in their stiff poses. Each of the character's sightline avoids all the others, giving the strange sense of disconnection to the group picture.

The scene in the novel, while it helps to explicate the painting, differs considerably from it. Indeed, the painting was completed in 1864, well before the novel was begun (in 1873), and it cannot be considered a dramatization of the scene. Jones, with his penchant for the directly anecdotal, misleads the unwary reader again. The novel carefully differentiates between the characters – Theobald, the servants, the mother, Christina (who is 'a little ashamed of the transaction to which I had been a witness', that is, the beating of Ernest, but goes on after the prayers to try to justify it), and Overton himself, who is both appalled and bored, and retails his methods of passing the time and diverting his attention during the prayer. Moreover, there is another, female figure in the painting who is not in the chapter in the book; she, like the narrator, is not within the circle round the table, and may represent the kind aunt who also opts out of the patriarchal system. Alethea Pontifex later in the novel befriends Ernest, but is not present in the scene of family prayers. The painting does not attempt this kind of characterological differentiation. It is rather as if the picture had caught and summed up the blighting freezing spirit of patriarchal religion which the novel then sought to show in its detailed development. The isolation, the different direction of the gaze of each character, is striking in the painting. There is no family, no community, here. The servants and the wife are simply subject to an unjust exercise of power. Whereas in earlier paintings in which the Bible is read, the Book has central power and significance – for example, in Nicolas Maes's *La Lecture*, portraying an old woman reading, the Bible suggests permanence and immortality over against the poor scrap of mortal flesh, and yet achieves it for her more powerfully than the art of the classical bust achieves it for the goddess on the shelf; or in Greuze's *Un père de famille qui lit la Bible à ses enfants* it conveys the power of authentic absorption in the Word for the unification, binding and 'harmonie' of the family group – in *Family Prayers* the Book marks merely the oblique direction of the father's solitary gaze away from the group.[87] The lack of light in Butler's painting becomes an incisive comment. The general sense in which the father is 'red-handed' is caught and memorialized in the painting, rather than the actual scene of the family prayers as described in the novel, or the narrative that lies behind it.

The novel nevertheless employs in its own way a number of visual elements and direct allusions to paintings and painters. The décor of the novel is not the same as that of the painting: the narrator stares minutely at the pattern of the drawing-room paper (bunches of red and white roses) in perhaps the best passage of the scene. In the painting the wall is

21. *Sketch of his own Head*, 1878

22. *Self-portrait, c.* 1873

23. *Self-portrait, 1866*

24. *Portrait of an Unidentified Woman, c.* 1873

25. Two Heads after Bellini, 1866

26. *Portrait of Thomas Cass, 1868*

27. *Portrait of John Marshman, 1866*

28. *Portrait of Alfred Cathie, 1898*

29. *Family Prayers*, 1864

30. *The Christening at Fobello, 1871*

31. *The Christening at Fobello, 1871*

32. *Mr Heatherley's Holiday, 1873*

simply green, a shade of green often used by Butler. The description of the pattern, and the bees attracted to it, catches the general feeling of the occasion (rather than this specific occasion only):

The drawing-room paper was of a pattern which consisted of bunches of red and white roses, and I saw several bees at different times fly up to these bunches and try them, under the impression that they were real flowers; having tried one bunch, they tried the next, and the next, and the next, till they reached the one that was nearest the ceiling, then they went down bunch by bunch as they had ascended, till they were stopped by the back of the sofa; on this they ascended bunch by bunch to the ceiling again; and so on, and so on till I was tired of watching them. As I thought of the family prayers being repeated night and morning, week by week, month by month, and year by year, I could not help thinking how like it was to the way in which the bees went up the wall and down the wall, bunch by bunch, without ever suspecting that so many of the associated ideas could be present, and yet the main idea be wanting hopelessly, and for ever.[88]

Thus the feeling is compounded of the mortal terror instilled by the threat and actuality of punishment in Scripture as in the life based on it, and the vacancy of mind of the listeners during a tedious repeated recitation in which 'the main idea' – sustenance – is lacking. This passage is probably itself an allusion to the classic case of the ancient painter Zeuxis who was noted for painting such realistic grapes that they attracted the birds: but the grapes, the flowers are in fact useless, inedible, sapless. Butler often expressed this distaste for sheer technique, 'finish'; thus in Rembrandt's *Esther, Haman and Ahasuerus* 'everything [was] subordinated to splendid slogging of a yellow dress'.[89]

The novel also specifies some of the paintings on the wall (which hung at Langar Rectory): 'The Carlo Dolci and the Sassoferrato looked down upon a sea of upturned backs, as we buried our faces in our chairs.' Dolci is undoubtedly short-hand for a vicious principle of painting: as Ruskin had put it, 'Some artists finish for the finish' sake'.[90] The last sentence in the chapter is also a reference to painting, though not to any of those hanging on the drawing room walls: 'All things must be crossed a little or they would cease to live – but holy things, such, for example, as Giovanni Bellini's saints, have been crossed with nothing but what is good of its kind.' The use of Bellini as a touchstone is frequent in Butler as in Ruskin.

The novel can thus be used to explicate the painting; but it would be more accurate to say the novel explicates the painting. The painting came, as Butler said, out of his own head in 1864; the novel was begun only in 1873. It too came from his own head; but the picture, supplying the epitome of his feelings about the family, was already there. The novel has its origin in Butler's visual memory. *The Way of All Flesh* is one of the most highly elaborate and original examples of ekphrasis we have.

Family Prayers has been called 'one of the few genuine naive paintings of the time', by Graham Reynolds, who sets Butler among the painters of the contemporary domestic scene, a mode encouraged by early Pre-Raphaelite book illustration, but in contrast to those who falsified, sentimentalized, and melodramatized it:

These paintings of the fifties to the seventies, and especially those made under Pre-Raphaelite influence, take us intimately into the ways of Victorian life. The dominant institution of the family is the theme of many of them. It is shown as a cheerful, happy entity by Hayllar [*A Family Group*]; and united in a festive occasion in Frith's *Many Happy Returns of the Day*. . . . But already there were men and women who suffered from the possessive restrictions imposed by family life. Samuel Butler's novel *The Way of all Flesh* summed up the views of all those who felt the cruelty, insensitivity and possessiveness inherent in Victorian family life. In one of the few genuine naive paintings of the time he has expressed a part of the same criticism in *Family Prayers*.[91]

Reynolds has underlined his affirmative view of Butler's contribution to naive painting in a note on the artist: 'As well as being one of the comparatively few worthy naive paintings of the English school, this is a pictorial expression of Butler's unending warfare against the narrow and cruel hypocrisy of Victorian family life.'[92]

There is, however, a world of difference between the Victorian 'painting of scenes of contemporary life' and the genuine 'naive' painting which Reynolds does nothing to explicate. In books on English naive painting, Butler does not appear. Undoubtedly, he fell between two stools: as a highly educated product of the upper middle classes, who also received an academic art training, he does not appear to qualify for inclusion among those 'naive painters' who were semi-professional sign painters, semi-literate or illiterate seamen, or wholly untrained amateurs. He could not be 'discovered' and patronized by other artists, as was 'Douanier' Rousseau in the 1890s or Alfred Wallis in the 1920s. He would not be eligible for admission to Dubuffet's striking collection of paintings by criminals and schizophrenics (among others), now hanging in a museum devoted to 'art brut' in Lausanne. He could not have gained a grant or been hung in the exhibition by the Arts Council of 'outsiders: an art without precedent or tradition'. One might ask further whether a painting with such a complex literary reference – even when the literary work originated with himself and post-dated the painting –

could be classified as naive. Yet the classification 'naive painting' also includes work by artists who are not untrained, nor of inferior social origin, nor illiterate. The first artist to organize an exhibition of such paintings in England was Hogarth, whose concern with contemporary scenes, 'low life', social criticism, and satire brought his own work close to some aspects of naive painting. The occasion, an exhibition in 1762 of a fictitious 'Society of Sign Painters', set up as a satire on the exhibition of the Society of Arts in the Strand, would have pleased Butler well; as with some of his own work, the reviewers were uncertain as to whether it was serious, an 'insult to understanding', or a joke designed to raise mirth.[93] Well-known artists often executed work otherwise associated with the 'naive', whether sign paintings (Hogarth himself painted signs, like the elder Crome, Millais and others), animal paintings, or folk art; others painted deliberately in a naive style, like Dubuffet himself. The association of Hogarth with an alternative tradition of the naive artist is a significant aspect of his reputation for the comic, the low-life, and the vulgar, and one that was vital for Butler. Often naive artists were championed, as Alfred Jarry championed Rousseau, by an avant-garde who used the style to lash convention and academic canons and to recommend an 'alternative art'. Some 'naive artists' have been promoted over time: 'mad' Blake began as a naive poet and painter, until he was taken up by Rossetti, lauded as a 'symbolist' by Yeats, and permitted in the twentieth century to enter the company of the Romantics proper. Butler was ahead of his day in regarding Blake as within the major Romantic tradition (a reason for holding him at bay). Blake's pictorial work, like that of more than one unchallengeably 'naive' painter, Adolf Wölfli, for example, whose paintings are closely linked to his extensive fantastic autobiography inscribed on the backs of his drawings, is associated in an intricate manner with his literary output.[94]

Butler's painting came 'out of my own head', not from studies, he said, out of his own visual memory of an experience that compacted into it an entire autobiography; this epitomizing inward visual faculty is an important characteristic of much naive art. As one critic has said of naive artists, they 'draw the important truths of the mind's eye rather than the details of observed fact'.[95] As Alfred Wallis wrote: 'what I do mosley is what use to To Bee out of my own memery what we may never see again.' Butler's 'out of my own head' is in striking contrast to his training in exact 'studies', whether of 'High Art' or, as recommended by Ruskin and the Pre-Raphaelites, of 'Nature'.

In one of the longest art notes from his early period, 'Relative Importances', Butler attempts a solution. He makes a positive assessment of 'impressionism', defined in such a way as to yield criteria for all good art (and literature) of whatever period, rather than to denominate a contemporary 'school':

It is the painter's business to help memory and imagination, not to supersede them. . . . His business is to supply those details which will most readily bring the whole before the mind along with them. He must not give too few but it is still more imperative on him not to give too many. . . .

He therefore tells best in painting, as in literature, who has best estimated the relative values or importances of the more special features characterizing his subject: this is to say, who . . . is at most pains to give those only that will say most in the fewest words, or touches. . . .

The difficulties of doing are serious enough . . . ; these however are small as compared with those of knowing what not to do – with learning to disregard the incessant importunity of small nobody details that persist in trying to thrust themselves above their betters. . . .

. . . When we look at a very highly finished picture (so called) unless we are in the hands of one who has attended successfully to the considerations insisted on above, we feel as though we were with a troublesome cicerone who will not let us look at things with our own eyes, but keeps intruding himself at every touch and turn, and trying to exercise that undue influence upon us which generally proves to have been the accompaniment of concealment and fraud. This is exactly what we feel in regard to Van Mieris and, though in a less degree, with Gerard Dow – whereas with Jean Van Eyck and Metsu, no matter how far they may have gone, we find them essentially as impressionist as Rembrandt or Velasquez.

For impressionism only means that due attention has been paid to the relative importances of the impressions made by the various characteristics of a given subject, and that they have been presented to us in order of precedence.[96]

'Impressionism', then, is in one sense simply the most economic employment of means for ends; but in another it is a writ of reduction or 'tersifying', even of minimalism, of ordered openness, non-academic, unobtrusive. It dictates no one particular style or technique (and we may read this as a deflation of the claims of the 'Impressionists' to be a school); it applies to literature as well as to painting.[97] Yet this view of 'impressionism', while in line with the critique of 'finish' for its own sake (as in Ruskin's defence of Turner, and in his doubts about the Pre-Raphaelites' 'habit of carrying everything up to the utmost point of completion',[98] and as in Baudelaire's defence of Corot in the 1846 Salon), resolves the conflict for the practising artist between 'studies' and 'out of one's own head' only at a verbal level.

The conflict is again strikingly expressed in another early art note on modes of seeing, 'Eyesight Wild and Tame':

If a man has not studied painting or at any rate black and white drawing, his eyes are wild; to learn to draw in light and shade tames them. The first step towards taming the eyes is to teach them not to see too much. Nothing tends so much to oversight as overseeing. Half close the eyes, or look through black crape. By seeing with the half we know what we can best dispense with.[99]

While ostensibly in favour of training, the whole tone of this passage expresses an underlying regret for the loss of the 'wild eyesight', and the tamed eye, the mere 'half' eye, is dressed in funereal black crape. Also a shaft directed at the excessive detail of 'studies', it opens the way for his later development of the idea of 'the ignorant eye', which will shed the training in seeing and valuing imposed on it by 'aesthetic terrorism' and find its own way to the naive. Thus the element of reduction is retained as essential to a new form of training which restores the wild eyesight.

Some of Butler's self-portraits also belong with the group of early 'naive' paintings, and show reduction as a technical possibility: they portray the young man's head in stark terms, with bold, flat masses of colour and little detail (illus. 22, 23). They are marked by the influence of the early calotypes, which encouraged the use of broad, flat, contrasting masses.[100] These early works are much more striking than his oil portraits in general, and bear out his later sense of having been misdirected. His direction lay in the exploration of the diverse forms of the naive and primitive latent in the terms and techniques of his time, which he would do much to explicate in his own criticism.

The Crisis: the 'Advertisement painting'

The crisis over the 'Advertisement painting' was the inward turning-point in Butler's career as a painter. Whatever the pressures of external developments in the art world, they were not the decisive factor. It is clear that he found it difficult to make ends meet as a painter; nevertheless, he turned down opportunities to take up commissions that did not please him. He preferred to please himself, to write – and these years are punctuated with his writings, from *Erewhon* (1870), to *The Fair Haven* (1873) and *Life and Habit* (1877), which took crucial time and energy in the years of withdrawal – and to live off his income and various business enterprises generated by it, rather than to accept work as an artist of a kind that held no interest. For example, he commented in 1901 on a letter from Miss Savage of 1875 urging him to take on work, painting panels for Gillow's – 'There are two very pretty ones in a shop round the corner': 'I called on Gillow's people, and found that the decorative panels they wanted were just of a kind that I did not see my way to do.'[101] He thus rejected commercial employment as an artist (later blaming his training again as impractical). At the same time Miss Savage told him that he might be employed 'if so disposed' by C. F. A. Voysey, the architect and designer associated with the Aesthetic Movement, on writing in his new magazine, but she hopes he will not as she detests Voysey; although Butler met him several times nothing came of it. He continued in this course even when it led to increased conflict with his father, which came to a head in 1879 when after some losses in his Canadian investments his father learned that he had run into debt through his support of Pauli. Butler responded only to an inner urgency, and often this called upon him against his will to do something other than painting:

I did not want to write *Erewhon*, I wanted to go on painting and found it an abominable nuisance being dragged willy-nilly into writing it. So with all my books – the subjects were never of my own choosing; they pressed themselves upon me with more force than I could resist.[102]

The 'Advertisement picture' was one that pressed itself upon him. In February 1877 he reported to Miss Savage that he had finished one hundred pages of *Life and Habit*, and at the same time he was working on the new painting:

I am also at work on my advertisement picture. I was three mornings studying in the street itself from 8 to 9, and shall do so again this week. I have also got on with the water colour at Thames Ditton.[103]

A later note supplies a 'narrative' title and describes the subject:

The advertisement picture was called 'The last days of Carey Street', and was simply the hoarding covered with advertisements and the Tower of St. Clement Danes – before the Law courts were begun.[104]

In March he invites Miss Savage to see the finished painting, describing it in more detail, adding that he has 'not written a line lately, and shall not till after the Academy':

I have made 'The Messiah' the central advertisement – between 'Nabob Pickles' and 'Three millions of money' – with 'The Messiah' much smaller than 'Mr. Sims Reeves, and Signor Foli'. It does not seem in the least pointed, and of course I copied the advt. from nature.[105]

Miss Savage replied that she could not come immediately but was sure she would 'see it in all its glory at the Academy'.[106] Apparently by the next week she had seen it in his studio, and had some reservations:

I have been thinking about your picture since I saw you; don't you think the figures are too much in a line? And I am still of the same mind about the blue which is always an obtrusive colour.[107]

His 1901 note recalls bitterly:

It was rejected for the Academy – the figures were bad. I painted much of it out when I got it back – got it into a thorough mess, and in the end gave it to Gogin, who I trust may have destroyed it.[108]

It seems clear from these descriptions that Butler was working with a subject that still had a link to contemporary genre painting, and that he was making painstaking studies rather than working 'out of my own head'; yet the scene is an emptied one, a demolished urban street with only the disembodied tower as a reminder of the past, and the whole overwritten with advertising graphics.[109] This has a prophetic note to it. It combines intensity of detail with intensity of a vision of nothingness; it could not be carried out by the traditional means of oil painting he was employing, but demanded the new graphics or photography. This was a modern equivalent of the naive sign-painters' art of Hogarth. 'An advertisement from nature' sums up the impossibility of the enterprise, and brings to a head the conflict between 'studies' – whether from the cast or from nature – and the inner eye. The anguish of his last, obsessed notes on it not long before his death shows that his failure to bring off this experiment in paint had the ring of finality for him. It called out a litany of exculpations and an explicit, despairing justification of his life in terms of his literary work:

As regards this picture – which it grieves me even to think of – I ought to have known that it was no good – and I did know, but was too jaded even to admit it to myself. What with Pauli, whom I believed to be even more in difficulties than myself, and who let me share with him down to the dregs of the capital which I was now eating (nay, he had the lion's share – I have written this story elsewhere so say no more.)[110] What with seeing ruin approaching, and finding both literature and painting to be broken reeds so far as selling was concerned; – what with the relations between myself and my father, and the really great anxiety that Life and Habit was to me, I was not myself – and though I could write I could not paint. Yet if I had been contented with simple water colour subjects, each drawing to take a fortnight's work, instead of fagging at an ambitious picture for months – I might have done fairly well – but after all I suppose the truth was that I felt literature to be a more tempting field, and one better worth trying to excel in than painting. Nor, in spite of the very great distress and difficulties of the years 1877–1886, do I think I was mistaken. I do not think that anything I could have done as a painter could have been as well worth doing as what I have done as a writer. So *finis coronat opus*. All's well that ends well. S. B., September 13th, 1901.[111]

Yet this crisis was not the end of the story of the 'Advertisement picture'. A number of his later photographs took up this theme, among them one of his best, with the title *Blind Man reading the Bible* (illus. 107), which sums up and fixes the paradox of the void with superimposed hieroglyphics. Moreover, the theme is invested in one of his finest pieces of comic word-painting. This vanished, botched painting epitomized his naive style at its most intense and obsessive, and enacted in his own terms the 'crisis of representation'.

After this turning-point, his own painting – which he by no means abandoned – became increasingly bound up with his travels and his art-historical researches in Italy. His search for the true primitive led him back to its sources. The richness and complexity of the literary context increased, as the circularity of his self-reference became fuller. The incorporation of his pictorial work into the text *Alps and Sanctuaries* (1881) in effect recognized this interdependence, although he certainly still cherished more ambitious plans for his painting. Butler held that book and periodical illustration was the one exception to the low standard of art, and most observers would now agree with him. The interdependence of literature and art here found its most natural and unforced expression; styles that failed to convince when projected onto lavish oil canvases worked on a more modest scale. The Pre-Raphaelites' wood-engravings (based on drawings) for Moxon's Tennyson (1857), especially Holman Hunt's *Lady of Shalott*, and Millais's illustrations for Trollope's novel *Orley Farm* were among their most successful works. Samuel Palmer's last etchings (1872), for his *English Version of the Eclogues of Virgil*, are among the finest works of the second half-century; the old Romantic living on into a new period produced the best of its Hellenism. Butler thought the best his period had to offer was the black and white magazine illustrations, of the type found in *Punch* – which had indeed published Thackeray, John Leech, Douglas Jerrold, and now with George Du Maurier led the attack against the Aesthetes (who naturally held that *Punch* had deteriorated). His friend Gogin

C · G

"Err.....er.....you're a Colonial bishop, I suppose."

33. Charles Gogin, *The Pan-Anglican Synod*, 1888

published cartoons, one of which, from *The Universal Review*, Butler preserved among his favourites (illus. 33). To sweep aside the art of the time in favour of the cartoon, of course, was to oppose the view not only of the Academy but of Wilde in 'The English Renaissance of Art' (1881). Yet the current cartoon was not so remote from the early Pre-Raphaelites as might appear; as Gombrich has said, 'the cartoon is the heir to the symbolic art of the Middle Ages, at a time when the didactic image was intended by the Church to teach the illiterate layman the sacred word.'[112] These techniques were gradually applied to secular wisdom in proverb illustrations and satirical prints. Butler's imagination specialized in such surprising leaps and apt juxtapositions.

Butler's integration of his own literary text and his pictorial illustration made the best use of his drawings and not surprisingly produced the most richly complex and oblique reverberation between text and picture – a reverberation which was in any case (as we have seen) a feature of his work even when overlaid by the simplistic anecdotalism of the commentators, or left void by the complete lack of comment. Most of his Italian paintings, whether landscapes, townscapes, the rare figure painting, are, moreover, closely related to his book illustrations. Technical limitations and the need to finance his own books led to restrictions on the quality of the reproduction; reference to his oil and watercolour works and his drawings (and to his photographs) can enrich the context of our reading of *Alps and Sanctuaries*, *Ex Voto*, and the substantial though unfinished *Verdi Prati*.

The Slade Professorship and essays in art criticism

In 1886 Butler applied for the Slade Professorship of Fine Art at Cambridge, on the resignation of Sidney Colvin. This had been seen by some merely as another gesture by the *enfant terrible*, but Butler may well have wished to draw attention to the serious intentions of his *Alps and Sanctuaries*.[113] He had, moreover, been working on his great favourite, Giovanni Bellini, having spent two summers in the museums of Northern Italy, and published 'Portraits of Gentile and Giovanni Bellini' in *The Athenaeum* (20 February 1886), attempting to reaffirm the traditional attribution to Gentile (sometimes to Giovanni) of the Louvre portrait of Bellini and his brother, then newly attributed by Crowe and Cavalcaselle (1871) to Cariani.[114] Between 1887 and 1914 the Louvre attributed the painting to Gentile Bellini, but denied that it represented the painter and his brother, as tradition maintained. But in 1924 the picture was called *Portraits d'hommes* and attributed to Cariani. The most recent Louvre catalogue (1983) repeats this attribution, but there is no agreement, even within the Louvre.[115] In any case, the current attribution cannot be our yardstick, for, as Francis Haskell has said, 'that is to make the (unprovable) assumption that today's connoisseurs must themselves be correct'.[116] Nevertheless, this is a case where Butler employed the weapons of scientific art criticism against connoisseurship, which he saw as typified by Crowe and Cavalcaselle's novel attribution on the basis of Cariani's 'melting and coloured tinting' alone.[117] There was and is no documentary evidence which could resolve the matter, and on these grounds the major authorities on Cariani today agree with Butler that there is no reason to assign it to Cariani rather than to Bellini.[118]

His letter to the electors gives his sense of his qualifications at the time:

I have the honour to offer myself as a Candidate for the Slade Professorship of Fine Art.

I took my degree in 1858, being bracketed 12th in the first class of the classical tripos.

I have studied painting for many years, and have exhibited on several occasions at the Royal Academy exhibitions. I am also well versed in the histories and methods of the various European Schools of painting, past and present.

Of late years, as the list of works herewith printed will show, I have given more time to literature, music and science than to painting pictures. I have, nevertheless, throughout continued to give my undivided attention, in the summer months, to painting from nature, and to the examination of foreign galleries.

During the last twenty years I have collected a large number of art notes, critical and historical, and should be very glad to find a motive for bringing them together, and a field for their employment.[119]

The other candidates were Harry Quilter (1851–1907), art critic for *The Spectator* and *The Times*, and J. H. Middleton, who had just published a book on Roman antiquities, *Ancient Rome* (1885), which had been well received. Middleton was the successful candidate. Butler was hardly surprised at not being selected; he wrote to his father, 'I have seen his book, and it is everything which is most grateful to the Academic mind – long, learned, dry, and handsomely got up.'[120] As he said on another occasion, 'we cannot expect a University Swell to know anything about art or music.' But the unsuccessful candidature led to his friendship with Quilter, and when Quilter launched *The Universal Review* in 1888, publishing his own substantial reviews of the French Salons and the exhibitions of the Royal Academy, Butler published nine articles, five of them on topics in art and art history, during the two years of its life. Most carry his own illustrations, mainly photographs; *The Universal Review* was lavishly illustrated with contemporary (and past) art.[121] Moreover, we know that he was gathering materials for *Ex Voto*. He found 'a field for their employment'.

In his later years, he often gave away his own paintings, scattering them broadcast as worthless. As he remarked, 'He is a great artist who can be depended on not to bark at nothing.'[122] Butler was certain that he was not a great artist; but he was determined 'not to bark at nothing'. The double negative, suggesting that by elimination there may be something to bark at after all, is characteristic. The process of elimination that would return him his 'wild eyesight' was to carry him very far afield, to the roots of European art.

65

34. *Primadengo, near Faido, c.* 1878

Resighting the Renaissance in Italy:
Alps and Sanctuaries, Ex Voto
and *Verdi Prati*

———

Alps and Sanctuaries

Butler was one of the important English travellers abroad for whom Italy
was not just a segment of a grand tour, or a holiday ground, or a
provocation for 'Home Thoughts from Abroad' but was, as he put it, his
'second country'.[1] In 1843 he had visited Italy for the first time, one of his
few happy childhood memories; during the rest of his life it offered him a
counter-image to the family life he had experienced. He visited Italy
twice more in the 1850s, once while still at Shrewsbury (in 1853) for half
a year (still with his family), once (in 1857) with a Cambridge friend, so
that fresh memories of Italy mingled with his New Zealand experiences
in *A First Year* and *Erewhon*.[2] Later he doubted he could have survived
without his several months a year there, and after his father's death his
Italian sojourns grew longer. As Byron declared he was a 'meridional'
man, happier in Italy than at home, so Butler was in some respects
'*méditerranéen*', as a French critic has called him.[3] Miss Savage, in a
letter praising 'the cherry-eating scene' in 'your Italian book', *Alps and
Sanctuaries*, recalled the first time she had perceived his true value after
some years of acquaintance – had, we might say less discreetly, fallen in
love with him (or, we might, with Larbaud, compliment Miss Savage on
her resemblance to 'nos grandes dames libertines du XVIIIe siècle'):[4]

One day when I was going to the gallery, a very hot day, I remember, I met you on the
shady side of Berners Street, eating cherries out of a basket. Like your Italian friends
you were perfectly silent with content, and you handed the basket to me as I was
passing, without saying a word. I pulled out a handful, and went on my way rejoicing
without saying a word either. I had not before perceived you to be different from any
body else. I was like Peter Bell and the primrose with the yellow brim.[5]

Italy became an imaginative and spiritual home for Butler, not merely
a counter-image or a refuge. 'They are the quickest witted people in the
world, and at the same time have much more of the old Roman

steadiness than they are generally credited with. . . . They have all our strong points, but they have more grace and elasticity than we have', he declared.[6] Italy became the locus of his own conception of art, as it had for Winckelmann, whose personal revival of classical art was sympathetically recounted by Pater in the key chapter of *The Renaissance*, as the groundwork for Pater's conception of the aesthetic style, which Butler was to undermine through his own delineation of the Renaissance. The 'Italian Journey', which had in the hands of Goethe become a literary genre at the end of the eighteenth century, he was able to adapt to his own purposes as a vehicle for his conception of the art of the past as a critique of the present and a call for an art of the future. The combined travel and art guide to Italy, suffused with the sensibility and personal stance of the author, was also developed by Stendhal in *L'Histoire de la Peinture en Italie* (1817) and did much to establish the other arts as a central presence in French literature. Ruskin's *The Stones of Venice* (1851–3) marks the English appropriation of the form; in his hands it became a 'moral drama', which is assimilated and skilfully deflated by Butler.[7] The genre falls into conscious decay with Henry Adams's *Mont St Michel and Chartres* (1903), which recognizes the incapacity of the modern 'tourist' to whip himself up, by whatever exertions of his ponderous fancy, into an understanding of the spirit that produced the great religious art of the past. The genre nevertheless takes a new lease of life, most notably in English in the hands of D. H. Lawrence, another writer-painter, whose *Twilight in Italy* (1913) owes much to Butler. Lawrence, walking from Germany to Lake Garda, catches Butler's combination of alp and lake, sanctuary and theatre, north and south, art and the community and, although without illustrations, *Twilight in Italy* produces word pictures close to his own paintings as, for example, in 'Italians in Exile' Lawrence describes the light and shadow, 'a pale luminousness, a sort of gleam among all the ruddy glow' of the group of displaced Italian anarchists rehearsing a play, and their doomed communality.[8] Lawrence's reworking brings out much in Butler that remains partly masked to the casual reader. In a recent reprint of Lawrence's three Italian travel books, the editor notes their debts to Ruskin's 'purple' prose and Pater's 'greenery-yallery' prose, but praises Lawrence for his colloquial language and 'low life' portraits as if they were all his own: the crucial forgotten intermediary here is Butler.[9] In this genre, whatever the particular proportions of history and art-guide, in the guise of personal travels, a world view is implied, and an archetypal cultural history is conveyed through encounters with land-scape, works of art, and individuals – past and present, real and imaginary.

Butler spent several months of each year in Italy and southern Switzerland, more precisely in the Ticino, the Piedmont and Lombardy, returning often to the same places. He formulated through his experiences there not only an *oeuvre* of sketches, drawings, watercolours and oil paintings, but also a distinctive view of the nature of the Renaissance. He put a case for a version of it that deserves to be placed in the context of the series of major statements of the nineteenth century on the Renaissance: those of the cultural historians Michelet, Ruskin, Heine, Arnold, Burckhardt, Symonds, and Pater; and those of critics who specifically dealt with the discovery or reassessment of the practitioners of the Renaissance in painting and sculpture, such as Pater on Giorgione and Botticelli; and those of the nineteenth-century artists who attempted their own reassessments through their own practice. More precisely, he represents a major phase in a 'historical cycle of discourse' which owing to his neglect has been thought absent from England.[10] He put his views in two major books of art criticism, in a substantial fragment of a third, and in periodical articles, essays, letters, and extensive notes, some still unpublished, and through his own illustrations. This body of work carried an assessment of art in Italy that broke new ground, and opened the way to the revaluation of a neglected group of artists and works. In European sources he figures as a pioneer. Butler's is a major example of 'canon-making' in the sense given it by Frank Kermode in his account of the 'discovery' and reassessment of Botticelli by Pater, Warburg, and Horne.[11] Butler drew attention not only to neglected artists and works, Gaudenzio Ferrari in particular, but also to a neglected region of Northern Italy, and to a form and a way of seeing: the Sacro Monte. At the same time, he ironized the myth of periodization itself. Yet his views have received almost no attention whatever from English art historians or literary critics.

The notion of the Renaissance was itself fully formulated only in the nineteenth century, although the simpler notion of the *renascità* or rebirth of the classics originated with the humanists, and was formulated for painting by Vasari (1550). The Renaissance as a period embodying a 'spirit' is of a piece with the triumph of historicism. The precise description of the spirit of specially defined ages, each of which has made a unique contribution to the history of civilization, was an approach to human experience that was first adumbrated by Vico in the early eighteenth century, and was developed by Herder and the subsequent generations of philosophical historians. Like every other 'age', the Renaissance did not exist except by reference to a theory of the relation of historical periodization to a totalizing conception of 'civilisation', which if not linearly progressive was seen as making cumulative contributions to the richness of the achievement of the human race. It also depended, for its definition as an 'epoch' with an ending as well as a 'rebirth', on a network of interdependent assessments of other times and places, crucially those just before and just after it, in relation to contemporary needs.

Butler's particular interests, in certain regions, art forms, and artists in Italy, stand out in relief against this larger backdrop as a considered polemic. The Italy that takes shape for us in his writings, and as we follow him through *Alps and Sanctuaries*, at once a traveller's notebook and a guidebook, an essay on art, and an integral gallery of his own drawings (and those of his friends), is entirely distinct from the world of the Grand Tour of the traditional traveller in Italy since the late seventeenth century, and while it belongs at first sight with the travel literature of the first half of the nineteenth century, it suggests new ways of seeing uniquely arising from his view of the Renaissance. Two modes of seeing predominated: the 'sublime', developed through the eighteenth century and culminating in the Romantics, in which a solitary, stationary individual undergoes an intense experience or 'aesthetic moment' in the face of an overwhelmingly great nature; and the 'excursive', in which a traveller passes through a landscape, pressing it into a variety of services.[12] These were theorized by Kant's account of the sublime, which draws a distinction between the linear (and endless) counting of phenomena, and the capacity of the human mind to impose the idea of 'the whole' on the phenomena. It is the culminating, unifying capacity that Romantics sought to demonstrate. In the travel books of the 1830s, especially Rogers's *Italy*, with illustrations by Turner and Stothard, the excursive view of the traveller was given pictorial as well as prose form. Ruskin increasingly turned towards the 'counting', towards the 'science of aspects', a critical rather than a poetic view, interpreting Wordsworth's long poem of *The Excursion* (1814) in this sense.[13]

This shift towards the empirical rather than the transcendental interpretation of the sublime set for Ruskin and the Pre-Raphaelites one of their main unsolved problems: the impossibility of calling a halt to the

35. *The Washing-place, Varallo, 1892*

36. *Wassen*, 1901

37. *Chiavenna*, 1887

38. *Tengia, c.* 1880

representation of particulars. Butler calls attention to an intermediate stage in this process of the degeneration of the aesthetics of the sublime when he notes in his copy of Felix Mendelssohn-Bartholdy's *Letters from Italy and Switzerland* that Mendelssohn's pose of contemplating certain views and pictures 'for hours' – six hours on the Righi Culm, 'a couple of hours a day at least' for three pictures of Titian – is ridiculous.[14] He deploys this ironically in *Alps and Sanctuaries* (in what Miss Savage referred to appreciatively as his 'Essay on Lying')[15]:

As for knowing whether or not one likes a picture, which under the present aesthetic reign of terror is *de rigueur*, I once heard a man say the only test was to ask one's self whether one would care to look at it if one was quite sure that one was alone; I have never been able to get beyond this test with the St. Gothard scenery, and applying it to the Devil's Bridge, I should say a stay of about thirty seconds would be enough for me. I daresay Mendelssohn would have stayed at least two hours at the Devil's Bridge, but then he did stay such a long while before things.[16]

Ruskin, of course, ever under his own 'aesthetic reign of terror', also represented himself in the Mendelssohnian manner, as if sheer length of time of contemplation could substitute for the Kantian instantaneous vision of wholeness. One of Ruskin's diary entries from Switzerland captures the pathos of this, and its link with a further claim to special moral and religious heroism:

I stood long [in contemplation of the Jungfrau and the two Eigers], praying that these happy hours and holy sights might be of more use to me than they have been, and might be remembered by me in hours of temptation or mortification.[17]

Butler, on the contrary, went out of his way to admit his omissions and his ignorance, and the accidents of circumstance that kept him from taking time or seeing properly, and the narrow escapes from such omissions that every traveller knows: 'the frescoes are somewhat damaged, and the light is so bad that if the *guardiano* of the sanctuary had not kindly lent us a candle we could not have seen them.'[18] Butler was more prone to admit candidly to the ignorant eye than to boast of the 'innocent eye' of Ruskin. This candour – which strongly implies his reader too should drop his pretenses at once – was also embodied in the style of the descriptions themselves. As Miss Savage remarked, 'the scenery descriptions [are] just what they ought to be not elaborate but complete – a delightful contrast to the interminable 'word pictures', that have been the fashion lately'.[19]

The 'ignorant eye' was given an important role in Butler's evolutionary cultural history. In 'The Etruscan Urns at Volterra', a Notebook entry intended for the sequel to *Alps and Sanctuaries*, he offers an amusing and well-turned excuse based on the race's evolutionary need to repeat itself to obtain 'fixity of type' (and thus to be exceedingly dull) for having looked at only three urns and 'hurried over the remaining 397 as fast as I could'.[20] He pursued the idea of the 'ignorant eye' more seriously in two essays which argue that the only way to find out what we 'really like and dislike' (as opposed to what the aesthetic tyrants have told us we ought to like) is at first to assume complete ignorance in front of a picture.[21] Cultural evolution depends on this rare moment of break-away from the repetition of the 'pabulum of the mind'. Paradoxically then, the road to the acquisition of the consciously 'ignorant eye' and thence to knowledge of what we really like and dislike – which contains the germ of the future – may be a longer road than ever the *poseur* in rapt contemplation of the second-hand sublime would care to take.

Alps and Sanctuaries and especially *Ex Voto* suggest a new solution to the problematic of the ways of the eye in both their prose and pictorial form. *Alps and Sanctuaries* is not 'confined to any one journey, but contains a resumé of our wanderings in Piedmont, Lombardy, and the Canton Ticino'.[22] At first the terrain appears deceptively familiar: the crossing of the Alps plays a prominent role, as it always had done in the tracing of the route from England across Switzerland, described by hundreds of travellers in prose and poetry and epitomized as a visionary spot of time in Wordsworth's *Prelude*. Butler's *Alps* begins at Faido, just the other side of the St Gotthard Pass, one of 'the easiest places on the Italian side of the Alps to reach from England'. Butler, however, walks up from Faido passing through a number of villages (illus. 34, 39, 42) into the Val Piora, where he has a visionary experience that vies not only with Wordsworth but with Ruskin's word-painting on the Pass of Faido painted by Turner.[23] Well off the carriage road employed by Turner and Ruskin, he had an encounter with the spirit of the Renaissance:

The first night I was ever in Piora there was a brilliant moon, and the unruffled surface of the lake took the reflection of the mountains. I could see the cattle a mile off, and hear the tinkling of their bells which danced multitudinously before the ear as the fireflies come and go before the eyes; for all through a fine summer's night the cattle will feed as though it were day. A little above the lake I came upon a man in a cave before a furnace, burning lime, and he sat looking into the fire with his back to the moonlight. . . . So after a while I left him with his face burnished as with gold from the fire, and his back silver with the moonbeams; behind him were the pastures and the reflections in the lake and the mountains; and the distant cowbells were ringing.[24]

39. *Dalpe, c.* 1880

40. *Calonico Church, No* 1, 1881

41. *Calonico Church, No 2, 1881*

42. *Campo Santo at Campiognia, 1881*

He wandered on to the chapel of S Carlo (illustrated in the text just after the introduction of the crowd of young peasants who have come up for the annual hay-making),[25] and by the lake went into a 'doze' and thought 'the burnished man from the furnace came up beside me and laid his hand on my shoulder'.

Then I saw the green slopes that rise all round the lake were much higher than I had thought; they went up thousands of feet, and there were pine forests upon them, while two large glaciers came down in streams that ended in a precipice of ice, falling sheer into the lake. The edges of the mountains against the sky were rugged and full of clefts, through which I saw thick clouds of dust being blown by the wind as though from the other side of the mountains.

And as I looked, I saw that this was not dust, but people coming in crowds from the other side, but so small as to be visible at first only as dust. And the people became musicians, and the mountainous amphitheatre a huge orchestra, and the glaciers were two noble armies of women-singers in white robes, ranged tier above tier behind each other, and the pines became orchestral players, while the thick dust-like cloud of chorus singers kept pouring through the clefts in the precipices in inconceivable numbers.

A precipice that 'rose from out of the glaciers shaped itself suddenly into an organ', and a familiar figure played a giant fugue, and then the people rose and sang 'Venus laughing from the skies'; but awaking, 'all was changed; a light fleecy cloud had filled the whole basin, but I still thought I heard a sound of music, and a scampering-off of great crowds from the part where the precipices should be.' Butler prints music in his text (from Handel's third set of organ concertos). He turned homewards:

When I got to the chapel of S. Carlo, I was in the moonlight again, and when near the hotel, I passed the man at the mouth of the furnace with the moon still gleaming upon his back, and the fire upon his face, and he was very grave and quiet.[26]

This reminds us of the strange musical statues at the border in *Erewhon* and in *Erewhon Revisited*, as the overture to the imaginary country, the prevision of the Sacro Monte. The full significance of this passage – its identification of Christian grace with the pagan joys of the young peasants – is made clear in the version of it Butler published in *Life and Habit*:

And grace is best; for where grace is, love is not distant. Grace! the old Pagan ideal whose charm even unlovely Paul could not withstand; but, as the legend tells us, his soul fainted within him, his heart misgave him, and standing alone on the seashore at dusk, he troubled deaf heaven with his bootless cries, his thin voice pleading for grace after the flesh. But the true grace, with her groves and high places, and troops

79

43. *Sacro Monte, Locarno No 2, c.* 1881

of young men and maidens crowned with flowers, and singing of love and youth and wine – the true grace he drove out into the wilderness – high up, it may be, into Piora, and into such-like places.[27]

This experience as a visual and aural characterization of the Renaissance vies with Rossetti's 'Hand and Soul' and with Pater's word-paintings and oblique reconstructions.

Equipped with this 'fable of perception' and visionary experience of the Renaissance, the traveller reaches Italy only in Chapter VII, by an alternative route across Switzerland from England, via Mont Cenis and Turin to San Michele. The traveller's first route is not in fact retraced; on the contrary, the reader follows a fantastic map by which the traveller's possible routes into Italy are superimposed, and we have again the effect of Erewhon: the descent into the country of the imagination. This imaginative simultaneity and the vision on the border underlies the apparently artless excursiveness of the account.

The grand pile of San Michele, the monastery on top of a mountain, begun in 900, the model for Mont St Michel, was one of Butler's favourite subjects; there are many illustrations of its architectural features taken from every angle in pencil, pen, etching, and at least one coloured one that has been lost. Some other familiar Italian places on the lakes make their appearance, such as Como, or the Borromean castle at

44. *Sacro Monte, Locarno, No 1, c. 1881*

Angera on Lake Maggiore; and at the end the reader will be returned to Locarno, a busy tourist intersection then as now (illus. 43, 44). But in between he will find himself straying off the familiar map, into regions 'unknown to the English public', as Butler leads him into a new erewhon in the midst of one of the most visited countrysides in Europe.[28] Even in Locarno his destination is in the hills high above the town and, on descending, his tour culminates in an unearthly comic vision. His use of the descent into the visionary landscape, rather than the sublime ascent of Snowdon or the Alps, is part of his ironizing of the well-worn convention. Butler's easy, familiar tone, his humorous anecdotes, his travellers' 'tips', do much to disarm the reader. He offers pithy descriptions of the people he encounters and germs of narrative: one of his landlords was set on marrying a third wife, and asked Butler to help choose among the six who had come up to be looked at: 'I saw one of them. She was a Visigoth-looking sort of person and wore a large wobbly-brimmed straw hat. . . .'[29] But should the reader leave his easy chair and follow Butler to Italy he will find himself not in the Milan of Stendhal, the Venice of Byron or of Ruskin, the Naples of Shelley, the Rome of Keats, the Florence of Browning and Landor and of countless lesser travellers, but in Varallo, Varese, Crea, Oropa, names little-known either to the grand tourist of the past or to the new breed of petty tourists that began to stream – and steam (once the St Gotthard railway tunnel was opened in 1881) – across the Alps in Butler's day.

Butler's reviewers remarked appreciatively on his discovery of new Italian territory: 'Why the beautiful hill country of Lombardy and Piedmont should have received so little notice up to the present is not easy to understand,' commented one.[30] Another pointed out: 'Mr Butler's Alps are the alps of Piedmont; his Sanctuaries are such old-world, remote, forgotten places as Graglia, and San Michele, and Oropa, and the Monte Bisbino.'[31] Still another remarked: 'Mr Butler differs from most of those who have of late written about Alpine regions in that he is no mountaineer, "nor cares to walk with Death and Morning on the silver horns"; but prefers, perhaps wisely, to make acquaintance with man and his works among the chestnuts and olive trees of the valley.'[32] Several dwell with interest on his chapter on San Michele as a place all too often familiar only from the train window.[33] Finally, he has not left the Alps after all – *his* alps; he is in the mountain sanctuaries, the 'holy mountains' where in 1481 a vision led to the founding of the 'New Jerusalem' at Varallo, and to other sanctuaries modelled on it in the ensuing two centuries. The unwitting traveller, taking the genial but paradoxical Butler as a companion, finds himself on a pilgrimage.

As he described the scene at Varese to his sister, 'the monde is exclusively Italian – no English ever stay here':

I got to Varese town the same evening and here [Hotel Riposo, Sacro Monte, about ten kilometres from the town] next morning. As usual it was a gran festa, but Alas! it was dreadfully wet both Monday & Tuesday, and the poor people, who came none the less, got such a drenching as many of them I am afraid will not soon forget. At five I got up & looked out of window – there they all were in thousands filling the broad road up to the Sanctuary, under a sea of 'humble brothers'. Today it is lovely and the mountain tops being covered with snow I think it bids fair to settle down. . . .

This is much the most beautiful of all the Italian Sanctuaries quâ place, and it is the most delightful place to stay at imaginable. There is a very nice Italian family here, an old gentleman his wife & daughter. The wife reminds me a little of Aunt Bather and the daughter is really very like Elsie. The old gentleman said to me today – 'Why shd one take walks at such a place as this? è inutile – it is enough to sit here in a chair without going so far as to say that it is quite useless to take a walk at all. I do think that this is about as good as any thing North Italy can do. This morning I saw Monte Rosa, Monte Viso, the mountains above Genoa and the Apennines as far as Bologna with Novara shrines. . . . Milan and the lakes of Varese, Gallarate & the Lago Maggiore all seen through chestnut trees & vineyards. I do not know any such panorama as this – & then on the other side the marvellous Sacro Monte.[34] [Illus. 45, 56.]

None of the early reviewers, nor the few early readers of *Alps and Sanctuaries*, it would seem, followed in Butler's actual or his mental footsteps;[35] even his sister May – who received his enthusiastic letters from the sites he visited over three years in preparation for *Alps* – the church at Giornico which is to be his '"magnum opus" of this summer [1878]'; the frescoes at Mesocco (illus. 48, 66); the 'stupendous santuario' of S Ambrogio, which he 'would like to make a whole book of' (illus. 46); and the Castle of Fénis (illus. 49), intended for *Verdi Prati* – never saw them.[36] It was left for his translator into French, Valery Larbaud, in the twentieth century to traverse and appreciate his route, and to find in Butler the ideal traveller, the modest English foil to Larbaud's narcissistic countryman Stendhal.[37] Butler suggests another mode of seeing: the sublime and excursive modes are still there, but they are unified in a theatrical experience in which the spectator is also a willing performer. Larbaud's phrase – with Butler 'Italian art appears on the same map as Italian life' – suggests again that superimposition of one imaginary country on another that characterized *Erewhon*. But unlike

45. *Sacro Monte, Varese,* 1892

46. *S Giorio – Comba di Susa, neighbourhood of S Ambrogio,* 1880

Erewhon and New Zealand, both these imaginary scenes bore the aspect of reality.

The 'Alps' and the 'sanctuaries' of the title are in fact inextricable. If the traveller is at first in Switzerland and then in Italy, the national boundary is not important; on the contrary, Butler (with the political map and the Baedeker of his day) defines an area, the Ticino, the Piedmont and parts of Lombardy, in which the northern or Germanic admixture with the Italian was vital. In the terms of art, he pursued the *intendo tedesco*, the 'German influence', through his intense interest in the Flemish influence on North Italian Renaissance art, in particular the Flemish sculptors who worked in the chapels of the sanctuaries. This opposition between and reunion of North and South is both historical and akin to the many such imaginative syntheses produced by the Romantics; and it is vital to the argument about the course of art in the fifteenth century, the moment of the onset of the Renaissance. It is part of the discovery of a 'Northern' art to match the Southern (the classical) art of Italy and Greece which was begun with the German Romantics Wackenroder, Tieck and, especially, Friedrich Schlegel, whose descriptions of his visits to the galleries of Paris and Dresden uncovered a new tendency and formed a new taste, leading to the large-scale purchases of Northern art by Ludwig of Bavaria and new collections in Munich and elsewhere.[38] In effect, the Italian primitives were seen by Schlegel as a continuation of the medieval art that the Romantics had reassessed and salvaged from the rationalist onslaughts of the Enlightenment. The nineteenth-century German 'primitives', the artists known as the Nazarenes, were directly inspired by Schlegel's formulations – as were, at one remove, the 'French Nazarenes' centred on Lyon in the 1830s.[39] In English, these ideas were represented by Lord Lindsay's *Sketches of the History of Christian Art* (1847), which Butler read at least in its later edition of 1882, and commented on very favourably.

Lindsay, an aristocratic amateur, devotee of religion, and collector, built on the work of the ultramontanist Alexis-François Rio (*De la poésie chrétienne, dans son principe, dans sa matière et dans ses formes*, 1836, and *De l'art chrétien*, 1851),[40] whose influence in England also led to the translation of Schlegel's *Descriptions of Paintings from Paris and the Netherlands* in 1848. As Schlegel was the major influence on the Nazarenes, so both Rio and Lindsay were major sources for Ruskin and the English Pre-Raphaelites. Lindsay sets the scene, replete with organic and religious metaphors, for the dramatic battle of good and evil forces

47. *S Ignatius Loyola, from a fresco near Ceres,* 1879

which Ruskin carried on: the new elements of the Renaissance in 'opening manhood' range themselves against the medieval primitives, the sides form up 'under the opposite banners of Christianity and Paganism'; the previous age 'may be compared to the peace of paradise, the latter to the turmoil that succeeded the Fall. . .'.[41]

Butler's apparently casual entry into the mountain sanctuaries takes place against the background of a far-reaching set of changes of taste and art-historical controversies. As he wrote – and surprisingly little has changed in this respect since his day – :

I cannot understand how a field so interesting, and containing treasures in so many

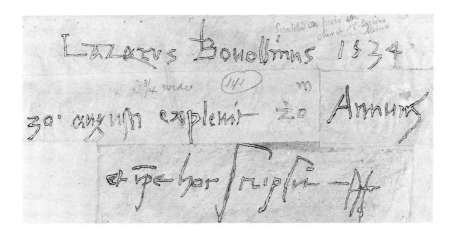

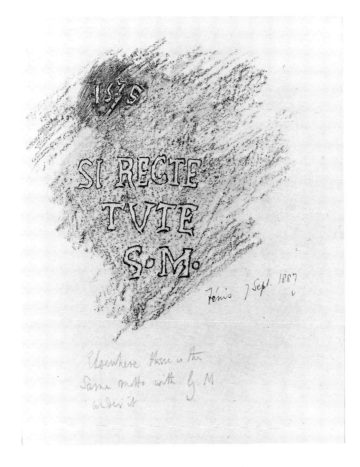

48. *Lazarus Bovollinus, 1534*, Mesocco, 1879

49. *Si Recte Tute S. M.*, Fénis, 1887

50. *Circumcision Chapel*, Sacro Monte, Varese, 1891

respects unrivalled, can have remained almost wholly untilled by the numerous English lovers of art who yearly flock to Italy. . . .[42]

These sanctuaries are large-scale works of art, which use the striking natural setting of mountain peak and mountain lake for an architectural complex incorporating a religious story into a series of chapels which mount the hill to the sanctuary proper, a church and often a monastery or convent. The chapels contain dramatic scenes from the story – often the life of Christ, or the life of Mary, or (as at Orta) the life of St Francis – recreated through life-size painted terracotta statues, and frescoes which extend the sculptured scene into the distance, and the architectural features of the chapel itself, which are often incorporated into the scene. The chapels vary in scale from very modest to imposing (illus. 50). The scenes are viewed through grilles or screens, sometimes of carved wood or wrought ironwork, with peepholes to position the viewers (illus. 51). The formats vary slightly at each site; sometimes, as at Varallo, there is a church at the foot of the *via sacra* as well as at the top; sometimes, as at

51. *Women looking into chapel*, Sacro Monte, 1891

52. Inner Court of Sanctuary of Oropa, c. 1880

Varese, there is a town at the top which houses the final chapel within its church; at Crea the sanctuary is near the foot of the Sacro Monte, which is crowned by the Chapel of the 'Assumption of Mary'; at Oropa the sanctuary is enclosed within a 'pile of collegiate buildings' which Butler likened to Trinity College set up on Snowdon (illus. 52, 53).[43] Often, in accordance with the original intention to map Jerusalem, there is a further ascent beyond the sanctuary into still higher mountains, the mountain of the *Tre Croci* – the Three Crosses of the hill of Calvary. Raising one's eyes from the sanctuary, or from the city at the summit, one may see the crosses on the skyline of a still distant mountain top. The 'Stations of the Cross', then, are set in motion in a *teatro monte*, a 'mountain theatre' in which the traveller, the pilgrim, is himself an actor. Ruskin's travelling beholder was likened by Proust to a pilgrim; but Butler's pilgrims do not simply proceed to a shrine, they 'read the book of the mountain', as he said, and they envision each complex drama-tized scene from the particular perspectives which most animate and unify it.

These extraordinary theatres were heirs and rivals to the spectacles

53. *Chapels of the Sanctuary of Oropa, looking down towards Lombardy, c.* 1880

and processions of the Italian fifteenth-century cities in which religious
ceremony, public holiday, and secular entertainment intertwined, beginning with the Mysteries themselves and embracing the *Trionfi* and the
Carnival.[44] They retain the element of extreme realism often found in the
Mysteries, and in the intermingling of the spectators – often masked –
with the actors in the street festivities. Fantasy was realized, both in
meticulous theatrical machines, like the tomb of the Virgin in the public
square at Perugia that opened after Mass at Corpus Christi to permit
Mary to ascend to heaven accompanied by singing angels, and in the
participation of the people in the events.

Varallo, this religious theatre in nature, as the site of the first invention
of the theatre mountain (and there is a close relation between these and
the Mystery plays of these regions, which were still performed, read
aloud, or alive in the common speech even in Butler's time)[45] engaged
Butler's attention most closely. There can be no doubt that the works of
art created in and through the Sacro Monte at Varallo are the most
significant: Varallo is the earliest Sacro Monte and founded on the
experience of an individual that has the ring of conviction about it; the

Fucine near Viù
S. Butler July 1880

Figures by
C. Gogin

54. *Fucine, near Viù*, 1880

92

other sanctuaries were later, outside the crucial period, their founding visions increasingly conventional (illus. 55).

Butler, it is clear, enjoyed the shock he was able to induce by embracing these images of popular Catholicism; nor can there be much doubt that this element of shock has played a role in the conspiracy of silence that has enveloped his art criticism. The Sacro Monte, so far as it was known, was seen as part of the machinery of the Counter–Reformation, as a piece of astute political theatre on the part of the Church, which carried on building them until well into the Baroque period – Orta, for example, was built a century after Varallo – and indeed is still adding to them, a modern *via crucis* at Oropa, a large-scale statue of the Pope at Varese rivalling the figure of Moses carved into the hillside at the top of the ascent to the Sanctuary. Butler went against a religious and political as well as an aesthetic prejudice that was deeply rooted in his countrymen, as none knew better than he. As he remarks, all of the Sacri Monti, built (except for Crea) on the last slopes of the Alps, have 'something of the spiritual frontier fortress about them'.[46] For all these reasons it is Varallo that holds the centre of his stage: the earliest, the most authentic of the Sacri Monti, at once the continuation of the 'primitive' and the expression of that verism that was the mode by which the new Renaissance spirit of realism made its way even into the most sacred of late medieval images.[47] Moreover, the ensemble of architectural, sculptural and painted elements of the Sacro Monte at Varallo may be seen as the high point of the realist tendency in the Quattrocentro and, far from being a byway or a backwater, as leading the way into the next age.[48]

The year 1486, Varallo's founding date – Caimi's vision is dated at 1481 – reverberates through the literature of controversy about the Renaissance: Ruskin chose 1480 as the watershed between the authentic art of the 'primitives' or true Pre-Raphaelites, and the corruption of the Renaissance. All the 'new effort and deadly catastrophe took place 1480–1520', he proclaimed.[49] 'Raphael, Michael Angelo, and Titian, together, bring about the deadly change, playing into each other's hands – Michael Angelo being the chief captain in evil; Titian, in natural force.'[50] The supporters of Raphael (like Burckhardt) saw it as the beginning of the greatest period of Italian Renaissance art, which embraced his lifetime (1483–1520). Even for those who adopted the Pre-Raphaelite position, prolonged controversy took place over which side of the divide Raphael himself belonged on. Holman Hunt declared that 'Pre-Raphaelitism is not Pre-Raphaelism.'[51] The ambivalence had begun with Schlegel himself, who felt that the spirit of the primitives was still at times discernible in Raphael.[52] Seen in the light of Schlegel's criticism as a whole, which placed the great break or 'world-historical caesura' between classical antiquity and Christianity, the Renaissance was simply a *Steigerung* or intensification of the medieval period, permitting Italian Renaissance literature to be a germ and a resource for Romanticism;[53] but in his art criticism (the *Descriptions*) his campaign for the recognition of early Northern art conveys the impression of a break. French and English critics were aware only of a fraction of Schlegel's criticism. Rio was prepared to countenance only the earliest of Raphael's Madonnas. Lindsay held that it was imitators of Raphael who had done the damage. To describe the great cultural shift, Lindsay adopted the metaphor not simply of the 'stopped traveller' or of the 'excursive beholder', but of the pilgrim's progress impeded and laid waste:

Pausing therefore in the midst of the fifteenth century, and looking mournfully round us, we feel as Mr. Greatheart might have done, if, starting in the morning with the Celestial City in view and Christiana and her children journeying promisingly at his side, he were to find himself all at once forsaken and alone, and all his efforts vain to reclaim his wayward companions into the path of progress and perfection.[54]

Varallo, then, Butler perceived, could serve as a crucial test case in the battle over the Renaissance. It was on the works created here, on the artists who worked here (together with their works elsewhere), and on the social conditions which made them possible, that Butler focused, and they form the centre of his view of the Renaissance. He came to know the town well, visiting it on nearly twenty occasions, and had many friends there; this was the capital of his 'second country'.[55]

In *Alps and Sanctuaries* Butler did not include Varallo, precisely because it was the most important site and merited a book in itself, which he wrote under the title *Ex Voto* (1889).[56] *Ex Voto*, translated into Italian in 1894, with an introduction written in Italian by Butler, is a more detailed and scholarly study of Varallo and its artists and, secondarily, of Crea, and on this study (together with supporting essays and notes) rests Butler's claim to have made a pioneering contribution to art history; but to understand the phenomenon of the Sacro Monte fully, Varallo must be reincorporated into *Alps and Sanctuaries*, and the form of that work recognized. Equally, the illustrations – Butler's drawings and watercolours of the sites in the Alps and on the Sacro Monte in *Alps*

55. *Plan of the Sacro Monte in* 1671

56. *Sacro Monte, Varese, c.* 1882

and Sanctuaries, and his striking photographs of the frescoes and statuary within the chapels in *Ex Voto* – must be brought together. His many photographs of the town and its inhabitants and the sites and their visitors capture the ambience in a more informal way. The outward and the inward views must be seen as part of one work. At the same time, Butler's strategy in separating them is an important part of his position: in *Alps* he deliberately appears as an excursive traveller, at times almost a guide, if as much in the manner of the 'cicerone' as of Murray or Baedeker; in *Ex Voto* he appears as an art historian, a critic. That is, although his position is in some respects that of a Pre-Raphaelite, in that he here defends a medieval or primitive art, he finds that here at least, in these mountain communities, the primitive persisted throughout the Renaissance. Moreover, a primitive form, the Sacro Monte, is created on the very eve of the Renaissance; and it holds the clues to a new art. He thus undercuts the melodramatic rhetorical oppositions of Lindsay and Ruskin. The grand battle between Christianity and Paganism, between Imagination and Reason, is off – because it was merely trumped-up. The sharp 'break' in time was non-existent. Yet to understand the thrust of Butler's argument and the significance of his tone it is essential to know that the battle had been presented as real and earnest in the strongest possible religious and moral terms. We see again the ambivalence of his relation to Pre-Raphaelitism: strongly attracted to it as an impressionable young man, an enthusiastic reader of Ruskin at Cambridge who came to feel 'decided dislike' for him,[57] an art student who had attempted to revive the style of Bellini in modern terms and produced in the vein of the Nazarenes two versions of his most important subject in an Italian setting, *The Christening at Fobello* (illus. 30, 31), Butler set out to demonstrate to them what primitivism really meant in a way that would scandalize them and show up their style as humbug.

Some vital elements of Pre-Raphaelitism were retained by Butler: the notion that there was a valuable school of primitives, that the Italian primitives were strongly linked with the Northern, especially Flemish primitives, and that there had been a decline of art from a variously specified date in the past down to the present. The notion of the decline of art was, of course, not confined to the Pre-Raphaelites. If the decline did not date from the 'Pre-Raphaelites' onwards, then it had taken place since the Renaissance, that is, from some time in the middle of the sixteenth century, from one moment or another in the life of Michelangelo. Burckhardt and others, following Michelet in holding the

Renaissance to be a relatively brief epoch rather than an open-ended revival or 'rebirth', ruled that its decline dated from the triumph of Michelangelo. As we have seen, the decline of art was an experience Butler felt along the blood, not a category of art historians. It was owing not to the onset of realism or 'the baroque', but to the triumph of imitation and the institutionalization of art. For Butler, Hazlitt's diatribe against the academies was reinforced by the personal certainty of the loss of a true spiritual aim in painting, an art in the service of God not of self-aggrandisement. Thus he held to the older view of the later date of the decline from the foundation of the Italian academy, reinforced by the newer argument of Schlegel, Rio and Lindsay from the loss of faith seen, however, as a gradual process not as an overnight event.

Butler, the unbuttoned, secular traveller, seems to find in the aesthetics of the 'mountain theatre', and the community that produced it, a new home for his houseless faith. This movement from religion into aesthetics was of course one of the most characteristic of the period, and had been formalized by Kant and Schiller before the turn of the century and carried out on principle by the Romantic imagination. The intense interest of the nineteenth century in the late medieval period and the Renaissance – a period of faith giving way to a pagan movement, a return to classical antiquity in a Christian context – is one aspect of this shift. The imaginative reconstruction of the past is the stuff of the artistic movements of the Nazarenes and the Pre-Raphaelites as it is of the art criticism of Ruskin and Pater. The epoch of 'the Renaissance' is invented and battled over before our eyes. The judgement of particular artists and their works is invested with an unusual significance and solemnity, as they come to represent not only culture but 'our culture', the uniquely great products and repositories of a past mythology. If that mythology is Christianity, the Renaissance increasingly becomes the repository of a new, secular European mythology. Lindsay found it expedient in his first volume to set out the elements of Christian mythology that it would be needful for his increasingly secular public to know; Burckhardt celebrated the 'individualism' of the Renaissance.

Yet Butler also uses his inquiries to press home his critique of late nineteenth-century art and criticism and, finally, of aestheticism itself. His choice of site, theme and artist is itself a running ironic commentary on the art criticism of his day and the solemnities of culture. In *The Fair Haven* he carried out not only a critique of all forms of Victorian religion, but also a critique of its still more pallid substitute, 'the aesthetic education of man', as Schiller called it, art as spilt religion. His final chapter on 'The Christ-ideal', an oblique attack on Hegel's secular version of the religious vision of Jesus which Strauss employed in his famous *Life of Jesus*, culminates in a stunningly ironic, almost Nietzschean image drawn from art: the corrupted Christ-ideals of Domenichino and Guido Reni. To read his irony aright, however, we must first be more complete adepts of Butler's personal history of art.

The approach to the main sites through the smaller chapels and isolated churches of the Alps contributes not only to the form of the book – it is like a *via sacra*, gradually approaching the heart of its subject through a pleasant meander – but to Butler's sense of the nature of the creative impulse which went into these shrines, an impulse which might still be seen in out-of-the-way places, in 'natural' artists, that is, the contemporary 'primitive', even in a day of decadent academic art like the late nineteenth century. In these out-of-the-way places he is able to find the clue to the future.

Varallo he reached by foot from Lake Orta over the Colma, the summit of the mountains, where a road was put in only recently; the descent through the rocky pinnacles into the town, the cupola of the sanctuary visible on the opposite peak, is magnificent:

There is nothing in North Italy more beautiful than this walk, with its park-like chestnut-covered slopes of undulating pasture land dotted about with the finest thatched barns to be found outside Titian. We might almost fancy that Handel had it in his mind when he wrote his divine air 'Verdi Prati.'[58]

From this juxtaposition, then, of his chosen Italian landscape with his favourite composer, Butler took the title of his third, unfinished book on Italy, 'Verdi Prati', Green Fields; indeed, he had originally intended to give this title to *Alps and Sanctuaries*. Announcing his departure the same week for Italy to begin the book that became *Alps*, he had written to his sister: 'It is to be about the Italian villages I go to on the slopes of the Alps & I have hit on a title which I think will do, to wit "Verdi Prati".'[59] Given his introduction, which associates Handel with Shakespeare in their love of England and Italy, perhaps it is not merely fanciful to suppose that he intended to allude also to the green fields of which Falstaff babbled on his deathbed.

Gaudenzio Ferrari and the Sacro Monte

At the crossroads entering Varallo one finds the chapel of the Madonna del Loreto, 'of singularly graceful elegant design'.[60] Since Butler's time the frescoes within as well as the fine statue of the Madonna have been attributed to Gaudenzio Ferrari and his associates.[61]

As Butler makes clear in the key chapter of *Alps*, 'The Decline of Italian Art', he saw as the hallmark of the early Renaissance, the high point of Italian art (which for him deteriorated after the founding of the Bologna Academy by the Carracci brothers), that union of individual imaginative power with the communal nature of the work of a group of varied artists, supported by the wider community of the town of Varallo and its smaller, allied communities in the Val Sesia. If the vision of the Franciscan monk was the starting-point, ratified by the Church's foundation of a monastery at Varallo in 1486, the work on the Sacro Monte was supported and organized by the *comune*, which in turn called upon patrician and well-to-do citizens to support it with funds. This may be seen as a classic form of early Quattrocento corporate patronage.[62] Often the work was anonymous, or participated in over time by so many artists and craftsmen that it is almost impossible to attribute it to any one 'master'. In this the Sacro Monte was for Butler the Renaissance equivalent of the monumental medieval cathedral that drew Ruskin's praise for the faithful labour of its many anonymous craftsmen over several generations. He explicitly opposed this ideal to the aggrandisement of the work of the 'great names', the *uomini d'oro*, Raphael, Leonardo, and Michelangelo.

Within this communal form, however, certain individual figures are discernible; individual craftsmen and the community are indispensable to one another. Just as the Sacro Monte was founded through the religious vision of one man, Bernardino Caimi, who was determined to realize his experience of Jerusalem in the mountains of his homeland, so the artistic vision was brought to its finest fruition in and through the work of Gaudenzio Ferrari. It is one of Butler's highest claims on our notice as an art critic that he perceived and championed Gaudenzio Ferrari. Butler's pioneering efforts, using the few available Italian sources, some scattered references in English, and his own eyes, led to the first full-length study of Gaudenzio in English; even in Italy his full recognition waited for the major exhibition in Vercelli in 1956.

Gaudenzio's talents did not go altogether unnoticed by Butler's contemporaries. Crowe and Cavalcaselle, it is true, the authors of the *History of Painting in North Italy*, hailed by Pater as the 'new Vasari', have next to nothing to say of him.[63] But he was belittled even by those who did discuss him through being labelled as a member of the Milan school, which was always placed firmly at the bottom of the ladder of Italian Renaissance art, and which tended to be disposed of simply as the pupils and imitators of Leonardo. Among these imitators Bernardino Luini and Gaudenzio Ferrari were sometimes singled out as being of more than usual ability. Jacob Burckhardt's brilliant *Cicerone, an Art Guide to Painting in Italy*, translated by Mrs Clough in 1873, with its lucid, committed, finely modulated overview of schools and individuals, shows clearly the magnitude of the task Butler set himself. It has been said that 'Our conception of the Renaissance is Jacob Burckhardt's creation.'[64] This book, together with his *Civilisation of the Renaissance in Italy* (1860), dominated thinking about the Renaissance for over half a century. According to Burckhardt, the great era of the Renaissance attained its 'full bloom' – the organic imagery is characteristic of the historicist mode – at the end of the fifteenth century:

[T]he short lifetime of Raphael (1483–1520) witnessed the rise of all that was most perfect, and . . . immediately after him, even with the greatest who outlived him, the decline began. But this perfect ideal was created, once for all, for the solace and admiration of all time, will live for ever, and bear the stamp of immortality.[65]

The metaphor of the organic era shapes Burckhardt's account. The blooming must needs be followed by the withering. Raphael duly receives by far the longest and most enthusiastic treatment of any individual artist. Leonardo and Michelangelo are given more measured praise, and Michelangelo's later works are themselves seen as expressive of the decline. The comparison is always with the standard of Raphael:

Whole vast spheres of existence which are capable of the highest artistic illustration remained closed to Michelangelo. He has left out all the most beautiful emotions of the soul (instead of enumerating them, we have but to suggest Raphael). . . .[66]

Ferrari, although discussed among a lengthy list of Milanese pupils of Leonardo headed by Luini, is presented as 'one of the most powerful masters of the golden time', but he is represented as torn between the available styles, 'widely distracted by the opposite teachings of the old Lombard and the Piedmontese schools, of Leonardo, Perugino, and Raphael, all of whose studios he must have attended at various periods of his life'.[67] Again Raphael is the point of comparison: the paintings of the *Presentation at the Temple* and *Christ among the Doctors* in S Maria delle Grazie, Varallo, are almost Raphaelesque in their mode of narration, perhaps the purest thing produced by him.[68] The great screen depicting the Passion in the same church – one of Butler's favourites, a reproduction of which hung permanently on the walls of his studio in Clifford's Inn – is seen as 'essentially a very free and powerful reproduction of a Peruginesque inspiration', with 'a reminiscence' of Signorelli. In his brief discussion of the Sacro Monte, he mentions the frescoes of the 'Procession of the Three Kings' in the chapel of that name, and singles out the 'Procession' round the walls of the Crucifixion Chapel 'of soldiers, knights, and ladies of Jerusalem, along with about twelve blond weeping angels on the dome' as 'a late masterpiece of very great fulness of expression, and most energetic breadth of representation'. But his sole comment on the statuary, which Butler was concerned to see as an integral part of Gaudenzio's work at the Sacro Monte, has an entirely dismissive and negative ring:

On the other hand, the groups in terra cotta which occupy the centre of the chapel cannot possibly be Ferrari's own work, even if he undertook them in partnership with some one else.[69]

Burckhardt does not, however, suggest that Ferrari was influenced by Michelangelo.

Symonds, in the volume of *The Renaissance in Italy* devoted to the 'Fine Arts', follows this model, and even more graphically and with considerable chronological distortion places the Milan school and Leonardo not simply at the beginning of a chapter on the sixteenth century, as does Burckhardt, but in his final chapter, pointedly entitled 'The Epigoni'. He places Leonardo, Raphael and Michelangelo among the masters of the fifteenth century, declaring 'What remained was but an after-bloom, rapidly tending to decadence'.[70]

Thus Butler, in order to do justice to Ferrari, had to combat Ruskin's arbitrary division into pure and impure (Pre-Raphaelite and Renaissance) and question the arbitrary dating of the 'Fall'; demonstrate the interest and value of the art of the Piedmont, Ticino, and Lombardy in general, and of the provincial sites as opposed to the major cities in particular; create in the mountain *comune* of Varallo another form and another centre of the Renaissance, in which Ferrari could take his place as the head of a school, and be free of the assumption that he worked in the shadow of Leonardo, or that he borrowed conflicting elements from the superior schools. Butler's reviewers, wondering why these regions of

Italy had remained so unexplored, answered their own question in echoing, however remotely, the views of the art historians on the hierarchy of the schools: the 'art and architecture of the country, though they have not reached a high classical standard of perfection and are developed only on the spot and without instruction, are picturesque and interesting in the extreme'.[71]

A major focus of the literature on the Renaissance was the great triumvirate Raphael, Leonardo, and Michelangelo, the *uomini d'oro*, names to conjure with. The entire tale could be told through the varied and dramatically expressed opinions of their intrinsic and relative merits, and their use as yardsticks against which all other artists are measured. Ultimately, it was the tendency to elevate these three, in whatever order, above the host of other artists, which Butler rebelled against, the reading of history through 'great men'; as he put it, 'The reputations of the great dead are governed in the main by the chicane that obtains among the living.'[72] In art criticism the tendency is perhaps summed up in the egotistic tradition of Stendhal, which claimed that the only true citizens of Milan were not the Milanese, but Stendhal and Leonardo.[73] Butler was convinced, on the contrary, that Leonardo did not constitute the School of Milan, and indeed that the art of Lombardy and Piedmont was rooted in the small communes rather than in Milan.

Butler opened *Ex Voto* with an attack on the false methods of art historians, in particular their tendency to work with the current 'counters' of received opinion rather than to see with their own eyes. Art historians' eyes were 'tamed' with a vengeance: often they did not even visit the places they described. Butler trains his attack on Sir Henry Layard, a leading art historian of his day, who translated part of Kugler's widely-read and much acclaimed *Handbuch der Geschichte der Malerei* (1837) into English. The *Handbook of Painting*, whose section on Italian painting was first translated in 1845, was said by Lady Eastlake on its revision in 1874 to have been 'the chief guide of the English traveller in Italy' for the past thirty years.[74] Butler's satiric method takes an individual as representative of his type, as in *The Way of All Flesh* he demolishes the well-known authority on Gospel harmonies, Dean Alcock, and with him the Church's current mode of fending off the unwelcome conclusions of the historical-critical movement. Butler's 'word-portraiture' is strongly linked to the seventeenth-century 'character', especially to (though no relation) his namesake Samuel Butler's thumbnail sketches of 'A Modern Politician', 'The Churchwarden', and

'The Horse-courser', and to Swift's monumental savaging of named public figures, from Marlborough to Steele, in the best tradition of 'learned' satire. In both cases (the Dean and the Professor Sir) the titles of honour are indicative of the wider reference of his attack; as Butler noted:

Title:
Records of a mis-spent life.[75]

In the egregious pair of Professors Hanky and Panky in *Erewhon Revisited* Butler combined the title of honour with an irresistibly significant name.

Butler demonstrates, from the false and misleading descriptions of the layout of sanctuaries and chapels and their contents, that Layard 'has evidently either never been at Varallo, or has so completely forgotten what he saw there that his visit no longer counts'.[76] Layard as translator is made conveniently to stand for the authorities responsible for the *Handbook*, and as art historian himself is indicted for his own remissness. This introduction shows not merely that Varallo has not received its due attention but, more crucially, that the 'lovers of art who yearly flock to Italy' must avoid seeing in the terms and categories laid down by the 'experts'. The experts would do better to avoid them too; as Butler remarks drily, the inaccuracies of second-hand seeing are such that 'I begin to understand now how we came to buy the Blenheim Raffaelle.' The whole of what follows in *Ex Voto* is an attempt to see for oneself and to evade the pernicious type-casting of 'Masters', 'Schools', 'periods', and 'isms'. Butler's efforts to open the eye and the mind merit comparison with Ruskin's grand educative efforts to teach the 'art of beholding' or 'the science of aspects'. What did Butler see, and how?

The road to the 'ignorant eye' passed through the available erudition. Always a quick scholar, Butler seized upon the main sources, read them with discrimination (and, as with his travels, with honesty about what he had skipped or not understood), and then moved off in his own direction. His 'idiosyncrasies' were always calculated. He used translations if they existed; otherwise he read the original. Nor should his tenacity in tracking down sources and new documentary evidence be underestimated. His earliest source was Gian Paolo Lomazzo, the first Renaissance writer to discuss Gaudenzio (who had been his own teacher), in the *Trattato dell'arte della pittura, scoltura et architettura* (1584), partially translated into English by Haydocke; the most recent was G. Colombo (1881). Lomazzo is of special interest, as he consciously set out to correct Vasari's scanty mention of Gaudenzio, and in his theoretical treatise *Idea del tempio della pittura* (1590) used Gaudenzio as the second of the seven governors of art (the others being Michelangelo, Caravaggio, Leonardo, Raphael, Mantegna, and Titian) who are visualized in architectural terms as a peristyle of caryatid columns at the centre of the Temple of Art. The styles of the seven governors are elucidated in terms of individual temperaments as understood by astrology. He was a major contributor to the emergence of an art criticism that had the capacity not merely to formulate art history through individual biographies but to describe artistic individuality.[77] The direction Butler's argument took was angled to the sources and the attitudes of his English audience.

Kugler, especially as revised by Burckhardt, gave considerable weight to the pre-Renaissance, although primarily sympathetic to classicism of a Goethean kind, and viewed the first quarter of the sixteenth century as a 'Golden Age' of art. The book gives an excellent account of the Lombard School, and in particular of Gaudenzio Ferrari, 'a painter of undoubted genius and originality, who takes one of the highest places in the Lombard school'.[78] Comparing him with Bernardino Luini, as do all the authorities, he quotes Morelli, who credits Gaudenzio with 'inventive genius, dramatic life and picturesqueness' which place him 'far above Luini':

In his hot haste *Ferrari* often loses his balance and becomes quaint and affected. Many of his larger compositions, too, are over-crowded with figures; but in his best works he is inferior to very few of his contemporaries, and occasionally, as in some of those groups of men and women in the great Crucifixion at Varallo, he might challenge a comparison with *Raphael* himself.[79]

While approving of this comparison as a measure of value, Layard rejects the tradition, apparently accepted by Burckhardt (in the *Cicerone*) and Symonds, and regarded as a source of damaging 'eclecticism', that Ferrari 'went to Rome, formed a friendship with Raphael, and painted with him in the Farnesina Palace'.[80] Butler quoted more at length and with some approval from S. W. King, *The Italian Valleys of the Pennine Alps*, whose account of his personal travels in an effusive 'picturesque' style (accompanied by his own illustrations) convincingly demonstrates his first-hand acquaintance with the entire region and with Varallo in particular;[81] but he quoted him in order to correct him, and combated with special care the repeated story of 'Gaudenzio's studies under Raphael'.[82] Here Layard, and Butler, follow

Morelli, who usefully challenged a number of inflated attributions, and wrote in no uncertain terms of works attributed to Gaudenzio in the Borghese Gallery in Rome, that they

supplied a further, if only a negative proof that he never crossed the Apennines, and that his supposed apprenticeship with Perugino and friendship with Raphael are pure fiction. At some future date I hope to prove this.[83]

Having succeeded in keeping 'Raphael's influence' at arm's length, Layard does, however, accept the view that Gaudenzio was later influenced by Michelangelo, and stresses the detrimental effect on his work:

He appears, like many other painters, to have fallen under the influence of *Michael Angelo*, whose works he may possibly have seen in Tuscany, although it is very doubtful whether he ever left the north of Italy. The proof of the existence of this influence is furnished by his frescoes in the church of S. Maria delle Grazie at Milan (1542), which are coarse, exaggerated, and Michael-Angelesque, with few of the fine qualities of his earlier works.[84]

Layard's treatment thus tends to split Gaudenzio's production into two halves, one half early, fine and worthy of comparison with Raphael though not through the direct 'influence' of Raphael, and one half late, degraded and resulting from the influence of Michelangelo. This represents an extreme example of the tendency to see Michelangelo as ushering in the period of 'degeneracy', and then to apply the general conception to the interpretation of individuals' works. The coherence of individual development was sacrificed to a procrustean period conception. For Butler's purposes, however, it had at least the advantage of identifying Gaudenzio's best 'first manner' as 'purely Lombardesque', while denigrating his work executed in Milan, thus bringing Varallo into prominence.[85] For Butler, it was important to make the finer distinction between Lombardy and Piedmont (where Varallo is situated).

Butler does not mention Michelangelo as an influence on Gaudenzio, and rejects the melodramatic view that a devastating decline set in under his sign, remarking only that in his art 'Michelangelo said the last word; but then he said just a word or two over'.[86] Butler also stresses Gaudenzio's independence from Leonardo (though he once attributes 'not a little mannerism' to Gaudenzio)[87] by pointing out that Stefano Scotto, probably Gaudenzio's 'chief instructor' in Milan, 'kept a school that was more or less a rival to that of Leonardo da Vinci'.[88] Scotto (it is now held) maintained the older Lombard traditions represented by Il Borgognone, whose presence in Gaudenzio's work is sometimes mis-

57. *Stefano Scotto with Mr S Butler*, Ecce Homo Chapel, Sacro Monte,
Varallo, *c.* 1882

taken by outsiders for Raphaelesque or Peruginesque. Butler's insistence on this point reflects his wish to combat the view expressed by his other main sources that all of Lombard art was to be regarded simply as imitative of Leonardo.[89] The tourist King too echoed this uncritically, assuming it to be the highest praise, in his description of the 'Crucifixion' at the centre of the screen at S Maria della Grazie:

The tranquil dignity and mournful resignation of the expiring Saviour, the eyes just closing, and the noble head drooping over the shoulder as if the agony were finished, remind one of Leonardo, in their pure and exalted religious tone.[90]

For Butler, not the great names but the small, unpretentious craftsmen were vital to that art. To regard them as 'anonymous' was itself a species of condescension. Butler's humorous photograph of himself with Gaudenzio's statue of Scotto shows his strong self-identification with the minor but highly individual artists, who were far from asserting their own grandeur, as well as the life-like particularity of the statues (illus. 57). The misapprehensions Butler points to in Layard's account of Tabachetti underline this, as Tabachetti is in turn seen as a 'local painter' (although he was a Flemish sculptor) who 'imitated' Gaudenzio and 'whose works only show how rapidly Gaudenzio's influence declined and his school deteriorated'.[91] Thus the masters' schools are like Chinese boxes, and within each, in descending order, the same pattern is imposed.

Bordiga, before Colombo the main nineteenth-century Italian writer on Gaudenzio, whose book Butler had in his library, did not present the later work of Ferrari as a Michelangelesque decline; indeed, he is particularly appreciative of the frescoes in S Maria delle Grazie, Milan.[92] These are now in poor condition; but Bordiga's discussion and Pianazzi's drawings show the powerful architectural conception that was also a feature of the Varallo chapels. Butler too rejected the notion of a decline, under whatever influences, except in the personal sense of family losses; he ends the story with Gaudenzio's departure from Varallo, in 1539, merely pointing out that he 'for the rest of his life resided in Milan, where he executed several important works'.[93]

On the all-important question of Gaudenzio's relation to Raphael, Butler cites Layard's quotation of Morelli, and goes on to assert:

Gaudenzio Ferrari was what Raphael is commonly believed to have been. I do not mean, that he was the prince of painters – such expressions are always hyperbolical; there has been no prince of painters; I mean that Gaudenzio Ferrari's feeling was profound, whereas Raphael's was at best only skin deep.[94]

We can see why even in his obituaries, Butler was taken to task for his bold criticisms of Raphael.[95] But this is to mistake his wish to '*épater les académies*' for his argument. Butler's account carefully rejects the views of his authorities wherever they submit to the dominance of the great trio of masters and subordinate the work of other artists to an ideological pattern expressed in terms of that mastery: Gaudenzio stands on his own feet in his community, and is not an imitator of Leonardo, nor of Raphael, nor of Michelangelo. Moreover, Butler rejects the normal 'pecking order' among the artists labelled as 'imitators of Leonardo', and as between Luini and Ferrari finds the latter 'the stronger man'.[96] Whereas Luini's work often recalls Leonardo's, Gaudenzio's bears no such obvious traces. Raphael is still a central concern, for Butler strongly associates Gaudenzio with that 'primitive' moment of the early Renaissance that Raphael had either represented (Lindsay), represented in part in his earlier works (Rio and Ruskin), or betrayed (or superseded) in the triumph of pagan classicism. Butler strives to free those values from their identification, in whole or in part, with one great name, by now not a man, nor an artist, nor a group of works, nor even a school, but a magical incantation, whether for good or evil.

This rejection of the notion that Ferrari had studied with or imitated one, two or all three of the great trio was supported by the first and only full-length treatment of Gaudenzio in English, by Ethel Halsey in 1904, who drew on Butler as well as his sources, and accompanied the text by a wider range of illustrations of the artist's work.[97] She rejected the notion that Gaudenzio had studied with or made the acquaintance of Raphael in Rome, and attributed the similarity of the *Dispute* to the *School of Athens* to a common source in the Lombard Bramante.[98] Leonardo is handled with diplomatic restraint; while making it clear that Gaudenzio was Scotto's pupil, and thus firmly within 'old Milanese tradition', she saw moments of Leonardo's influence, which did not affect Gaudenzio entirely for the worse.[99] She did not, however, reject the notion of a late 'decline', and thus still belongs in the tradition of Layard, although she attributed the decline to the influence of Correggio rather than Michelangelo, placing the turn for the worse in 1527.[100] This may have owed something to Ruskin's negative view of Correggio:

Correggio, in the sidelong grace, artificial smiles, and purple languors of his saints, indicates the inferior instinct which would have guided his choice in quite other directions, had it not been for the fashion of the age, and the need of the day.[101]

Burckhardt's treatment of the reasons why 'to some people he is absolutely repulsive' and 'the first quite immoral painter', including a comparison with Michelangelo, is particularly illuminating; he himself concludes that 'there is an entire lack of moral elevation: if these forms should come to life, what good would come out of them, what kind of expression of life would one expect from them?'[102] Recent critics have found a point of contact between Gaudenzio and Correggio in their work for the Borromeo family at Isola Bella. In general, however, the association of the late Gaudenzio with the decline into realism appears to confuse the tradition of dramatic and architectonic representation inherent in the *donnée* of the Sacro Monte with the influence of Michelangelesque foreshortening.

Bernard Berenson writing *The North Italian Painters* after 1905 conceded in one brief paragraph that Gaudenzio was 'less than his fellows under the direct influence of Leonardo or his works' (and so superior to Luini), yet only by virtue of his being a remote provincial, 'by temperament an energetic mountaineer, with a certain coarse strength and forcefulness'.[103] Yet in effect by discussing, as Symonds had done, the whole of Milanese and Lombard painting with reference to Leonardo (while stressing Leonardo's superior Florentine origins), he reinforced the denigration of Lombardy and Piedmont, and the association of Gaudenzio and Leonardo. Even today the brief summary of Gaudenzio Ferrari's significance included in the London National Gallery's listing of its holdings concludes simply: 'His art was much affected by the Milanese followers of Leonardo da Vinci.'[104] This affects the observer who has carried out the double itinerary proposed by Butler, through the sites where Gaudenzio worked, and through the art critics who spoke of him, with a considerable shock.

Butler's book concerned itself not with Ferrari's complete *oeuvre*, but with what he took to be its nerve centre: his work at Varallo. Nevertheless, he in fact saw nearly if not all of that *oeuvre*,[105] then as now (with a few shifts) in the galleries and libraries of Milan and Turin, and in churches in a number of towns of the North including Milan, Vercelli, Novara, Arona, Lugano, Como, Saronno, and villages in the neighbourhood of Varallo (a number of which Butler describes), such as his birthplace Valduggia (where Butler attended a *festa* in his honour 'in a whirl of *discorsi* and flags flying and processions in which we took part of course'[106]), Borgosesia, Fobello, Morbegno, La Rocca and Gattinara. At Montrigone is one of his most moving and arresting works, the figure of *St John the Baptist*, at once wild and ethereal, which Butler photographed more than once (illus. 81). Gaudenzio executed large fresco cycles not only at S Maria delle Grazie, Varallo (1513), but also at S Cristoforo, Vercelli (the 'Life of Mary' and the 'Life of Mary Magdalen'), which exquisite little church also contains the fine painting known as *La Madonna degli Aranci*, 'The Madonna of the Orange Tree' of 1529 (properly speaking, it is of St Christopher, who appears in the foreground; illus. 58); and at S Maria dei Miracoli, Saronno, where (from 1534) he painted the superb cupola of singing angels, 'carrying diversity of most strange instruments in their hands'.[107] This brilliant 'angel concert' in a cupola had only one major predecessor, Correggio's very different *Assumption of the Virgin* in the Cathedral at Parma. The depiction of musical instruments has a place in the history of music as well as painting; some of the instruments are authentic, others fantastic, and some, like the double bagpipe and the fiddle which could be both blown and bowed at the same time was a playful possibility (illus. 89, 90).[108] At Saronno his work adjoins that of Bernardino Luini. Further major fresco cycles were executed at S Maria della Pace, Milan (illus. 87); and at the Sacro Monte, Varallo. Vercelli was in fact of particular importance as an art centre at the time, and many of his contacts and his commissions came from there, including his first teacher and later his pupils and his second wife; he lived there from 1528–36. His work is also to be seen in the Galleria Sabauda in Turin with works of the Piedmont and Lombard schools, especially his *St Joachim expelled from the Temple* (illus. 86) and his *Crucifixion*, which has many resemblances to his Sacro Monte, Varallo, work;[109] and at the Brera, Milan, where his large and striking (and controversial) painting of a favourite subject of Lombard art, the *Martyrdom of St Catherine of Alexandria*, now hangs, and his last frescoes from S Maria della Pace, Milan, have been preserved. The National Gallery in London has three works by Gaudenzio, including the early *Annunciation* and the later fragments of the larger work of which parts are in Turin (illus. 59).

The concentration on Varallo, however, allows Butler to consider both early and late works, among them some of Gaudenzio's finest productions, and to stress the unity of his work with itself and with that of the communal artistic enterprise of Varallo. There Gaudenzio executed a number of works apart from the Sacro Monte, including his fine *Pietà* in the Church of S Gaudenzio, the Chapel of the Madonna del Loreto, and the famous fresco reputedly painted by moonlight (already

58. Gaudenzio Ferrari, *The Madonna of the Orange Tree*, 1529,
S Cristoforo, Vercelli

59. Gaudenzio Ferrari, *The Annunciation*, before 1511

in a ruinous state in Butler's time). Butler's intense interest in and long familiarity with Varallo give his photographs of the Sacro Monte a quality unsurpassed by any modern renderings of these works, and it is here that his own art finds one form of fulfilment (illus. 82, 83).

Butler examined in some detail the confused evidence as to the earliest date of the chapels and their gradual development, still a matter of controversy. He concluded that the earliest chapels were probably of the 1490s or very early sixteenth century, and contained wooden statues, without frescoed backgrounds. Gaudenzio's role was decisive, for 'the daring scheme of combining the utmost resources of both painting and sculpture in a single work' was evolved by him. Butler stresses the gradual evolution of the conception; Gaudenzio began by painting frescoes over the entrance of one of the chapels just above the grille through which visitors gaze:

Probably the original scheme was to have sculptured figures inside the chapels, and frescoes outside; by an easy modification these last were transferred from the outside to the inside, and so designed as to form an integral part of the composition: the daring scheme of combining the utmost resources of both painting and sculpture in a single work was thus gradually evolved rather than arrived at *per saltum*.[110]

The idea of 'turning the full strength of both painting and sculpture at once on to a single subject' is so daring, indeed, that it might suggest the name of Leonardo; but this view is 'based solely on the fact that both Leonardo and the scheme were audacious'.[111]

Gaudenzio's contribution was decisive too, in that once he arrived at

114

the combination of internal frescoes and terracotta statues in an architectural setting, the conception did not change. A recent critic, bearing out the leading role assigned to Gaudenzio, cites the instruction contained in the contract to artists engaged on the Sacro Monte a hundred years later, to attain to the greatest possible perfection 'by imitating the hand of the painter Gaudenzio'.[112]

Butler singled out the work of Gaudenzio among the many scenes and figures of the Sacro Monte, not an easy task, especially given the practice over the centuries of renewing the figures and repainting. The chapels of most interest are the Crucifixion Chapel, the last – a crowded, lively and various scene comparable to his several Crucifixion paintings; the 'Adoration of the Shepherds'; the 'Adoration of the Magi'; and the 'Journey to Calvary' (where Butler also saw Tabachetti's hand).

A number of these he photographed. He wrote to his sister on Christmas Eve, 1887, as he excitedly departed for Varallo to take the pictures for *Ex Voto*:

I shall start for Varallo on Xmas eve – with Camera & dry plates – It is absolutely impossible for me to finish my book without going there. I have written 200 pp and am purposely leaving the rest till I have been there. They are very much pleased with me for coming.[113]

In *Ex Voto* he included five photographs of works by Gaudenzio, one showing two statues identified as 'portraits of Scotto and Leonardo' (Scotto appears twice; see illus. 57 for photograph of Butler with Scotto), and three of the Crucifixion Chapel from different positions (*General view looking towards the Bad Thief*, *General view looking towards the Good Thief*, and *The Bad Thief*).[114] Among his effects are a number of published and unpublished photographs of the interiors of the chapels, including a group from Varallo and a group from Crea. Of these, several are of Gaudenzio's Crucifixion Chapel (illus. 82, 83).

Gaudenzio's stock has undoubtedly risen in the century since Butler championed him, and in ways that confirm Butler's analysis. The handicap of not having been taken up by Vasari has almost been overcome. New attention paid to Lombard art in the past half-century has given it a new, independent value and facilitated the comparison of Gaudenzio with other artists and centres in the North. The exhibition held at Vercelli in 1956 was the sign of the progress of his fame, indeed is seen as having brought about a 'revolution' in Gaudenzio criticism and ushered in a new period of intense and detailed study of his work.[115] A recent account of Lombard art perceives him as a true representative of it, not as a follower of Leonardo, but as a pupil of the *mal noto* Scotto, and in the line of Il Borgognone and Bramantino. He is linked not with Raphael but with Perugino, whose actual presence and work in Lombardy 1494–9 is stressed; the legend of a journey to Central Italy, 'perhaps to Rome', is referred to as suggesting an opportunity for him to have made the acquaintance not of Raphael but of 'Pre-Raphaelite proto-classicism'. Moreover, his contribution to the Sacro Monte is stressed, and his essential traits linked with the nature of the Sacro Monte – scenic, theatrical, yet inward – and with the religious genius of his community. If in some of his works, notably the *St Catherine*, he succumbed momentarily to the lure of new styles, and in Milan sometimes permitted his pupils too much scope, he by no means went into decline but returned in his final frescoes in S Maria della Pace, Milan, especially the *Adoration of the Magi*, to the spirit of his best works.

'To say Sacro Monte is to say Gaudenzio':

For not a few years, then, to say Sacro Monte will be to say Gaudenzio Ferrari: and that is not only because of the high quality of his pictorial imagination, but, more particularly, because of a radical intervention of the painter in the conception itself, architectonic and scenographic, of the sacred drama, as recent criticism has clearly shown; in addition, many sculptural groups are directly inspired by Gaudenzio, when not from his own hand, and there one has an idea of the intensity with which our artist participated in this grand apotheosis of the expressive spirituality of his people.[116]

This summary reflects an immense amount of detailed scholarly work by a number of hands in the last half-century, and especially since the Vercelli exhibition in 1956. In this new work, quite apart from its quantity, quality and density, we can see all the signs of the rise of Gaudenzio's reputation: new works discovered through restoration (at Borgosesia[117] and Valduggia) and through reattribution (for example, the *Two angels in prayer*, now said to be his earliest known work, appropriately in Varallo, in the Chapel of the 'Tomb of the Virgin' in S Maria della Grazie, the earliest chapel, still within the church, and dating from before the death of Caimi in 1499;[118] and the rare polychrome wooden statue of *St Bartholomew*;[119] his graphic work in part published and commented on;[120] the diminution of reference to the 'great names' and the increase in detailed comparisons with a range of other artists and specific works, especially the earlier sculpture of the Piedmont, and the work of other artists of Lombard tradition, especially Spanzotto (at

Ivrea), and of other artists of the North, especially Lotto at Bergamo; the study of his colouration as comparable with the Venetians; and the detailed study of his teachers (Giovenone in Vercelli and Scotto in Milan) and his pupils (Lanino, Giovenone the younger, and others). Butler's interest in Scotto is pursued by recent critics, who stress the sense in which Scotto and Gaudenzio replied to Leonardo (or his imitators) rather than succumbing to him.[121] Not least, we observe the translation of negative judgements into their positive equivalents – 'conflict of influences' has become 'openness to new currents', 'eclecticism' has become 'versatility'. Especially interesting from Butler's point of view is the tendency to value the Sacro Monte phenomenon not simply as devotional, but as a new form of art; and to attribute its real originality of conception as well as execution to Gaudenzio himself. Gaudenzio brought about the transformation, soon after Caimi's death, from the chapel representing a 'devotional theme' or 'narrated fable' envisaged by Caimi into the dramatic progression through successive moments of ensemble of fresco, sculpture, and chapel architecture.[122] The early wooden statuary traditional to the valleys of the Alps – the earliest at the Sacro Monte, now identified as a *Pietà* – developed a new form. Gaudenzio's birthdate is variously placed but is now thought to have been earlier than the traditional 1481, probably about 1475, thus giving him sufficient maturity to have shaped the entire conception shortly after the turn of the century.

Perhaps most interesting of all is the change not in the 'rating' attached to Gaudenzio (such shifts in expert opinion, and market prices, might have elicited Butler's scepticism about 'art bullying'), but in the general conception of the Renaissance. Gaudenzio has come to serve, as he did for Butler, a larger art-historical conception, representing the maintenance of an older tradition throughout a period seen by others in melodramatic terms of cataclysmic change tagged with extravagantly moral and contradictory labels of 'good' and 'evil', and at the same time introducing a decisive innovation. Whole ages – and whole men – had been dragged into and chopped to fit the rationalizing and dialectical schemata of the newly defined conception of the Renaissance, whether employed by the defenders of the Middle Ages, or by the defenders of the old idea of the rebirth of the classics. Gaudenzio has come to be a powerful example of an individual artist who was able to reshape his regional tradition through the absorption of a rapid series of new departures and at the end of his life to appear as a 'proto-mannerist' capable of speaking to the best of Mannerism and Baroque without having betrayed his 'Pre-Raphaelite' heritage or fallen into decadence. The scepticism of our own time about 'origins' and 'ends' of periods and movements chimes with Butler's; we now have, a hundred years later, Butler's Gaudenzio, the crucial figure of a first-rate artist, who successfully negotiated a transition, stepping deftly across the imaginary Pre-Raphaelite cleft. The juggling with period conceptions which was an aspect of the fertile imagination of Friedrich Schlegel, the founder of Romantic criticism, hardened into literalism in the hands of the epigoni – Rio, Lindsay, Ruskin – and the 'scientific' art historians; Butler resisted it earlier than most. He was able to employ the Pre-Raphaelite idea to capture the moment of 'primitivism' independent of Raphael in Gaudenzio and to give full value to the communal element in his work, while rescuing his individuality from the crippling schematizations of the theorists of whatever stripe. Gaudenzio's full stature emerges, and a new biography of a Renaissance artist joins the company of Vasari's *Lives*. No one who follows Butler's invitation to look with his own 'ignorant' eye can resist the unique combination of grace, fluency, *vezzosità* ('blitheness'), and drama in Gaudenzio's works.

It is ironic that Butler's contribution to this result, both the specific art-historical re-evaluation of the work of Gaudenzio and his fellow artists at the Sacro Monte and elsewhere which led to the extension of the canon, and the more searching inspection of the cultural-historical categories that distort viewing, should go unnoticed in his own country, and be misrepresented on occasion even by those who have made more recent contributions to the same effect. Butler's works are ensconced in the permanent bibliography of the development of Gaudenzio's critical reputation; the English edition of *Ex Voto*, the Italian translation, and the Shrewsbury edition (including the translation into English of his introduction to the Italian edition), all appear in the standard Italian bibliography. Yet Mallé's account of Gaudenzio's reception holds that Butler succumbed to precisely that form of Pre-Raphaelitism from which he laboured to extricate himself, Gaudenzio, and cultural history:

In 1894 Butler dedicated a volume to the Sacro Monte and one would expect from the great writer if not critical insight at least poetic participation. But it doesn't occur. He ranges himself with the prejudices of Pre-Raphaelitism which condition his approach but permit him to love the emotional qualities in Ferrari. Natural sympathy, but judgements as far as possible from the right track. Even the comments on the 'theatricality' of the chapels fail to bear fruit.[123]

To understand this we must register the fact that the recent critical reassessment of Gaudenzio in Italy, which has granted him his independence from Raphael, Leonardo, and Michelangelo, has done so through a celebration of the long misprized art of Lombardy and Piedmont. If Gaudenzio is the vital link between the art of Lombardy and the art of Piedmont, neither stops with him. Butler's favourite after Gaudenzio, Tabachetti – Jean de Wespin the Fleming – has been dispossessed in favour of Tanzio da Varallo and Il Morazzone, who lead directly to Lombard Mannerism and Baroque.[124] The Northern influence is accepted, but as having acted on Gaudenzio through no less a figure than Dürer. These attributions may or may not be correct. The point is that the tendency that has led to the full recognition of Gaudenzio has also led to the view that Gaudenzio left materials for the rank and file of Lombard mannerists. The theatricality of the Sacro Monte is also a part of the later history of art in the region, and the notion that Mannerism and Baroque necessarily represented decline – an article of faith with both the Pre-Raphaelites and the advocates of the Renaissance – is naturally rejected by Italian art historians.

Tabachetti and grotesque realism

Apart from Gaudenzio, Butler's major interest among the artists of the Sacro Monte was Tabachetti, or Jean de Wespin, a Flemish sculptor born in Dinant, who worked in the North of Italy, and settled there in 1588 with several members of his family. 'Great and fascinating as Gaudenzio was', he found Tabachetti 'a still more interesting figure', for 'if Gaudenzio has never received anything like his due meed of praise, Tabachetti may be almost said never to have been praised at all.'[125] Butler laboured to ascertain the still obscure facts about his life and works, and to establish the value of the vivid, lifelike statuary that appealed to him. The early reviewers of *Ex Voto*, and Butler's obituarists, stressed the achievement of his 'discovery for the English world' of a virtually unknown artist in an age of such discoveries, as Vasari's thumbnail sketches, primarily of Tuscan artists, were extended.[126]

There has been much controversy and uncertainty over the attributions to Tabachetti, and other artists and craftsmen who took part in the decoration of the chapels. Some of Butler's favourite groups and individual figures at Varallo were attributed to Tabachetti, including the graphic rendering of 'the Little Old Man', *Il Vecchietto*, which he used

60. Tabachetti, or Giovanni D'Enrico, *Il Vecchietto*, Chapel of the Descent from the Cross, Sacro Monte, Varallo

as frontispiece to *Ex Voto* (illus. 60), and the scene of *The Dream of Joseph*. The former is still attributed to him by some; but in other sources it is now attributed to Giovanni D'Enrico.[127] *The Bad Thieves* (and other figures) in Chapel XXXV and 'The Journey to Calvary' (Chapel XXXVI) are still considered to be his: two dark, thin, bent and skulking figures, which nevertheless bear a resemblance to Gaudenzio's intense figure of *The Good Thief* (Chapel XXXVIII, 'Christ on the Cross').[128] Butler singled out 'The Journey to Calvary' and included four photographs in *Ex Voto*: a *General view to the right, St John and the Madonna with the other Maries, St Veronica and Man with goitre,* and *The Two Thieves and their Driver* (illus. 69, 70, 77).[129] Some of his attributions of figures in chapels at Varallo have been disputed, and the works attributed rather to Tanzio da Varallo, Giovanni D'Enrico or Il Morazzone.[130] Butler also had a strong interest in the D'Enrico brothers, Giovanni (c. 1560–1640) and Antonio (also known as Tanzio da Varallo), and by and large his attributions have been borne out by further inquiry, which has tended to increase their *oeuvre* – sometimes at the expense of Tabachetti. Butler included in *Ex Voto* four illustrations of the work of Giovanni D'Enrico: *Caiaphas* (Chapel XXV); *Herod* (in Chapel XXVIII); *Laughing Boys in the Herod Chapel* (Chapel XXVIII); and (by either Tabachetti or D'Enrico) *Man in background in Flagellation Chapel*. It is often difficult to be certain which of the attributions to accept as the authorities conflict, and sometimes the scholarship does not accord with the local guidebooks; even within a single museum or gallery the catalogue may disagree with the attribution on or near the work, as at the Pinacoteca, Varallo. Tabachetti's presence at Varallo is well documented, but the number of works given to him has diminished. As a recent Italian work on the art of the region puts the relationship between Tabachetti and the others, Tabachetti's 'sharp delineations of movement and character', especially in the 'Journey to Calvary' Chapel, led to the 'second splendid phase' of the Sacro Monte in the hands of Giovanni (who worked there for nearly forty years) and his brother (illus. 78–80).[131]

Butler's attributions at Crea were tentative, partly because the chapels had just been restored and repainted when he visited; these were some of his best photographs, in which the intensity of his interest in Tabachetti is registered. Only the Chapel of the 'Martyrdom of St Eusebius' seemed to him certainly to contain work by Tabachetti. The chapels of 'The Birth of the Virgin', 'The Marriage at Cana', and 'The

61. *Jones and Professor Voglino in the Presentation Chapel*, Crea, 1891

Marriage of the Virgin', where he found some signs of his work, have now been attributed to Tabachetti (illus. 72, 74, 75, 76).[132]

Butler would be the last, however, to stake any artist's or critic's reputation on the correct attribution of what he rightly saw as a communal enterprise. The more successful that enterprise was the less easy or appropriate it would be to prise any individual artist out of the collaborative work. The longer the Sacro Monte continued the more difficult it became to extricate the original artist from the renovators. The important fact for him was the joint endeavour in which individuals might remain anonymous but be none the less great artists. The variety of names by which these artists were known – by their place of origin, their family name, their teacher's name, their place of work, or the works they executed – merely demonstrates the negligible importance of the soubriquet. To show this in an age dedicated to aggrandisement of the 'Masters' he had to isolate and give a name, a biography and an *oeuvre* to individual artists; but his contention was that in the communal work in which religion and society were one the name of the artist was unimportant to himself as to others. Anonymity was one of the hallmarks of the authentic 'primitive'. This contention, never more eloquently expressed than in Ruskin's *Seven Lamps*, was certainly one of his early guiding lights. For him, however, it was not a function of the medieval only, but also of futurity: it was an aspect of his evolutionary theory that the small and unknown might labour alone or without recognition and in places unfrequented by the Academies to maintain a style or to create a new one which might eventually bear fruit. At the same time, as Butler strove to specify the histories of the anonymous he added their names to the historical rolls; and the result of work of this kind has been to draw the medieval workmen also out of the reverential obscurity in which Ruskin was content to leave them.[133] The *Annales* histories of the inarticulate, the mute, and the unconscious in our own time have had similar results.

Butler's interest in Tabachetti was nevertheless part of his polemical view of the Renaissance, and again we find him intervening subtly but decisively, setting out from Pre-Raphaelite premises to undermine their position. To the Pre-Raphaelites inheriting Schlegel's rediscovery of the Northern artists, the early Renaissance was marked by the intermingling of Northern or Flemish and German art with Italian art. Lord Lindsay had put the case for 'looking on the early Teutonic school as of equal importance with the early Italian' with his usual rhetorical flourish:

The one [the Italian], it is true, walked with its gaze fixed on heaven, the other on earth, but, like the astronomer and geologist, two distinct worlds were thus revealed to them, and they gave glory to God accordingly. But as heaven and earth must be wedded ere children can be born to Abraham, so the Ideal and the Real, Imagination and Reason, must be reconciled and blent in union ere Art can attain maturity.[134]

The School of Cologne, and the Flemish, in particular van Eyck, influenced Italy both through the visits of Italian artists to Flanders and especially through the visits of Northern artists to Venice, Florence and Naples; despite his rhetoric Lindsay gives a workmanlike brief account of these movements in the final section of his book, 'Influence of Teutonic on Italian Painting – and Conclusion'.[135] It is important to remember that at the time Lindsay wrote almost none of these works were visible in England; van Eyck's *Arnolfini*, acquired by the National Gallery in London in 1842, was virtually alone. It has been remarked that 'the Pre-Raphaelites knew almost nothing of the painters before Raphael'; this was as true of the Northern as of the Southern painters.[136]

The first large exhibition in England of early Northern art was the Manchester Exhibition of Flemish Art in 1857; in the wake of this Butler made his third visit to Italy, travelling via the major galleries of the Netherlands and Belgium. Thus well before his immersion in the sites of Northern Italy – even before his voyage to New Zealand – he had seen a range of major examples of Flemish art.

Jean de Wespin and his family, then, known in Italy as 'Tabachetti', represented the movement of Northern art into the Piedmont and Lombardy, and the association of Gaudenzio as the heir of the truest tendency of local art with the intense realism of the sculptor of the North, is Butler's version of the 'union of opposite' elements in the early Renaissance. That Tabachetti was not contemporary with Gaudenzio, but worked on the Sacro Monte sites after 1580, underlines the community of place over time, and demonstrates the ideality of the 'moment' of fusion of Northern and Southern art which, in fact, as Lord Lindsay pointed out, went on over two centuries. Recent work on Gaudenzio has pointed to a 'Northern' moment in his own work as on the one hand part of the traditional inheritance of the Alpine valleys in close touch with Northern art, and on the other hand as specifically absorbing the best of the new art from the Northern Renaissance through the importation of Dürer's graphic work. Thus the presence Butler identified with Tabachetti has been lodged within Gaudenzio's own work – completing the picture of an artist who absorbed all the best of his time. Finally, the stress on the values identified with 'Tabachetti' allows Butler also to suggest a new phase of realism that was not a 'decline', and to open a path to the future.

His main work is now seen to be at Crea, and Butler devoted a separate section of *Ex Voto* to Crea, as well as discussing it in his chapter on Tabachetti. The scene in Italy's finest wine-growing country is still as he described it:

the rich *colline* [hills] of the Monferrato district begin to rise immediately outside [the town of Casale], and continue in an endless series of vineclad slopes and village-capped hill-tops as far as the eye can reach. These *colline* are of exquisite beauty in themselves, and from their sides the most magnificent views of Piedmont and the Alps extend themselves in every direction.[137]

Having ascended in zigzags from the little station at Serralunga, he describes the scene that greeted him:

The piazza of the sanctuary is some two thousand feet above the sea, and the views are in some respects finer even than those from the Sacro Monte of Varese itself, inasmuch as we are looking towards the chain of the Alps, instead of away from them.[138]

It is here that he carries out his boldest challenge to accepted canons of taste.

Although this general story of the reconciling of the best of North and South was accepted and promoted by Lindsay and Ruskin, it is noticeable that they are still ambivalent about Northern art, still at times not willing to concede it equality with the Italian. There are certain worrying features: the extreme realism, the vulgarity, the grotesque humour. Despite waxing eloquent about Cologne and Nuremberg, and adhering to the general parallel that 'Cologne stands in fact in nearly the same relation to the North as does Giotto to the South',[139] Lord Lindsay exhibits curious lapses, blind spots, and hesitations. The tomb of the Emperor Maximilian at Innsbruck he praises enthusiastically – 'no bastard offspring of Grecian allegory, but thoroughly real and Teutonic'[140] – but the great sculptor Veit Stoss at Nuremberg he dismisses as 'very inferior', and as for 'other curious wood-carvings' he passes them by as 'a minor branch of the fine arts'.[141] Moreover, despite his espousal of the primitive he is concerned for anatomical correctness and for the aerial perspective 'they wholly lacked', and he doesn't like the 'angularity' of the later German and Flemish painters.[142] Worse still, and here he draws the line, is 'the innate Teutonic tendency to caricature'. This unfortunate tendency, which 'led to so many vulgarities in the later schools', peeps out at Cologne, as in 'a picture of Our Saviour before Pilate, where one of the false witnesses, in his embarrassment, scratches his head'.[143] But for the most part he is relieved to find that the deplorable tendency to caricature is still subordinated to 'the higher considerations of expression and propriety'. He is a little worried by the fact that the same minute degree of finish as employed for gems, and rich draperies, is devoted to 'broken thatch, wattled fences' and the like. Even more revealing is that he continues to insist on the distinction between 'High' and 'Low' art; and the champion of Northern art damns 'Jerome Bosch and his imitators', 'a tribe whose characteristics, however original and meritorious in their way, exclude them from consideration under this first department of high and serious Christian art'.[144]

Ruskin too softens down aspects of Northern art that make him uncomfortable. Ruskin spoke slightingly of Correggio's 'low instinct' for the sensuous; yet in his hierarchy of schools of art according to the criterion of the 'love of beauty' in his chapter 'Of Greatness of Style', he placed him no lower than in the second rank, as 'intensely loving physical and corporeal beauty'; whereas 'Albert Dürer, Rubens, and in general the Northern artists, apparently insensible to beauty and caring only for truth, whether shapely or not', are consigned to the 'third rank'. Below this come such as Teniers, and 'other such worshippers of the depraved', who are 'of a certain order in the abyss'.[145] Ruskin's hierarchies change as his criteria change – Teniers rises into the 'third rank', when the criterion is subject matter ('Choice of Noble Subject'), where any artists belong who are concerned with matters such as 'the sports of boys or the simplicities of clowns';[146] but his negative tone towards Northern art is often apparent even when it contradicts the tendency of his argument as, for example, he speaks dismissively of 'Dutch trivialities' even when the argument is that the relation of 'plain facts' may conduce to a 'noble' history painting.[147]

Nowhere is Ruskin more self-contradictory than about the grotesque. The eighteenth-century development of the theory of the Sublime which in the hands of the Romantics overturned and replaced the Neo-classic doctrine of the beautiful had brought the grotesque into prominence as having a strong connection with the powerful but less savoury ranges of the Sublime. This had been dealt with in a variety of ways by theorists from Burke to Schlegel and Victor Hugo. Ruskin, in his two major treatments of the grotesque, in *The Stones of Venice* and in *Modern Painters*, retains the link with the 'terrible sublime', but renders the grotesque at once more harmless and less admissible.

The grotesque is permitted to take its place as the third form of the 'true ideal' (with 'purism' and 'naturalism'), especially in sacred subjects (Holbein's *Dance of Death* or Dürer's *Knight and Death*), but at the expense of its negative aspects. Just as he consigned the treatment of 'immoral subjects' to an entirely negative scale, or 'the abyss', so he read the diabolic, the bestial, the inhuman, and the immoral out of the grotesque. The 'true grotesque' became a measure of 'moral aspiration' in the perceiver.[148] Even Lamb, despite his championship of Hogarth, drew the line at the series of engravings *The Four Stages of Cruelty* as 'mere caricature'; the last in particular, which shows the murderer receiving *The Reward of Cruelty* by the dissection of his body in an anatomical theatre, is clearly related to Rembrandt's *The Anatomy Lesson*.[149] Lamb defends Hogarth's 'grotesque physiognomies' as for the most part 'permanent abiding ideas' rather than mere 'sports of nature'.[150] Whereas for Victor Hugo it was Shakespeare who represented the grotesque most fully, and thereby became the quintessentially modern writer, Ruskin admits only Shakespeare's Ariel and Titania, as the grotesque arising from 'healthful but irrational play of the imagination in times of rest'.[151] Moreover, according to Ruskin, the grotesque must be expressed only 'imperfectly', in order that it should always be clear that it is only thought, not reality. Most telling for Butler is the inferior place assigned to humour: 'So far as it [the 'jesting grotesque'] expresses any transient flash of wit or satire, the less labour of line, or colour, given to its expression the better; elaborate jesting being always intensely painful.'[152]

Butler deliberately chose the Fleming Tabachetti as exemplifying precisely those elements of realism that even the purveyors in England of the Romantic affirmation of Northern art found it hardest to accept and which showed up their self-contradictions most glaringly.[153] He battled against the distinction between 'High' and 'Low', and in favour of the everyday, the characteristic, the gritty, the grotesque (not least the 'jesting' grotesque), and the satiric. His intense interest in figures like 'the Goitred Man' shows that he was prepared to give house room in art to 'sports of nature'. His work in Basel on Holbein drawings was strategic: it was by this route that Northern graphic art had entered Italy; and the English link to the visual tradition in which 'caricature' was an authentic art reached back beyond Hogarth to Holbein.[154] The subject of the drawings was *La Danse des Paysans*, 'The Peasants' Dance', and the drawings were realized in the fictive architecture of the façade of the *Haus zum Tanz*, the House of the Dance, in the early 1520s.[155] Butler cast his article in the form of an attribution, holding that a drawing (illus. 62) that was identified as a copy of the Holbein drawing of the façade was in fact also by Holbein.[156] The attribution question has obscured the reason for his interest in the *Haus zum Tanz*. Holbein's design presents a similar challenge to the 'goose-step' of *Stilgeschichte* as does Gaudenzio's: far from representing simply the Renaissance-classical taking over the Late Gothic, the façade as a whole with its *trompe l'oeil* effect has a strong Mannerist element.[157] What interested Butler was the retention of the earlier 'Peasant Dance' motif in the assemblage of stylistic elements in Holbein's innovative façade. The combination of a homely motif painted as a bas-relief within a complex architectural setting had strong resemblances to the Sacro Monte.[158] A model of the house (now destroyed) shows clearly the position of the

62. Hans Holbein the Younger, or copyist, *The Peasants' Dance* (detail),
drawing of the façade of the *Haus zum Tanz*, Basel, *c.* 1525

63. Model of Hans Holbein's designs for the *Haus zum Tanz*, Basel, 1878

motif (illus. 63). Butler stressed the elements that embarrassed Lindsay and Ruskin. Were the sculptures of the Sacro Monte life-size? Ruskin had declared that 'in the best works of Raphael and Leonardo the figures are almost always less than life'. [159] Did the statues have 'real hair', as King reported? Butler is delighted to compound the offence by pointing out that it is not human hair, but horse hair.

The form of the grotesque most closely related to the visual is Friedrich Schlegel's *Bilderwitz*, defined as anatomical and physical, and employing 'reversed relationships', '*verkehrte Versetzungen*', as in 'breeches parts' for women. For Schlegel this was related to the role-changes required in hermeneutic interpretation, the process of 'self-creation' and 'self-destruction' which is part of the endless cycle of re-reading and which defines irony.[160] The critic who did so much to establish 'Northern' art as equal and opposite to classical art not surprisingly brings us closest to the art of the grotesque. For Schlegel the grotesque is a deliberate, not a naive, play with paradoxes and strange reversals of form and matter. Butler exemplifies this visual form of the grotesque with exceptional clarity in his anecdote, almost a parable of the grotesque, about the search within the chapels (Butler liked nothing better than to penetrate behind the illusionistic framework) for 'the original Adam and Eve' among the statues of the Sacro Monte. There had been, he was told, an old Adam and Eve, who had been replaced by newer and superior figures by Tabachetti, and rather than waste the old statues they were 'now doing duty as Roman soldiers in Chapel No. 23, the Capture of Christ' (illus. 64):[161]

On investigation, we found, against the wall, two figures dressed as Roman soldiers that evidently had something wrong with them. The draperies of all the other figures are painted, either terra-cotta or wood, but with these two they are real, being painted linen or calico, dipped in thin mortar or plaster of Paris, and real drapery always means that the figure has had something done to it. The armour, where armour shows, is not quite of the same pattern as that painted on the other figures, nor is it of the same make; in the case of the remoter figure it does not go down far enough, and leaves a lucid interval of what was evidently once bare stomach, but has now been painted the brightest blue that could be found, so that it does not catch the eye as flesh; a little further examination was enough to make us strongly suspect that the figures had both been originally nude, and in this case the story current in Varallo was probably true.

Then the question arose, which was Adam, and which Eve? The farther figure was the larger and therefore ought to have been Adam, but it had long hair, and looked a good deal more like a woman than the other did. The nearer figure had a beard and moustaches, and was quite unlike a woman; true, we could see no sign of bosom

130

64. *The Old Adam and Eve*, Sacro Monte, Varallo,
photograph by Samuel Butler, 1889

131

with the farther figure, but neither could we with the nearer. On the whole, therefore, we settled it that the nearer and moustached soldier was Adam, and the more distant long-haired beardless one, Eve.[162]

The story has already succeeded in suggesting a change of sex for one figure (from Eve into Roman soldier) and a physical role reversal (the small figure is male, the large female), and has envisioned each figure in turn as both male and female. But the grotesque effect does not end there. In the evening they (Butler and Jones) were allowed to enter the chapel to examine the figures more closely:

The drapery showed that curiosity had been already rife upon the subject, and, observing this, Jones and I gently lifted as much of it as was necessary, and put the matter for ever beyond future power of question that the farther, long-haired, beardless figure was Adam, and the nearer, moustached one, Eve. They are now looking in the same direction, as joining in the hue and cry against Christ, but were originally turned towards one another; the one offering, and the other taking, the apple.[163]

Here the male and female identities are once again reversed, causing a further scanning of each figure as each sex, and turning the inanimate animate (an aspect of the grotesque) as the sexes shift; still more surprising is that the matter can be settled by anatomical inspection. So 'finished' were these ambiguous statues that their sex could be settled beyond doubt. This serves as a parody of Ruskin's celebrated passage in *The Stones of Venice* damning the Renaissance sculptors of Venice for failing to finish their statues and carve them down to the last invisible detail, the failure that announced the onset of corruption. The joke is given a further turn here by the story of the original sin itself: is not the sin to look for and recognize the difference of sex? The sign of sin, emblematized by the fig leaf, at the Fall of Man and Woman is to know sex when they see it, not to have or to commit it. It is Ruskin who commits the sin, not the Renaissance. Ruskin, who would have turned in distaste from this vulgar anecdote and from these highly 'finished' statues exemplifying his doctrine, is mocked by them. Further, the case confronts him with his own confusion: the grotesque, according to him, must always be left 'unfinished'; yet not to finish is corrupt. The statues are naive grotesques – and here Butler wickedly recalls Ruskin's praise for the anonymous 'Lombard craftsman' who saw a griffin;[164] his critical exemplum is a deliberate grotesque.

This form of extreme realism, extending to anatomical details, exhibited especially by costumed or polychrome statuary, automata and panoramas, with its power to create uncertainty and discomfort in the viewer as to whether what he is seeing is real or not, was identified by Freud with 'the uncanny'.[165] This element in Butler's account of the Sacro Monte may well be one of the factors that has prevented its discussion for so long. Butler's *Bilderwitz* is comic, but its anatomical grotesque joins the uncanny discomfort of the ambiguity of detailed realism in a deliberate and very modern offence against the elevated idea of 'Art'. Adam's and Eve's doubled gender-swapping is in a class defined for the twentieth-century by Duchamp's moustache on the Mona Lisa.

While the comedy of the grotesque was well within his repertoire, Butler did not embrace all forms of extreme realism; like Schlegel,[166] like Lindsay,[167] and like Burckhardt,[168] he was uncomfortable with the Bologna school.[169] There were several schools of extreme dramatic realism in Renaissance Italy north of Florence in the last third of the Quattrocento: in Bologna the work of Nicola d'Apulia initiated the tendency, especially the extraordinarily expressive polychrome terracotta *Bewailing of the Body of Christ* in S Maria della Vita; Mazzoni is associated with this *Bewailing* through a number of terracotta groups on this subject or that of the Nativity in the area just to the north of Bologna. Mazzoni's work was based at first on life-casts of hands and faces and even torsos, glass was used for eyes, and as at the Sacri Monti the statues were dressed in real clothes and given real props and impedimenta; later a mask-like representation of emotion was used.[170] Butler did not accept any link between them, however; it is in the context of the Sacro Monte that Butler attempted to come to terms with realism.

Under the general heading of 'Tabachetti', as he approached the nerve of his own style, Butler was roused to some of his most characteristic, richly comic expressions of his point of view, and of his art-critical method. The brilliant essay on *The Sanctuary of Montrigone* – which forms the second half of his *Universal Review* article on Tabachetti, entitled *A Sculptor and a Shrine* (1888) – is an extended essay on one composite work, a Chapel of the 'Birth of the Virgin', and on one particular statue in it (illus. 65). The statue is again an example of sexual ambiguity: is it St Anne's mother? or is it her husband, St Joachim? Is it the Virgin's grandmother? or is it her father? The reader focuses with increasing intensity on this figure sitting by the bed as it is redescribed, first as the saintly father (like Joseph, whose ambiguous role evokes considerable sympathy in Italy), then as St Anne's mother – this identification confirmed by Butler's Italian friend, 'one of the leading doctors

65. *The Virgin's Grandmother*, Chapel of the Birth of the Virgin, Montrigone, photograph by Samuel Butler, 1889

at Varallo', who recognizes her instantly as not only a woman but '*una suocera tremenda*', 'a mother-in-law of the first magnitude', then again as Joachim (who as the sacristan says, 'looks like a woman but isn't a woman'). Each identification opens into a suggested drama ('Dear Mamma has come. We knew that she would, and that any little misunderstandings between her and Joachim would ere long be forgotten and forgiven'), which as the reader begins to imagine the next scene is halted by the counter-identification. The riddling relationships add to the number of apparent reidentifications – for St Joachim's mother-in-law is, of course, none other than the Virgin's Grandmother. It is this title Butler settles on, for where else has one met her, clearly an important person in the Family Romance of the Virgin's life? The result of this focussing on a minor figure in the composition – 'attribution' and even identification are finally irrelevant – is that it is permanently fixed in the reader's mind. It may be fixed in precisely the form given it by his photograph and his description, which are inseparable; or, as his essay suggests, it may have a further life in the imagination.[171] The rapid shifts of narrative perspective create radically different alternating images like the duck-rabbit optical illusion. This intensely expressive, homely, forceful yet ultimately enigmatic figure by an anonymous artist in an obscure mountain village chapel forms the basis of a comic set piece of 'word-sculpture' which deliberately challenges Pater's famous passage on the Mona Lisa. Butler's essay deserves to be equally famous.

The subject, the Birth of the Virgin, is one that occupied him in his consideration of Tabachetti at Crea:

It is not always easy for us English to tell the Birth of the Virgin from the Nativity, and it may help the reader to distinguish these subjects readily if he will bear in mind that at the Birth of the Virgin the baby is always going to be washed – which never happens at the Nativity; this, and that the Virgin's mother is almost invariably to have an egg, and generally a good deal more, whereas the Virgin never has anything to eat or drink. The Virgin's mother always wants keeping up.[172]

He passes in review a number of treatments of the subject in Lombardy, including Gaudenzio's fresco at S Cristofero, Vercelli, where 'the Virgin's mother is eating one egg with a spoon, and there is another coming in on a tray, which I think is to be beaten up in wine. Something more substantial to follow is coming in on a hot plate with a cover over it and a napkin.'[173] The homely, practical scene reminds us of Gerard David's refreshing painting *Virgin and Child with a Bowl of Milk* in which Mary for once is not breast-feeding an infant Christ but carefully spooning up milk (probably gruel) for a large, prospering child of several months old. The two capable, absorbed nurses who prepare the bath are executed with the kind of dramatic verve and anatomical bravura verging on comic exuberance that Gaudenzio displayed in his famous portrayals of angels (illus. 89, 90).[174] For Butler not only Gaudenzio but Shakespeare's Nurse in *Romeo and Juliet* is the inescapable analogy. He makes it explicit in his treatment of another instance of this scene, in his essay 'A Medieval Girl School', on the chapels at Oropa: of the 'head nurse', who has the infant 'in full charge', he says: 'I am afraid Shakespeare was dead before the sculptor was born, otherwise I should have felt certain that he had drawn Juliet's nurse from this figure.'[175] Shakespeare was not only paired with Hogarth as exemplifying English comic genius, he was the prime example of an anonymous craftsman emerging from humble circumstances for whose Life only scanty materials were available; in his book on Shakespeare's sonnets Butler constructed an individualized Life of the Renaissance Artist from his works.[176] The link between his English and his Italian Renaissance studies is a close one. Butler adduces another work of Gaudenzio's, at Milan, where two eggs are coming in on a tray, 'and they too, I should say, are to be beaten up in wine'. In *Montrigone* he grounds the whole scene in local custom: 'The Virgin's mother does not, I believe, get eggs east of Milan. I am told that the custom of giving eggs either raw, or beaten up with wine, to women immediately after their confinement, is a Valsesian one. . .'.[177] Butler, of course, is deliberately keeping at bay any 'symbolic interpretation', while amply suggesting 'renewed life'. At this crucial point, then, where he is conveying his sense of the presence of 'Flemish' realism in Northern Italy, Tabachetti disappears (Butler does not attribute this chapel to him), and it is Gaudenzio's renderings he draws on. Gaudenzio's last work brought the two stories together – those of St Anne and of the Virgin Mary – in the church of S Maria della Pace, Milan (illus. 87). That some critics now see it as reverting to his earliest manner, and others see it as having traces of 'mannerism', need not detain us.

The Sanctuary at Montrigone displays Butler's art-critical method at its sharpest (and funniest): provoking to surprise, opposition, mirth, and (in those who can stand the pace) dawning recognition and complete overhauling of opinion and feeling. This casts light on his use of the 'false attribution' and the 'dubious identification', as well as the insult to the great name: it draws shocked opinion's attention to the object. In his essay on *The Genesis of Feeling* he outlined in Lamarckist evolutionary terms the rationale of this critical method: feeling, originating as undifferentiated 'shock', is progressively differentiated and refined by use, and the fact of its conventionalization (Butler's view of language is radically Saussurean before its time) becomes lost to consciousness. The evolution of human culture – always his concern even in his biological speculations – depends, then, on an analogous process which his critical method epitomizes: beginning in shock, which gives rise to progressive reconsideration of opinion, it ends in a fresh differentiation of feeling. The challenge to stock responses always produces pain, which is a growth point in the differentiation of feeling. The 'ignorant eye' begins to learn what it really likes and dislikes.

Natural artists

We are now perhaps in a position to understand the chapter on 'The Decline of Italian Art' that stands at the very centre of *Alps and Sanctuaries*, and the suggestions Butler makes for reversing the decline. Butler reports at first hand from exhibitions of Italian art: 'Modern Italian art is in many respects as bad as it once was good . . . The Italian painters, with very few exceptions, paint as badly as we do, or worse . . .'[178] The notion that a decline had taken place from the founding of the Italian Academy was, as we have seen, a familiar one; Butler found it in Layard, to look no further afield. Lindsay and Ruskin he assimilated in such a way as to present one aspect of the work of Gaudenzio – his traditional spiritual grace – in the best available light; in order to salvage his work as a whole, the Pre-Raphaelite thesis of a radical break at the inception of 'the Renaissance' had to be rejected. The Sacro Monte's extreme realism led forward as well as back. In this context his argument against the art of his contemporaries, and his prescription for the future, is clarified.

Many of those who praised the past demanded a return to it. Butler's merit lay in understanding that any attempt to ape the past would fail; Schlegel's call to return to the 'tranquil pious spirit of early Christianity' was doomed from the start. But those who rejected the revaluation of the Italian primitives for fear that it would have only a negative impact on current painting were also mistaken in the long run.[179] The originality of Butler's conception by comparison with the Pre-Raphaelites and with both the German and the French 'Nazarenes', who moved towards symbolism (culminating in Puvis de Chavannes), is startling. The idea of the 'primitive', once acquired through imaginative insight, and affirmed through historical research – uncovering the sites, rewriting the canon, and re-stocking the museums – had to be reinterpreted from scratch, if art was to achieve a renascence. The evolutionary mental leap required to conceive the 'primitive' in a secular industrial society could only be achieved by retrieving 'the ignorant eye'.

He set off from the offence to 'High Art' and the recall to local 'Low' tradition:

This [black and white periodical illustration] is the one kind of art – and it is a very good one – in which we excel as distinctly as the age of Phidias excelled in sculpture. Leonardo da Vinci would never have succeeded in getting his drawings accepted at 85 Fleet Street, any more than one of the artists or the staff of 'Punch' could paint a fresco which should hold its own against Da Vinci's Last Supper.[180]

In 'The Decline of Art' and at the end of the previous chapter ('Lanzo') he published some examples of the kind of art and art training he would like to promote – the work of 'natural artists', or as we would say, 'primitive' or 'naive artists', the untrained artist expressing himself freely. We are now in a position to understand his grouping. He gives two examples of the work of an 'untrained Italian amateur',[181] and a third by a 'self-taught Italian', showing 'unaffected archaism'.[182] There are English 'natural artists', the progeny of Hogarth, such as the obscure artist ('Mr Pollard') of a cheap lithograph, *The Funeral of Tom Moody*, and unpretentious sporting prints.[183] Talent is not lacking, in Italy or elsewhere. The work of children and untutored adults is vital: the potential artist may learn to express himself, if only he is not hampered by being made to copy the classics, or nature, or any prescribed object. In 'Decline', as a cautionary tale he offers the work of a twelve-year old Italian boy who had been overtrained and highly praised by an 'eminent sculptor' as a credit to his school.[184] His call for a society of artists in which the beginner would help the beginner, and the child the child is a satiric comment on Ruskin's Guild of St George, where the great man condescended to dispense art instruction to the humble, and echoes in a new key Hogarth's insistence that the Academy should remain a society of equals, without offices or emoluments. The question 'By doing what may we again get Bellinis and Andrea Mantegnas as in old times?' cannot be answered by the injunction: 'Copy them'. The 'imitation' of the 'primitives' recommended by Schlegel and Ruskin is a contradiction in terms. An artist might still flourish in the Vals of the Alps who worked

66. Henry Festing Jones, *Fresco at Mesocco – 'March'*, 1879

in the spirit of the old; Butler adduces the example of Dedomenici da Rossi (*d.* 1840) whose traces he has found in the neighbourhood of Varallo. But it cannot be uprooted from its milieu, exported to the academies or reduced to rule. Butler collected examples of the work of the whole range of 'natural artists'. The colour, the spontaneity, the unconscious comedy, the simple expressive power he wanted he tried to convey in the examples he published; colour is a strong element in the originals lost in his black and white reproductions. He collected several intended for *Alps* which were excluded in the final selection on grounds of cost; and these are the most striking (illus. 67, 68).

Having retraced Butler's long road to the Italian Renaissance and

67. 'Natural artist', *The Windmill*

68. 'Natural artist', *Blowing up a mine*

back to England in the late nineteenth century, we can now see that this collocation of the true naive, the grotesque, the realistic and the comic, once melded with entire coherence and confidence into the art of Gaudenzio Ferrari, is liberated through his history of culture and projected into the future as an entirely new set of possibilities. Butler 'blows up a mine'. This apparent unexpectedness, the sense of something rich and strange at last understood, the result of long effort of thought and personal pain, which at first appears a birth of a new period, in the still longer course of evolution comes to be woven into the seamless fabric of human experience. As Butler put it in the biological perspective that lay behind his cultural and art history:

All that can be said is that there is a nisus in the right direction which is not wholly in vain, and that though tens of thousands of men and women of genius are as dandelion seeds borne upon the air and perishing without visible result, yet there is here and there a seed that really does take root and spring upwards to be a plant on the whole more vigorous than that from which it sprung.[185]

69. Tabachetti (1567–1615), *Chapel of the Journey to Calvary, c.* 1599,
Sacro Monte, Varallo, photograph by Samuel Butler, 1888

70. Tabachetti, *Chapel of the Journey to Calvary*, Sacro Monte, Varallo.
Detail: *St Veronica and Christ with the goitred Man and Flagellator*,
photograph by Samuel Butler, 1888

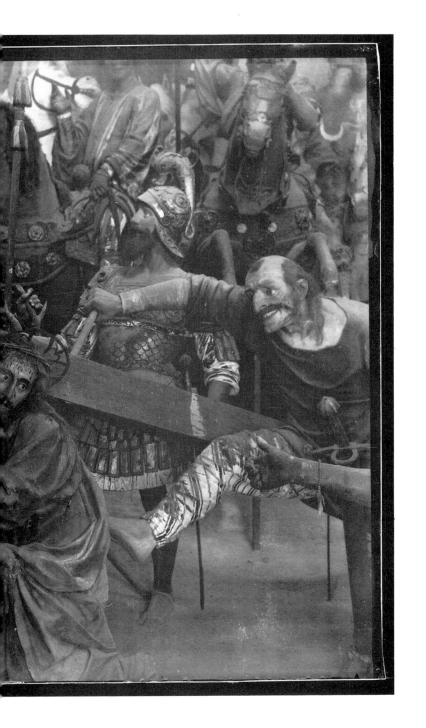

71. *Chapel of the Birth of the Virgin*, Crea, photograph by Samuel Butler, 1891

72. Tabachetti, *Chapel of the Marriage at Cana, c.* 1605, Crea,
photograph by Samuel Butler, 1891

147

73. Tabachetti (attrib.), *The goitred Man*, Chapel of the Journey to Calvary, Sacro Monte, Varallo, photograph by Samuel Butler

74. *Chapel of the Birth of the Virgin*, Crea, photograph by Samuel Butler, 1891

75. Tabachetti, *Chapel of the Martyrdom of St Eusebius*, *c.* 1598, Crea,
photograph by Samuel Butler, 1891

76. Tabachetti, *Chapel of the Martyrdom of St Eusebius*, *c.* 1598, Crea,
photograph by Samuel Butler, 1891

77. Tabachetti, *Chapel of the Journey to Calvary*, Sacro Monte, Varallo. Detail:
St Veronica, photograph by Samuel Butler, 1888

78. Giovanni D'Enrico (*c.* 1560–1640) (attrib.), *Ecce Homo Chapel*, *c.* 1608, Sacro
Monte, Varallo. Detail: *Man with two children*, photograph by Samuel Butler, 1888

79. Giovanni D'Enrico (attrib.), *Ecce Homo Chapel*, *c.* 1608, Sacro Monte, Varallo. Detail: *Man with staff*, photograph by Samuel Butler, 1888

80. Giovanni D'Enrico (attrib.), *Ecce Homo Chapel*, *c.* 1608, Sacro Monte, Varallo. Detail: *Stooping man*, photograph by Samuel Butler, 1888

81. Gaudenzio Ferrari (*c.* 1475–1546), *St John the Baptist in the Wilderness*,
Montrigone, photograph by Samuel Butler, 1890

154

82. Gaudenzio Ferrari, *Crucifixion Chapel*, 1518, Sacro Monte, Varallo,
photograph by Samuel Butler, 1889

83. Gaudenzio Ferrari, *Crucifixion Chapel*, 1518, Sacro Monte, Varallo, photograph by Samuel Butler, 1889

84. Gaudenzio Ferrari, *Chapel of the Adoration of the Magi*, 1528, Sacro Monte, Varallo, photograph by Samuel Butler

85. Gaudenzio Ferrari, *The Marriage of the Virgin, c.* 1528, S Cristoforo, Vercelli

86. Gaudenzio Ferrari, *St Joachim expelled from the Temple*, before 1510, Turin

87. Gaudenzio Ferrari, *Two Nurses preparing the Bath*, detail of *The Birth of the Virgin*, 1546, S Maria della Pace, Milan

88. Gaudenzio Ferrari, *King*, 1528, Chapel of the Adoration of the Magi, Sacro Monte, Varallo

89. Gaudenzio Ferrari, *Cupola of S Maria dei Miracoli, Saronno*, 1534–7

90. Gaudenzio Ferrari, *Three Angels with musical instruments*, 1534–7, detail of Cupola, S Maria dei Miracoli, Saronno

91. *La Musa Polinnia* ('Authoress of the Odyssey'), 1st century AD

Victorian Hellenism
and *The Authoress of the Odyssey*

————

Butler's passion for Italy found another expression, again one which engaged with a major topic of contemporary taste in literature and art and cut a swathe across received opinion. Once again he appears as an explorer, an adventurer on new terrain, topographical and intellectual. If his explorations in the North of Italy, in the Ticino, Piedmont and Lombardy, led to a quite fresh interpretation of the Renaissance which differentiated him sharply from his contemporaries, his explorations in the South, in Sicily, led to an equally pungent indictment of Victorian Hellenism and the opening of a new perspective.

Authorship of the 'Homeric' epics

His book *The Authoress of the Odyssey* was published in 1897, illustrated with a striking portrait of the Authoress, an anonymous painting on a wooden panel of a young Greek girl (illus. 91), with maps of Ulysses' journey, and with photographs Butler took on site. It was the climax of a group of works related to Homer, including the oratorio 'Ulysses' (which sent him back to the *Odyssey* for the libretto, on which he collaborated with Jones, and set to music); his lecture on 'The Humour of Homer'; and his prose translations of the *Iliad* and the *Odyssey* and of Hesiod's *Works and Days*. This group of related works took him several times to Sicily, as well as to Greece and the Troad, to see Schliemann's excavation sites during the 1890s. *The Authoress of the Odyssey* is one of his most characteristic productions, whose revolutionary implications and sheer impudence led the Establishment to receive it in dignified silence, broken only by the occasional parenthetical sneer. To this day the scope and aim of Butler's irony has not been recognized. Even less has it been registered that Butler's position leads to a revision of the traditional iconography of Homer and his epics, both the representations of 'the blind bard' himself from ancient times, and the illustrations of scenes from the poem, in particular the meeting of Odysseus with Nausicaa.

Yet David Grene in his introduction to a new edition of *The Authoress of the Odyssey* in 1967 pointed out that two out of three of Butler's main contentions would now be accepted by classicists: the first, that the *Iliad* and the *Odyssey* were composed by different authors; the second, that some time elapsed between their composition. The third contention, however, was that the celebrated epic was written by a woman, who lived at Trapani and drew the locale of the poem from Sicily.[1] What Grene labels the third contention needs to be broken down into two: first, that the poet was a woman; second, that the locale of the poem is primarily Sicilian. For on the Western orientation, topography and archaeology of the *Odyssey* – like everything relating to the poem, much disputed matters – Butler has received a good deal of support and indeed figures as the modern founder of one line of Homeric research. It is only the contention that the author of the *Odyssey* was a woman which has remained anathema, and excluded him from the circle of reputable critics of Homer. As one of his supporters from within the ranks of classical scholarship described the reaction:

The scholars who heard of his view were shocked. More, they were huffed. The Poet Laureate could take the suggestion sensibly. But of the scholars a few turned nasty, while most adopted instinctively an attitude of Hush. It was not until sufficient time had elapsed for them to suppose the theory dead that they even began to joke about it.[2]

Even the sympathetic Larbaud pronounced his view 'un peu inattendu'.[3] That his best-known English disciples were Shaw and Graves (who incorporated the Authoress into *The Greek Myths*) has only served to reinforce his reputation for impertinence and idiosyncrasy. Yet the prime beneficiary of Butler's Odyssey is James Joyce's *Ulysses*.

To enumerate Butler's contentions separately and to attempt to assess their accuracy according to the current views of classical scholars, however, is completely to miss the significance of his book. Taken as a whole – and it can only be understood as such – *Authoress* is a brilliant polemic aimed not merely at classical scholarship but at the whole phenomenon of Victorian Hellenism, the set of attitudes that he saw to be founded upon a false principle that had misdirected his own training and was producing a meretricious art. It aims at that complex of patriarchal and authoritarian assumptions which the corpus of his work met in head-on collision, and as with *The Fair Haven* the audience was so immersed in its values that it was unable to recognize the tone or the target.

The Authoress, according to Butler, was the young unmarried woman who included herself in the *Odyssey* in much the best episode, as Nausicaa. Book 6 of the poem centres on Nausicaa, who is the first person to encounter Ulysses after his landing on the Phaeacian shore, washed up in the storm, wholly bereft of men, ships and possessions. It is the dramatic moment of the lowest point in his fortunes, and the beginning of his homecoming. Athena appears to Nausicaa in a dream, in the form of her best friend, to suggest that as the time when she will be ripe for marriage is at hand, she should prepare her wardrobe. Nausicaa goes to her parents, offering to wash her brothers' clothes to conceal her embarrassment at being seen to prepare for the coming of a husband, and is granted a wagon and mules to go to the washing place. She sets out with her maidens, and on arrival they do the washing and then proceed to picnic and play ball. Meanwhile their voices wake Ulysses from his deep exhausted sleep on a pile of dry leaves, and he ventures forth, covering his nakedness with a branch. Nausicaa is not frightened, and he addresses her in a polished speech, comparing her with a young sapling he has seen growing by the temple of Apollo, and throwing himself on her mercy. She commands her maidens, who have fled, to return, and encourages him to bathe and dress in clothes she lends him. She then instructs him to follow her wagon, but not to return with her, as it might give rise to gossip – had she taken a foreign husband, then, for she had always scorned the lads of her acquaintance? – but to follow after and to appeal to her mother for help. She sets off for home, Ulysses following after. In the subsequent books, Ulysses is well received (Books 7 and 8), and tells the whole tale of his wanderings since Troy (Books 9–12). The Phaeacians offer to take him home. She meets him once more, as he departs, and he promises always to remember how she saved him.

Butler's Nausicaa, the Authoress, was at home in Sicily, had never travelled, knew little of Greece and nothing of navigation or war. She focussed on the domestic side of the story; the first four books tell of Telemachus and Penelope at home, hoping for Ulysses' return, and the whole of Books 13–24 describe Ulysses' homecoming; Ulysses himself enters only in Book 5, and only five books are devoted to his famous adventures on the way. She lavished her interest on women throughout, both on the human women, Penelope, Helen, Nausicaa, and the old nurse Eurycleia who alone recognizes Ulysses, and on the mythological women, Athena, Circe, the Sirens, Calypso, and the parade of legendary ladies in Hades, including the ghost of his mother. She is jealous of female honour and power, insisting on the faithfulness of Penelope and Ulysses' sole wish to return home, even at the sacrifice of the immortality offered him by Calypso. Her Ulysses is a passive figure, imprisoned, bullied, protected, and salvaged by women; of his ten years of wandering after the fall of Troy in fact no fewer than eight years are spent simply in the captivity of Calypso and Circe. The topography is taken almost exclusively from Sicily: both the land of the Phaeacians and the home-land of 'Ithaca' are based on the geography of Trapani and Mt Eryx, as well as serving traditionally as the land of the Cyclops, while Scylla and Charybdis are by common consent located in the straits of Messina. Thus Ulysses' much vaunted journey to the outer bounds of the known world is in fact a little cruise round Sicily from Trapani to Trapani.[4] Such is Butler's provocative case.

To understand why this was so offensive one must look at the view of Homer which was inculcated in the great Victorian public schools and ingrained in public life and speech, a view which Butler had been forced to imbibe at first hand throughout the sound classical schooling which had issued in his good Tripos results at Cambridge. One must also look more specifically at the scholarship of his day, in particular at the 'Homeric question' as it had been raised and pursued since F. A. Wolf's *Prolegomena ad Homerum* (1795). Grene has oversimplified Butler's position, in the interests of aligning him with current views. Butler had no illusions as he declared war, saying, 'How can I expect Homeric scholars to tolerate theories so subversive of all that most of them have been insisting on for so many years?'[5] His position opposed both the extreme wing of the Wolfian 'disintegrators' of the Homeric epics, and the rearguard action fought against them, as against the closely related critical analysis of the composition of the Bible, by the guardians of Victorian classicism.

The great Victorians did not always agree with the scholars of their own day, instead vigorously defending the unity, personality, and grandeur of the poet Homer against the German school and its English adherents, who held that 'Homer' was a fictional authorial attribution representing a complex process first of gradual accumulation of oral epic songs over a considerable time, then a later phase of 'editing' or 'composing' the materials into the form in which they were finally written down, probably in the time of Peisistratus in the sixth century BC. It is the latter position which emerged as the mainstream of classical scholarship, and with various adjustments, has remained so to this day. Only very recently has the tide begun to turn against the more extreme formulations of the case for the 'oral' nature of the epics. Butler cunningly uses points from each school against the other, and placing both of them over against his bold reinvention of the epic debunks both.[6] His creative rereading leads him to produce the first modern translation, and to rewrite the poem in critical terms as a novel that puts us – as it put Joyce – well on the road to Ulysses the Dubliner.

The epitome of the Victorian attitude towards Homer, what has been called the 'Boy's Own view of classical history', is Gladstone's three-volume *Prolegomena: Studies on Homer and the Homeric Age* (1858). In a plea for the extended study of Homer in the universities, he wrote: 'He is second to none of the poets of Greece as the poet of boys; but he is far advanced before them all . . . as the poet of men.'[7] For some, like Andrew Lang, this required the 'Surge and Thunder' interpretation of the *Odyssey*.[8] For Gladstone it meant the preference for the *Iliad* over the *Odyssey* (to which he pays scant attention); and his reliance on Homer's evidence as supplying historical and geographical fact as well as moral instruction gives the epics an almost scriptural precedence. Homer's testimony must be treated as 'paramount, and as constituting a class by itself, with which no other literary testimony may compete'.[9] He canvasses Homer for testimony, on ethnology, on religion, on politics, on geography, and only at the end of the last volume, on poetry. Just as the German school of historical criticism broke down the seamless unity of Biblical inspiration, so it fragmented the unity of the author 'Homer' and undermined his 'witness'. Homer for him is the Bible of the Greeks. Gladstone will not have either scriptural or scripture-like authority questioned, and inveighs aginst the 'Homeric bubble-schemes' of the 'piecers', who argue that there were originally a number of Iliadic and Odyssean songs, afterwards made up into the poems; the 'amplifiers', who look on the epics as expanded by gradual interpolations and additions from a brief original; and the 'separators', who 'will have just two Homers and no more, one for the *Iliad* and one for the *Odyssey*'.[10] Thus Homer ranked with the Bible – and the translation most widely used in Victorian times, that of Lang, Leaf and Myers of the *Iliad*, and Butcher and Lang of the *Odyssey*, was modelled on the Bible.

92. *Head of Kore* (Greek maiden; type of Nausicaa), 6th century BC

In these terms, Butler took up the position of a 'separator', attributing the *Iliad* to a male author, the *Odyssey* to a female author, thus whittling away at the massive indivisible grandeur of Homer:

Phenomenal works imply a phenomenal workman, but there are phenomenal women as well as phenomenal men, and though there is much in the 'Iliad' which no woman, however phenomenal, can be supposed at all likely to have written, there is not a line in the 'Odyssey' which a woman might not perfectly well write, and there is much beauty which a man would be almost certain to neglect.[11]

His pert young Authoress of the *Odyssey* was calculated to infuriate those who saw Homer as a manual of war, religion, and politics, for the education of the male ruling class. His very defence of the personality of the Authoress was a deliberate travesty of their defence of the person-ality of the patriarchal Homer, represented since antiquity as a grave, bearded man, if not an old, blind sage.[12] Recent paintings such as Ingres's *The Apotheosis of Homer*, showing a dark, bearded and balding man enthroned in front of a classical temple, being crowned with the laurel wreath by a winged muse, carried on the tradition, and served as a model for many 'Tributes to the Old Masters' on public monuments across Europe, including the podium of the Albert Memorial.[13]

The Hellenism of Victorian artists like Frederic Leighton and G. F. Watts was grounded in such attitudes. As Christopher Wood has amusingly sketched it in *Olympian Dreamers*:

So every Victorian schoolboy enjoyed the tales of the *Iliad* and the *Odyssey*, suitably expurgated of course, much in the same spirit in which they enjoyed the novels of G. A. Henty and Rider Haggard, or joined the Boy Scouts. This Boy's Own view of classical history is reflected in many Victorian pictures of the period, especially in the work of J. W. Waterhouse and Herbert Draper, who both painted Homeric subjects.[14]

Nausicaa appears among the Homeric subjects of contemporary artists, extending a long iconographical tradition that begins in the 8th century BC (illus. 92, 93, 94, 95). Nausicaa was a relatively common nineteenth-century subject, both explicitly, as in paintings by Edward Poynter (*Nausicaa and her Maidens*, part of a series including the equally popular *Andromeda* and *Atalanta*), G. D. Leslie, and Frederic Leighton (illus. 96), and in related subjects grouped as 'Females mourning dead or departed lovers', such as Leighton's *The Last Watch of Hero*, *Lachrymae*, and *Clytie*, the latter nymph also in a contorted Michelangelesque bust by Watts.[15] The Kore or type of Greek maiden

173

93. *Odysseus making his appearance to Nausicaa and her companions*, Attic red-figure pyxis and lid attributed to Aison, late 5th century BC

94. Pieter Lastman, *Ulysses and Nausicaa*, 1609

95. John Flaxman, *Ulysses following the car of Nausicaa*, 1805

96. Frederic Leighton, *Nausicaa*, 1878

appears in a wide range of Victorian paintings of nubile girls under the name of Syrinx, Psyche, Pandora, and the like. A striking example of the debased use of the Kore for aesthetic titillation is Jean-Léon Gérome's *Greek Slave*.[16] Butler's portrait of Nausicaa, the elaborate and subtle verbal construction that lies behind the image of the *Musa Polinnia*, is a critique of their art and the attitudes that informed it.[17]

Gladstone was not amused by the separators' suggestion of different authors for the two 'homeric' epics, which he saw as a threat to serious moral values. Nor was Matthew Arnold, whose lectures *On Translating Homer* (1861) adopt a similar stance, setting Homer up as the model for the 'grand style', and castigating those like Wolf who by regarding the epics as a series of folk lays had given rise to the pernicious balladeers' Homer.[18] He singled out some well-chosen examples of the ballad style at its worst, in the actual collections of folk ballads such as Percy's *Reliques*, and in their imitators like Walter Scott and Macauley's 'pinchbeck' *Lays of Ancient Rome*, and in the translators of Homer such as William Morris, whose verse *Odyssey*, in a pseudo-hexameter line that infuriated Arnold, was closely linked to his interest in renderings of other early poetry like the Icelandic *Eddas*, the *Nibelungenlied*, and the Finnish *Kalevala* collections, and was associated with the style of the homeric 'Epic cycle' by scholars like Karl Lachmann, the most extreme of the followers of Wolf. Moreover, according to Arnold, while inferior poets may write composite works, the great masters stand alone: 'So the insurmountable obstacle to believing the *Iliad* a consolidated work of several poets is this: that the work of the great masters is unique; and the *Iliad* has a great master's genuine stamp, and that stamp is *the grand style*.'[19] Homer's speed, simplicity, and moral weight – Homer is 'sustainedly noble' – had been compromised by the German school of thought.[20] The grand style itself was jeopardized. The importance of any threat to Homer's high seriousness can be gauged by Arnold's belief that Homer's only equal in modern European literature was Dante; only Homer and Dante could show moderns what the grand style was, by their example. 'I may say that the presence or absence of the grand style can only be spiritually discerned. . . .'[21] Arnold's style of *ex cathedra* pronouncement, his telling yet obscurantist use of literary 'touchstones' by which to test for grandeur, and his ferocious attacks on his opponents, is the literary equivalent of Gladstone's moral rhetoric. The foundations were under attack, and must be defended.

Butler's mischievous intention is plain enough: his Authoress, his teen-age Nausicaa, is the very reverse of 'grand'. He could have found no more effective way of epitomizing the contrary of all the values that Gladstone and Arnold wished to defend under the aegis of 'Homer' than to make the poet a woman. Gladstone figures as one of his prime satiric targets throughout his writings, especially in the letters to Miss Savage.

'Let the reader note', he says playfully, 'how Nausicaa has to keep her father up to having a clean shirt on when he ought to have one (vi, 60), whereas her younger brothers appear to keep her up to having one for them when they want one.'[22] Far from being a master mariner, she tended to be a bit vague about how rudders and suchlike worked.[23] If traditionally the aged Homer had been thought to nod towards the end of the Odyssey – he was 'like the sinking sun, whose grandeur remains without its intensity', as Longinus put it, grandly – Butler opines that Nausicaa had perhaps found the husband she so clearly craved.[24] If scholarship had rendered the name 'Homer' increasingly empty and open to all comers – bards and strolling minstrels over several centuries, editors both self-appointed and institutionally installed, a community of epigoni on the island of Chios – this new *carrière ouverte aux talents* had not yet been opened to women candidates. Butler deliberately confirmed the worst fears of the Victorian defenders of Homer of what 'disintegration' might bring.

He was not seeking merely to offend, however, but to point to real difficulties in the Wolfian hypothesis as well as in the thunderous indignation of its opponents. His choice of the Nausicaa episode in Book 6 as the focus of his reading shows his unerring critical sense, for this episode continues to present difficulties for recent commentators on Homer too, who have followed in the main the path opened by Wolf. The analyses of the affinities of Homeric poetry with the practice of oral epic throughout the world which have been carried out since the work begun by Milman Parry in the 1930s, summarized by Albert Lord in *The Singer of the Tales* (1950), and extended and revised more recently by Ruth Finnegan, represented a refined version of the notions of composite authorship over time in a traditional style handed down from minstrel to minstrel, in which 'unity of tone' resides not in the hand of the master but in the shared, conventional, formulaic language itself. Yet while the single author has receded, patriarchal prejudices are still largely intact. To see why the Nausicaa episode remains so worrying gives us an insight into Butler's methods. G. S. Kirk, a contemporary Homeric scholar, wonders whether we can really attribute to the composite author of epic such subtle psychological insights into the feminine character as Book 6 of the Odyssey offers us; is not this to bring a 'modern' view to bear on the ancient poem? Indeed, Kirk is worried by all the feminine elements in Homer, by Helen and Andromache, by Penelope. Are they not – and especially the Nausicaa episode – in a remarkably '*un*heroic tone'? For 'the traditional hero sleeps with his women, or uses them as servants, rather than engaging them in delicate conversation.'[25] The great Victorian defenders of the unity of Homer were better readers of Homer than this, with their stress on Homer's refinement as well as his manliness. Moreover, this bears on the textual question as well; for Parry argued that in certain places such as the depiction of Helen – and Kirk thinks the Nausicaa episode is even more testing – the original hand of a great poet showed itself, however overlaid or interwoven with other materials; here, if anywhere, we must recognize the 'marks of the great composer's *ipsissima verba*'.[26]

The 'scandalous versions'

If the integrity of the poet and his works had to be defended against the fragmenters, Gladstone and Arnold agreed too in deploring the decline in the stature ascribed to Homer's characters. Mure devoted many pages to a description of the heroic attributes of Achilles and Ulysses, arguing that the unity of Homer resides in the unity of character of the two epics' respective heroes. Gladstone complained of the 'mutilation' of Homer's main characters, especially Ulysses and Helen, as well as Achilles:

Ulysses and Helen stand out in the Iliad from among others with whom they might have been confounded; the first by virtue of his self-mastery and sagacity, the second, not only by her beauty and her fall, but by the singularly tender and ethereal shading of her character. The later tradition, laying rude hands upon the subtler distinctions thus established, has degraded these two great characters, the one into little better than a stage rogue, the other into little more than a stage voluptuary. . . .[27]

Gladstone laments that 'the entire primitive and patriarchal colouring has gone' from the Homeric characters. This 'degradation', of course, was scarcely of recent vintage; indeed, it began in ancient times. Ulysses himself has had a particularly bad press, on account of the 'ethical ambiguity of his main characteristic: intelligence', as W. B. Stanford, the chronicler of his reputation, has said.[28] Ancient materials provided other stories of Ulysses; the Greek dramatists used him as a comic figure (as in Aeschylus' fragment *The Bone-gatherers*, where a chamber pot is emptied over Ulysses' head) and a villain (as in Euripides' *Hecuba*, where he is made responsible for the bloody sacrifice of Hecuba's daughter), as well as a highly ambiguous hero (as in Sophocles' *Philoctetes*, where his unscrupulous cunning is employed on his suffering comrade in order to ensure Greek victory). Dante gave a negative reading of the venturer beyond the limits of the civilized world. Shakespeare in *Troilus and Cressida* shows us Ulysses the stage villain and Helen the stage voluptuary, as an aspect of the tragedy of disillusionment.

But this degeneration only made it the more essential to preserve the 'primitive and patriarchal' Homer (note the Biblical terminology). The Victorian 'Ulysses' was, after all, Tennyson's, who bade his comrades put out to sea once more, and 'sitting well in order smite / The sounding furrow':

> One equal temper of heroic hearts,
> Made weak by time and fate, but strong in will
> To strive, to seek, to find, and not to yield.

Instead – and Tennyson is another of his favourite targets – Butler set out to provide a new chapter in the degradation and mutilation of Ulysses: a passive character, subject to women's powers and desire.[29]

Butler's handling of other characters also belongs to the history of the decline in moral stature. Perhaps his most striking chapter is 'On the Question whether or no Penelope is being white-washed'. For here, having set up his Authoress as the stout defender of women's honour and privilege, he questions her and undermines the portrait of the noble and faithful wife Penelope that he has shown the Authoress painting for her readers' edification. And here the full scope of Butler's critique is brought home to us. Butler is attacking not merely the male-dominated version of the Hellenic tradition, but also the over-refined 'feminine' version of it that had gained currency in the Neo-classical period and been formulated most memorably by the German art historian Winckelmann in the middle of the eighteenth century and was now in its decadence. Victorian Hellenism suffered from 'Boy's Own' classicism; but it suffered equally from effeminacy. Its combination of muscular heroics and feeble prettification produced a meretricious art, inflated, lax, and partial to nubile nudes. Butler perceived what had to be done.

Penelope, according to him, was not the virtuous lady wife that the Authoress made her out to be. She is dangling herself before the suitors, leading them on by writing each one of them encouraging notes in private, and receiving their presents. She could have got rid of them had she really wanted to. Butler's shrewd sense of human motive, his gift for the ludicrous, and his artful deployment of a 'low' rather than a grand style, are displayed:

Sending pretty little messages to her admirers was not exactly the way to get rid of them. Did she ever try snubbing? Nothing of the kind is placed on record. Did she ever say, 'Well, Antinous, whoever else I may marry, you may make your mind easy that it will not be you.' Then there was boring – did she ever try that? Did she ever read them any of her grandfather's letters? Did she ever sing them her own songs, or play them music of her own composition. I have always found these courses successful when I wanted to get rid of people. There are indeed signs that something had been done in this direction, for the suitors say that they cannot stand her high art nonsense and aesthetic rhodomontade any longer, but it is more likely she had been trying to attract than to repel.[30]

'In all Penelope's devotion to her husband there is an ever present sense that the lady doth protest too much.' Butler draws on the alternative tradition of the epic *Telegonus*, which shows Ulysses finally killed by Telegonus (his son by Circe), having put Penelope off on his return and married another woman, Callidice, Queen of Thesprotia. As Butler puts it: 'He must, therefore, have divorced Penelope, and he could hardly have done this if he accepted the Odyssean version of her conduct.'[31] Even in the *Odyssey* itself, if we attend to the suitors' stories, it is clear the Authoress is whitewashing Penelope. 'Roughly, then, the Authoress's version is that Penelope is an injured innocent, and the suitors', that she is an artful heartless flirt who prefers having a hundred admirers rather than one husband.'[32]

In short, in 'these scandalous versions', as Butler calls them, the noble Ulysses did not return to his wife, and his noble wife was not faithful to him. These versions are derived from the ancient sources of the ironic, debunking treatment of the Homeric heroes and heroines. Butler's attributing of the noble sentiments beloved of his own contemporaries to his young, unfledged Authoress effectively undermines the sentiments, and makes his contemporaries ridiculous, while preserving sympathy for the young girl to whom they are appropriate.[33] Here again we see the emerging outlines of Joyce's Molly, a Penelope still sighing after her suitors, and putting the fear of Buck Mulligan into the heart of her husband, who can never expunge the last trace of their unwelcome presence in his house.

The domestic version of the *Odyssey* had begun to gain currency early in the eighteenth century. As Butler points out, the great classicist

Bentley had said that the *Iliad* was composed for men, and the *Odyssey* for women.[34] Though the perception of the difference did not carry with it any claim to female authorship, it could be used to make such a claim plausible. Pope's translation itself had something of the refinement and grace about it that became favoured over ruder versions, indeed, was sometimes expressed as a preference for the *Odyssey* over the *Iliad*. Even in ancient times critics like Longinus expressed the view that the *Iliad* was for men, the *Odyssey* for ladies. One eighteenth-century expression of this may be found in Lady Mary Wortley Montagu's lively letters from Asia Minor. She wrote that she was reading over Pope's Homer with 'infinite Pleasure', and found much in the surroundings that explained customs and beauties in the poem that she had not grasped:

It would be too tedious to point out all the passages that relate to the present customs, but I can assure you that the Princesses and great Ladys pass their time at their Looms embroidering Veils and Robes, surrounded by their Maids, which are allways very numerous, in the same Manner as we find Andromache and Helen describ'd. . . . The Snowy Veil that Helen throws over her face is still fashionable; . . . Their manner of danceing is certainly the same that Diana is sung to have danc'd by Eurotas. The Great Lady still Leads the dance and is follow'd by a troop of young Girls who imitate her steps, and if she sings, make up the Chorus. The Tunes are extreme Gay and Lively, yet with something in 'em wonderfull soft. The steps are vary'd according to Pleasure of her that leads the dance, but always in exact time and infinitly more Agreable than any of our Dances, at least in my Opinion. I sometimes make one in the Train, but am not skilfull enough to lead.[35]

A little later in the century we find the preference for the *Odyssey* expressed by Joseph Warton in conjunction with praise for the exquisite manners of simpler times, and singling out the Nausicaa episode as expressive of it:

But besides its variety, the *Odyssey* is the most amusing and entertaining of all other poems, on account of the pictures it preserves to us of ancient manners customs laws and politics, and of the domestic life of the heroic ages. The more any nation becomes polished, the more the genuine feelings of nature are disguised, and their manners are consequently less adapted to bear a faithful description. Good-breeding is founded on the dissimulation or suppression of such sentiments, as may probably provoke of offend those with whom we converse. The little forms and ceremonies which have been introduced into civil life by the moderns, are not suited to the dignity and simplicity of the *Epic Muse*. The coronation feast of an European monarch would not shine half so much in poetry, as the simple supper prepared for *Ulysses* at the Phæacian court; the gardens of *Alcinous* are much fitter for description than those of Versailles; and *Nausicaa*, descending to the river to wash her garments, and dancing afterwards upon the banks with her fellow-virgins, like

Diana amidst her nymphs, "Tho' all are fair, she shines above the rest" is a far more graceful figure, than the most glittering lady in the drawing-room, with a complexion plaistered to repair the vigil of cards, and a shape violated by a stiff brocade and an immeasurable hoop. The compliment also which Ulysses pays to this innocent unadorned beauty, especially when he compares her to a young palm-tree of Delos, contains more gallantry and elegance, than the most applauded sonnet of the politest French marquis that ever rhymed.[36]

Here, then, the 'primitive and patriarchal' is equated with this refined pastoral presided over by the maiden Nausicaa.

In this praise of the natural we see the taste for the *Odyssey* being strengthened by the movement towards the Rousseauan retreat from the corruption of *les lumières*. The four different types of ancient portraits of Homer had been augmented by a type of Homer as poetic bard, as popularized by late eighteenth-century poetry, a more graceful, pastoral figure. Corot's *Homer and the Shepherds* (illus. 97), an important painting in the battle against 'finish', was singled out for praise in Baudelaire's 1846 Salon.

Goethe, with his instinct for the conception of works that would epitomize the age, planned a play centering round the meeting of Ulysses and Nausicaa, to be entitled *Nausikaa*. Moreover, it was Sicily itself which summed up for him, as for Butler, the spirit of Nausicaa, and with her, the *Odyssey*. His *Italian Journey* – the journey he had waited for all his life – contains a number of enthusiastic new insights into Homer, which climax in his Nausicaa drama, inspired by the Sicilian landscape. He wrote:

A word about Homer. The scales have fallen from my eyes. His descriptions, his similes, etc., which to us seem merely poetic, are in fact utterly natural though drawn, of course, with an inner comprehension which takes one's breath away. Even when the events he narrates are fabulous and fictitious, they have a naturalness about them which I have never felt so strongly as in the presence of the settings he describes.

The settings themselves he describes first in a general way, as encompassing all the scenery of the poem:

Now that my mind is stored with images of all these coasts and promontories, gulfs and bays, islands and headlands, rocky cliffs and sandy beaches, wooded hills and gentle pastures, fertile fields, flower gardens, tended trees, festooned vines, mountains wreathed in clouds, eternally serene plains and the all-encircling sea with its ever-changing colours and moods, for the first time the *Odyssey* has become a living truth to me.[37]

97. Camille Corot, *Homer and the Shepherds*, 1846

Here Goethe carries on the tradition of the German traveller who, like Winckelmann, never arrived in Greece, but found his Greece in Italy, or like Hölderlin, came no nearer to Greece or Italy than the south of France, but found himself in the Mediterranean landscape 'struck by the arrow of Apollo' and enabled to create a new awareness of the Hellenic spirit.

But Goethe goes further: for it was here too, in Sicily, in Palermo, in the Public Gardens, amid the profusion of vegetation, that he had his vision of the *Urpflanze*, the primal plant that he held to be the model for all plant life. This morphological vision was at one with his sudden insight into the natural form of epic. As with Butler, whose Lamarckist views on evolution gave him a sense of the growing point of the collective consciousness, Sicily supplied both the primordial landscape and the landscape of the next phase of human growth.

This 'enchanted garden', which 'transports one back into the antique world', conjured up the *Odyssey* again:

The enchanted garden, the inky waves on the northern horizon, breaking on the curved beaches of the bays, and the peculiar tang of the sea air, all conjured up images of the island of the blessed Phaeacians.[38]

It was here too that he conceived the *Nausikaa*:

There could be no better commentary on the *Odyssey*, I felt, than just this setting. I bought a copy and read it with passionate interest. It fired me with the desire to produce a work of my own, and very soon I could think of nothing else: in other words, I became obsessed with the idea of treating the story of Nausicaa as a tragedy.[39]

Goethe never finished the play conceived in this enchanted spot; in 1827 he published one act and some fragments of *Nausikaa*. But the outline he left of it in the *Italian Journey* is suggestive:

Act I. Nausicaa is playing with a ball with her maids. The unexpected encounter takes place. Her hesitation about accompanying the stranger personally into the city is the first sign that she feels drawn towards him.
Act II. The palace of Alcinous [her father]· The characters of the suitors are revealed. The act ends with the entrance of Ulysses.
Act III. The importance of the adventurer is brought out. I planned to produce an interesting artistic effect with a narration in dialogue of his adventures. Each listener responds to this with a different emotion. As the narration proceeds, passions run higher, and the strong attraction which Nausicaa feels for the stranger is at last revealed in action and counter-action.
Act IV. Off stage, Ulysses gives proof of his prowess, while on stage, the women give free expression to their sympathies, hopes and tender sentiments. Nausicaa cannot control her feeling and compromises herself irrevocably before her own people. Ulysses, the half guilty, half innocent cause of this, is finally forced to announce his determination to depart.
Act V. Nothing is left for the good girl but to kill herself.[40]

Goethe's dénouement is pat, unpersuasive. One can hardly imagine Butler's (or, for that matter, Homer's) Nausicaa committing suicide. Goethe tended to view himself as a romantic Ulysses:

I too was a wanderer; I too was in danger of arousing sympathies which, though not perhaps of the kind which end in tragedy, could still be painful and destructive; I too was far from my native land, in circumstances where one entertains an audience with glowing descriptions of distant objects, adventures while travelling, incidents in one's life; where one is considered a demigod by the young and a braggart by the sedate; where one experiences many an undeserved favour, many an unexpected obstacle. It was facts like these which gave the plot its particular fascination for me. I spent all my days in Palermo and most of the time I was travelling through Sicily dreaming about it.[41]

Whatever the reason Goethe left the play unfinished, the tragic form was inappropriate to his own romance. It was left for Butler – and his professed dislike for Goethe was strong – to see that one form for

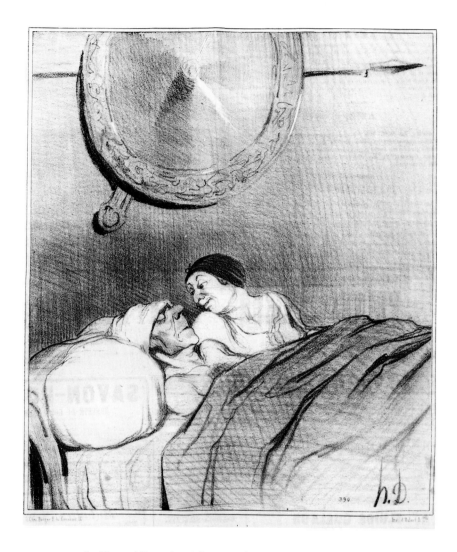

98. Honoré Daumier, *Ulysses and Penelope*, from *Charivari*,
'Histoires Anciennes', 1842

Nausicaa was comic fiction; and its time, the present. The modern development of the classical epic into the novel, begun for the *Odyssey* with Fénelon's *Télémaque* at the beginning of the eighteenth century, was decisively forwarded by Butler. If occasionally he too cast himself as Ulysses, it was again in a comic vein:

I am elderly, grey-bearded, and, according to my clerk, Alfred, disgustingly fat; I wear spectacles and get more and more bronchitic as I grow older. Still no young prince in a fairy story ever found an invisible princess more effectually hidden behind a hedge of dullness or more fast asleep than Nausicaa was when I woke her and hailed her as Authoress of the *Odyssey*. And there was no difficulty about it either – all one had to do was go up to the front door and ring the bell.[42]

That his visual medium for his Sicilian journey was the photograph and the map, not the conjuration of a reimagined antique world, is the measure of the leap he had taken.

Mapping the periplus of Ulysses

Butler's photographs of Sicily fall into several groups: those which were taken for the *Authoress* to illustrate the close fit of certain landscapes in and near Trapani to specific scenes in the *Odyssey*; those which illustrate the nature of megalithic architecture as representative of Odyssean society, an important element in his own argument for the primitive in art as a value; and his sharp, humorous photographs of contemporary Sicily which extend the idiom of the Victorian 'street scene'. Some of these explicitly identify modern scenes with Odyssean ones.

Butler's maps and photographs of the sites stand at the beginning of the modern phase of the search for Ulysses' route (illus. 99). It is here that one can trace the explicit reception of the *Authoress* – although not one of his successors had any time for his contention that the poet was a woman, and most do not even refer to it. Given the cool reception of his book at home, it is again abroad that we must look to find his influence.

Butler's contribution is praised in a recent scholarly study of the geography of Homer: he was the first to place the legendary voyage against an accurate map; and he returned to the Mediterranean theory against a number of suggestions in the 1870s and '80s that took Ulysses to the Canary Islands, round the coast of Africa, and even to the North and South poles.[43] The Wolfs' geographical study reproduces the major modern mappings, beginning with Butler and proceeding to Dörpfeld, Herrmann, Bérard, Pocock, Moulinier, Zeller and Bradford. Dörpfeld, Schliemann's successor, disappointed at the lack of archaeological evidence, had himself argued against Ithaca as the site of Ulysses' homecoming, and roused a good deal of discussion in the 1920s and '30s.

According to *The Voyages of Ulysses: A Photographic Interpretation of Homer's Classic*, combining a selection of the early illustrations of the Ulysses story beginning from the 8th century BC with recent photographs of the alleged sites, if Thucydides and Strabo were the most important commentators among the ancients on Ulysses' route and the 'periplus' or round-trip in the Mediterranean, among the moderns 'the four most important commentators are: Samuel Butler . . .; Victor Bérard, with photographer Fred Boissonas . . .; Jean Bérard; and Ernle Bradford'.[44] A more sedentary localizer was L. G. Pocock, professor of Greek in New Zealand, who in several publications brought fresh evidence and photographs to the support of Butler's Sicilian thesis.[45] And as recently as last year the intrepid Tim Severin, geographer, ship's captain, and author of *The Jason Voyage* and *The Brendan Voyage*, set out once again on *The Ulysses Voyage*.

The most weighty of these successors is Victor Bérard, a French classicist who wrote extensively on Homeric topics and produced a new translation of the epics into French, and in 1913 undertook a voyage in search of the sites of the *Odyssey* which resulted in the four-volume study *Les Navigations d'Ulysse* (1927–9) and, after his death, in the photographic retracing of his Mediterranean voyage by his son, Jean Bérard, in the handsome volume *Dans le sillage d'Ulysse* (1935).[46] Lessing's photographs in *The Voyages of Ulysses* follow Bérard's route (illus. 100). The Bérards in effect produced a celebration of what Fernand Braudel in our day has called '*la longue durée*' of the civilization of the Mediterranean.[47]

Ernle Bradford, geographer, keen sailor in Mediterranean waters, and amateur of Homer, makes frequent mention of Butler, supporting several of his Sicilian locations, including 'Goat Island' (now Favignano) off Trapani as the island from which Ulysses sighted the land of the Cyclopes. He agrees with Butler that whoever wrote the *Odyssey* was not a seaman – any more than the author of 'The Ancient Mariner' was a seaman – but need not have been a 'woman, or a citizen of the mainland who had a landsman's dislike of the sea', for in his experience the Italian,

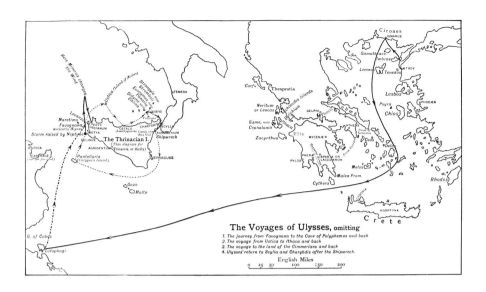

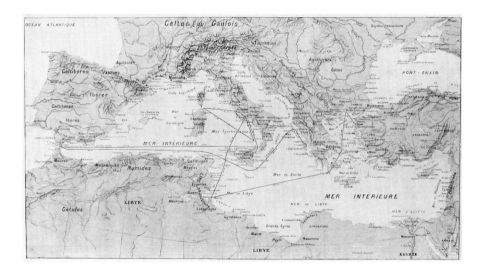

99. *Map of the voyage of Ulysses*, from *Authoress of the Odyssey*, 1897

100. *Itinéraire d'Ulysse*, from Victor Bérard, *Les navigations d'Ulysse*, 1929

Greek and Sicilian seafaring men go to sea not from love of it, but from necessity. 'Love of the sea', he finds, is 'a Nordic trait.'[48]

Tim Severin undertook *The Ulysses Voyage* in the 'Argo', the reconstruction of an Aegean sailing ship in which he had retraced Jason's route. He conceals his debts to all those who have preceded him in this voyage, referring to them only in the most oblique way. Butler appears anonymously: 'Homer was a woman – so runs one theory';[49] Bérard is named, but only as a dusty scholar who mistakenly considered the Phoenician routes through the Mediterranean important, whereas recent research shows the Mycenaeans had their own trade routes.[50] Severin's acknowledged sources are rather the archaeologists and the nineteenth-century British map-maker, the naval man Thomas Spratt, whose map of Troy – 'Spratt's map' – was used by all the archaeologists from Schliemann onwards. He relies on the Royal Navy, the 'premier map-making organization in the world' in the nineteenth century, on whose 'Sailing Directions and meticulous hand-drawn charts which the Naval Hydrographer's office engraved beautifully on steel plates the descendant maps still depend'. Their maps of the Mediterranean, prepared in 1872, are unsurpassed in 'many out-of-the-way corners of the Mediterranean'.[51] While his course purports to follow Homer's directions, he is forced to admit that in many cases the homeric measures of time and distance are 'symbolic'.[52] His ship being much smaller than Ulysses' ship would have been and also undermanned, Severin produces, like Butler, a 'domestic' voyage, in which most of Ulysses' adventures, including his visit to Hades (which he interprets simply as a visit to a local 'entrance to Hades' on the mainland near Ithaca), cluster round his home island of Ithaca off the west coast of Greece, as in Butler's version they cluster round Sicily.[53] Thus the solemn smallboat derring-do of the twentieth-century reconstructors has an unintentionally miniaturizing effect, just as Butler's irony consciously does.

This hilariously inappropriate fruit of his labours is in itself an irony that Butler would have relished: his stay-at-home Authoress and his inactive Ulysses gave rise to a new spate of explorations by boat, plane and professional photographer and geographer culminating in aerial photographs of the Mediterranean from a NASA satellite in which the Mediterranean is finally lost to view.[54] In order to take *au pied de la lettre* the geographical search for Ulysses' route it was necessary to ignore Butler's point, which was precisely that the Odyssean poet had – *pace* the manly celebrators of Homer's technical prowess – no knowledge whatever of wind and weather, rigging and rudders. Those who followed Butler's lead, as they fondly imagined, were baffled, as when the Wolfs took him to task for failing to follow Homer's precise nautical indications,[55] while those who dismiss the geographical localizers dismiss Butler with them, wholly failing to grasp the significance of his strategy.[56] That all the geographical localizers disagree among themselves, and always had done, gave Butler his opportunity: each of his Sicilian locations finds support from some commentator. His lilliputian odyssey, which cuts the heroic Ulysses down to size, can be given a solemn gloss of factuality. His real heir is Joyce, maps of whose anti-hero Leopold Bloom's odyssean wanderings around Dublin – his routes carefully established and photographed by scholars – sell in all sizes and prices at the Morello Tower to tourists who religiously follow them.

We are reminded again of Butler's ingenious use of his family background and inheritance: his grandfather had written atlases of ancient and modern geography for school use, and his father had re-issued them. In Samuel Butler, DD's *Atlas of Antient Geography*, the *Orbis Veteribus Notus*, the 'World as known to the Ancients', the flat Mediterranean-centred world, was projected onto the modern system of latitudes and longitudes, yet it faded off into nothing at a cerulean Aethiopia Interior, and to the north a yellow Scythia gave way to the Shakespearean 'Anthropophagi?' (the question mark is Grandfather Butler's).[57] While doubtless his grandfather's concern was for accuracy and clarity rather than imagination – as Butler liked to point out, 'the main use of a classical education consists in the check it gives to originality, and the way in which it prevents an inconvenient number of people from using their own eyes' – such a map could not fail to pique his imagination. The very mapping of the 'World as known to the Ancients' onto the modern grid of latitudes and longitudes – in effect a fiction precisely situated in terms of modern scientific system – is suggestive of the method underlying his mapping of Erewhon, the 'New Jerusalem', and the world of Odysseus. Not only had he much of the incisive, accurate, and graphic in his own make-up, the map-maker's art has been seen as a distinctively Northern or Dutch art of describing.[58] His native gifts and his art criticism reinforce one another, and the map may be seen as a fundamental form of his visual imagination.[59]

Gladstone had inveighed against all claims to a western Mediterranean locale for the *Odyssey*, for his Homer continued to be at home near Troy. His own very interesting map, which traces Odysseus' route

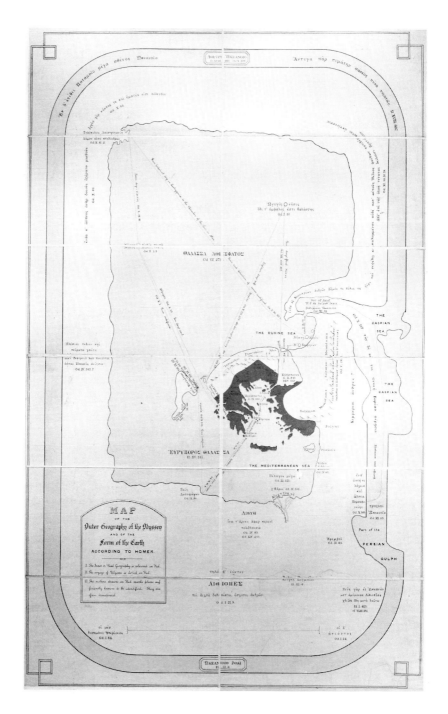

101. *Map of the external geography of the Odyssey and the form of the earth according to Homer*, from William E. Gladstone, *Studies in Homer*, 1858

on a map that attempts to reconstruct the ancient view of the geography of the world, begins and ends the journey in Ithaca (illus. 101). Latin tradition, in its attempts to glorify Rome had, he held, falsified Homer:

This geography of the Odyssey has been thoroughly vitiated and obscured by the action of spurious Latin tradition, which forcibly accommodated Homer to the exigencies of a Roman dynasty and a South Italian poem.[60]

Butler, on the contrary, enforced the Italian claim, the claim of the Greek colonial settlement, the claim of the periphery against the Arnoldian centre, against a false and posturing Hellenism. This support for the provincial, the outlying region, is of a piece with his argument for a ruder but more authentic Renaissance.

To make good his claim, he brings into play the new archaeological evidence from the excavations of Mycenaean palaces by Schliemann and Dörpfeld, not only at Troy, but at Mycenae itself, and at Pylos, the home of Nestor visited by Telemachus at the beginning of the *Odyssey* to gain news of his father from his old comrade at Troy. No one can look at the reports and the pictorial record of these excavations even now without excitement. The pictures from the excavations at Troy were not in the first instance photographs, but engravings from drawings, and they capture the romantic aura and the sense of Schliemann's own faith that this was indeed the Troy of Homer.[61] It was left for others to find the sites mean, too small to be Troy, and lacking in evidence of destruction by fire; the interpretation of the archaeological evidence is still controversial. Butler speculates that the Greeks did not take Troy, but gave up, burnt their tents and sailed away; and Troy fell later, from quite other causes. Butler was prepared to set off to see for himself. Out of these inquiries has grown a revised portrait of the Mycenaean age, and the altogether less grand and wealthy world of the 'heroic age' that followed the fall of the Mycenaean civilization, and which is held to be the age of 'Homer', that is, of the Trojan story as it came down to the next generations. The 'heroic age' became an 'unheroic age', neither the age of gold nor of silver of ancient legend; even the place of bronze in it has been subject to controversy. The Homeric epics attempt, not always successfully, to recall the former age of greater prosperity and display in which Agamemnon's fleet set sail; but the world in which the epics were formulated was an altogether reduced one.[62] As Butler put it, to 'Homer' the time of the Trojan Wars was 'much what the Middle Ages are to

102. *Erice walls*, 1892

ourselves'.[63] Whereas Gladstone insisted that only a generation could have passed between the fall of Troy and the *Iliad* – just as the writing of the first Gospel had still to be placed as close as possible to the Crucifixion – on the basis of the archaeological evidence Butler suggests a date of about 1350 BC for the fall of Troy, about 1150 BC for the composition of the *Iliad*, and would prefer a later one, to leave time for the formation of the Epic cycle; in any case, the *Odyssey* must be dated about one hundred years later than the *Iliad*.[64] Present estimates would place the *Odyssey* even later, in the 8th century BC. As with the Bible, the 'testimony' was seen to be remote from the eye-witness accounts they had once been considered.

Whatever the truth of the matter, Butler grasped the opportunity given him by the new scholarship to paint an altogether ruder and homelier scene than had been customary as the homeric world of the Authoress, a world of the early emigration of the Greeks to Sicily as outlined by Thucydides, a world of crumbling megalithic walls, not of

103. *Henry Festing Jones in flute of column*, Selinunte (Sicily), 1896

the former grandeur of Mycenae nor of the later grandeur of the great classical temples of Selinunte and Segesta. The anonymous portrait of the Authoress found by a man ploughing a field fitted this scene of provincial settlement.[65] His photographs underline this story,[66] with his views of megalithic walls not only at Hissarlik (the site of Troy, according to Schliemann), but in Sicily (such massive rough stone walls became one of his favourite photographic subjects; illus. 102). He slashes at the grand style, photographing Jones in the flute of a column at Selinunte (illus. 103), to show the overblown excesses of the attempts at grandeur which dwarfed the human, as D. H. Lawrence in *Etruscan Places* undercut the marble monuments of Rome with his praise of the modest evanescence of Etruscan architecture. He offers photographs of a Sicilian farmhouse with courtyard to suggest the modest scale of Odysseus' 'palace', which Schliemann had sought in vain in Ithaca. The unpublished photographs include 'The kind of thing that I suppose Laertes villa to have been', a tiny cottage with well-tilled fields terraced

104. Jones inside the Grotto del Toro, Trapani, 1896

up the steep hill behind it.[67] How contrary all this ran to the current academic iconography can be seen in Achille Benouville, *Ulysse et Nausicaä*, cited as typical of the 'Landscape of the Ecole des Beaux-Arts', and showing 'all the conventional features of the historical landscape – classical buildings, winding stream, large massive trees, and an imposing mountain on the horizon'.[68] In particular, Butler banishes the classical temple so prominent on the distant mountain. His 'heroic age' was thoroughly unheroic. It was in this provincial, unvarnished, down-to-earth world that the Authoress was able to find the independence to carry out her work. The many women poets of Greece, he points out, belong to the early period of Greek development, not to the supposed high classical age of fifth century B C Athens; the Authoress was merely the first of them. The position of women then was 'much what it is at the present, and incomparably higher than it was in the Athenian civilization with which we are best acquainted'.[69] If these pictures of the Odyssean milieu render up a barer and a humbler world than the genuflecting centuries had supposed, they, like Butler's snapshots of life in Italy and elsewhere, with their intense interest in the comedy of individualism, strip off all pretence without degrading their originals. The Authoress as the vivid focus of Butler's new perceptions of a long loved poem embodies – in all its full unexpectedness and contrariness – what Pater called 'the freshness which belongs to all periods of growth in art, the charm of *ascésis*, of the austere and serious girding of the loins in youth'.[70]

Butler explicitly drew attention to the way this representation of the Odyssean world of the Authoress extended the tradition in painting that he affirmed, and undermined the 'grand style' and its hollow and distorted idealization:

No artist can reach an ideal higher than his own best actual environment. Trying to materially improve upon that with which he or she is fairly familiar invariably ends in failure. It is only adjuncts that may be arranged and varied – the essence may be taken or left, but it must not be bettered. The attempt to take nature and be content with her save in respect of details which after all are unimportant, leads to Donatello, Giovanni Bellini, Holbein, Rembrandt, and De Hooghe – the attempt to improve upon her leads straight to Michael Angelo and the *barocco*, to Turner and the modern drop scene.[71]

Modern illustrations of Homer move in the directions pointed to by Butler, for example, Kokoschka's *Odysseus meets Nausikaa*, with its shaggy, stripped Odysseus expressive of utter wretchedness casting

105. Oskar Kokoschka, *Odysseus meets Nausikaa*, 1965

himself on Nausicaa's mercy, her ball at once plaything, womb, and world (illus. 105).

This cautionary tale of misinterpretation of Butler's Homeric writings reminds us forcibly that Butler's medium was not the photograph and the map if these are taken literally in the manner of his successors on the trail of Ulysses, but rather an imaginary construct as powerful as Goethe's, in which the 'factuality' of his visual realization is fused with his fantasy. The landscape, the geographical verity, opens again on an erewhon. This fusion of inner and outer in an 'objective' form supplied by modern technology is characteristic of modern interpretations of photography such as Walter Benjamin's. If we tend to see these projections onto a map as, typically in modern times, onto an urban landscape, as in Baudelair's Paris, the Christiana (now Oslo) of Hamsun's *Hunger*, the Venice of Raymond Roussel,[72] and of course the Dublin of Joyce, Butler produced a dystopic pastoral of the new primitivism in which the use of the new medium by the self-styled painter *manqué* was itself an irony. Finally, Butler's form here was the harbinger of a major twentieth-century genre: literary criticism as creative invention on demythologized sites. Butler's extraordinary *tour-de-force* reveals the truth of the Odyssean journey, that it too, with its sharply realized localities, its epic superimpositions, and its mythic and folkloric perspectives, also opens on an erewhon.

At the centre of his *Odyssey* – in the mythic encounter of Ulysses with the dead in Hades, which most observers, even the most fanatical devotees of the Admiralty Pilot, have agreed is 'off the map' – Butler places his own Authoress, at the head of the list of the great dead he would most like to meet. Naming among others, Homer, Shakespeare, Sappho, Handel, Giovanni Bellini, Rembrandt, Holbein, de Hoogh, Donatello, Jean de Wespin (a not unexpected addition to his list of artists), he concludes: 'Yet the writer of the "Odyssey" interests me so profoundly that I am not sure I should not ask to see her before any of the others.'[73] This brilliant use of the *mise-en-abîme* creates not merely an infinitely receding series, but a unique form of closure. It is the triumph of the 'imaginary portrait': Pygmalion meets his Galatea at the heart of his own re-reading.

Translating the 'Odyssey'

Butler's prose translation of the *Odyssey*, which embodies his fresh conception of it, marks the beginning of a new era in the handling of that much translated poem. 'Finding no readable prose translation', he remarked, 'I was driven to the original.'[74] This is a well-aimed blow against the prose translation of Butcher and Lang, much used in the Victorian period, which even gained a guarded commendation from Arnold. It is hardly surprising that Lang reviewed Butler with a certain asperity. In his Notebooks Butler explicitly attacked Lang:

The difference between the Andrew Lang manner of translating the *Odyssey* and mine is that between making a mummy and a baby. He tries to preserve a corpse (for the *Odyssey* is a corpse to all who need Lang's translation), whereas I try to originate a new life and one that is instinct (as far as I can effect this) with the spirit though not the form of the original.[75]

Before Lang, of course, the translations of Homer had been in verse: the great landmarks in English translation, from Chapman's Homer, Dryden's *Iliad* Book I, and Pope's Homer to Cowper's *Odyssey* were poetry, and often stood with the best original poetry of their authors and the age. Each period required its own translation, just because these translations succeeded in summing up the quintessence of the style of their time. Chapman's is one of the great achievements of the Elizabethan age, and the Romantics had rediscovered it; if Arnold castigated it as over-ingenious and impeding the flow of Homer with its own added felicities, the reader can only embrace it, as Keats did. Pope, though his ornamental couplets are far from our own taste, still reads brilliantly well. Cowper's blank verse has much of the easy movement that Arnold demanded, though it is often full of eighteenth-century diction of the kind Wordsworth denounced as 'gaudy and inane phraseology'. Butler, a novelist in the age of novelists, saw the compelling need for a translation into a new form of the mock-epic or burlesque using a prose medium. If verse is to be translated into prose, he saw, 'great licence must be allowed to the translator in getting rid of all those poetical common forms which are foreign to the genius of prose'. He went on: 'If the work is to be translated into prose, let it be into such prose as we write and speak among ourselves.'[76]

Butcher and Lang were far from any such prose. Although they were praised for accuracy – and even today are reckoned the most faithful English versions, 'to which all subsequent English versions are much indebted'[77] – their Biblical style was laden with archaisms. In the epic simile describing Ulysses as a lion coming out to meet Nausicaa they write:

And forth he sallied like a lion mountain-bred, trusting in his strength, who fares out blown and rained upon, with flaming eyes; amid the kine he goes or amid the sheep or in the track of the wild deer; yea, his belly bids him to make assay upon the flocks, even within a close-penned fold. Even so Odysseus was fain to draw nigh to the fair-tressed maidens, all naked as he was, such need had come upon him.[78]

In the heightened context of the epic simile, this is passable. But as Ulysses speaks to Nausicaa the style seems clumsy, verbose and repetitive, and the archaisms and unnecessary inversions obtrude:

But he is of heart the most blessed beyond all other who shall prevail with gifts of wooing, and lead thee to his home. Never have mine eyes beheld such an one among mortals, neither man nor woman; great awe comes upon me as I look on thee. Yet in Delos once I saw as goodly a thing: a young sapling of a palm tree springing by the altar of Apollo. For thither too I went, and much people with me, on that path where my sore troubles were to be. Yea, and when I looked thereupon, long time I marvelled in spirit, – for never grew there yet so goodly a shoot from ground, – even in such wise as I wonder at thee, lady, and am astonied and do greatly fear to touch thy knees, though grievous sorrow is upon me.[79]

The distance between this and Butler's prose tells even more in Nausicaa's reply, as Butler gives us a relish of his Authoress's character. Butcher and Lang render her opening thus:

Then Nausicaa of the white arms answered him, and said: 'Stranger, forasmuch as thou seemest no evil man nor foolish – and it is Olympian Zeus himself that giveth weal to men, to the good and to the evil, to each one as he will, and this thy lot doubtless is of him, and so thou must in anywise endure it: – and now, since thou hast come to our city and our land, thou shalt not lack raiment, nor aught else that is the due of a hapless suppliant, when he has met them who can befriend him.'[80]

Butler's Nausicaa replies directly, aptly, and above all colloquially:

Stranger, you appear to be a sensible well-disposed person. There is no accounting for luck; Jove gives prosperity to rich and poor just as he chooses, so you must take what he has seen fit to send you, and make the best of it. Now, however, that you have come to this our country, you shall not want for clothes nor for anything else that a foreigner in distress may reasonably look for.[81]

The pithy, low mimetic style of Butler's Notebooks is distinctly audible here, pricking the bubbles of rhetoric and clearing away the underbrush of the false Biblical. The 'Sample Passages' from his translation of the *Odyssey* which he published in 1894 announce it on the title page as 'freely rendered into modern colloquial English for the use of those who cannot read the original', whereas the completed version of 1900 bears the more neutral description 'English prose'.[82] The use of prose for those who could not read the original is also a departure from the terms of the 'quarrel between the ancients and moderns', in which prose versions such as that of Anne Dacier in France had been intended for those who did know the original, whereas the classically unlettered could have recourse to the inaccurate but poetic versions. His reviewers at the time, while making play with 'Miss Homer's Poem', 'The Odyssey in Slang', the 'Ulysseid', and 'How to Vulgarize Homer', perceived what was at stake, and gave him considerable praise for his pungent colloquial rendering, while registering the full force of its startling incongruity with the Homer they knew.[83] The favourable case was summed up by *The Spectator*:

One can imagine Mr Butler pleasing people who would not care for the admirable work of Messrs Butcher and Lang. Admirable it is, but it is not actual human speech; no one ever talked it; no one would ever write it, except for the one purpose of helping a learner to understand Homer. But Mr Butler's version is actual speech; it is sometimes prosaic, but it is vivid; it gives a picture of life painted without any conventional lines or colours.[84]

Butler was prepared in other contexts to carry his linguistic experiments with the vernacular even further, for example in the outrageously vulgar and very funny essay in epistolary form, 'The Aunt, the Nieces and the Dog'. Again a woman is the source of the 'finest word I know in the English language', the spontaneous, expressive, and original colloquial epithet – 'rampingest-scampingest-rackety-tow-row-roaringest boy in the whole school' – coined, as Butler points out, not 'by my poor old grandfather, whose education had left little to desire' but by an old matron at school, Mrs Bromfield.[85]

Ironically, Butler was strongly chastised by two significant women: his sister May, who had only half dared to disagree with his views on art, here felt on home ground, and roundly took issue with his renderings, descrying no relation between 'Homer' and 'humour', and declaring that 'the ghost of our grandfather will haunt you';[86] and more importantly, Jane Harrison, a noted classical scholar, whose book *Myths of the Odyssey in Art and Literature* (1882) is a deeply-felt and refined study, was outraged by Butler's apparent flippancy.[87] He thought (wrongly) that the review 'How to vulgarize Homer' was by her.[88] He enjoyed the row, however, and thought it was his 'best gesture' – because for once it was in terms the public readily understood.[89] Even the intended savagings showed some insight: 'If Mr Butler could discover the mock epic of which Thersites was hero (and surely he could), it might be worth his while to rewrite it.'[90] The same reviewer remarks on 'his self-given role of Sam Weller Thersites'. Butler described his role in terms that hark back to his perception of the grotesque in the early Renaissance setting and suggest a new form of the ancient masks of tragedy and comedy:

There is a tomb at some place in France, I think at Carcassonne, on which there is some sculpture representing the friends and relations of the deceased in paroxysms of grief with their cheeks all cracked, and crying, like Gaudenzio's angels on the Sacro Monte at Varallo-Sesia. Round the corner, however, just out of sight till one searches, there is a man holding both his sides and splitting with laughter. In some parts of the Odyssey, especially about Ulysses and Penelope, I fancy that laughing man as being round the corner.[91]

Here we see again Butler's condensation of a complex literary and art-historical analysis into a visual image which is itself a free invention from diverse literary, pictorial and sculptural materials. If he is cast as the laughing man, yet the link with Gaudenzio's weeping angels creates a mask for tragi-comedy.

Against the tradition of poetic renderings, and against the archaizing prose of the Victorian version, the shock value of Butler's enterprise is still considerable. It retains its freshness, its verve, and its readability when placed over against the twentieth-century's standard translation, Richmond Lattimore's plain verse 'in the language of contemporary prose', aiming at Arnoldian directness and speed, but disclaiming 'nobility'. Butler was aware, however, that more would be needed for the modern prose rendering than he could bring to it himself. His best translation is probably of Hesiod, whose composition comes through powerfully and clearly. He expressed his doubts humorously, calling for a new Authoress who alone would be capable of a new translation of Homer:

I am male, practised and elderly, and the trail of sex, age and experience is certain to be over my translation. If the poem is ever to be well translated, it must be by some high-spirited English girl who has been brought up at Athens and who, therefore, has not been jaded by academic study of the language.[92]

If it was left for Joyce to invent a new prose in which to bring over the *Odyssey* into English for his time, and to a new Authoress still to come in our own, yet Butler brought Homer alive and kicking and speaking 'the language we write and speak among ourselves' into the twentieth century.[93] His 'imaginary portrait' of the Authoress – for it is an egregious example of that Victorian genre while suggesting the novel-as-criticism of our own day – his 'Portrait of the Authoress of the *Odyssey* as a young girl' epitomizes the shift of focus from 'high seriousness' to the high irony of modernism.

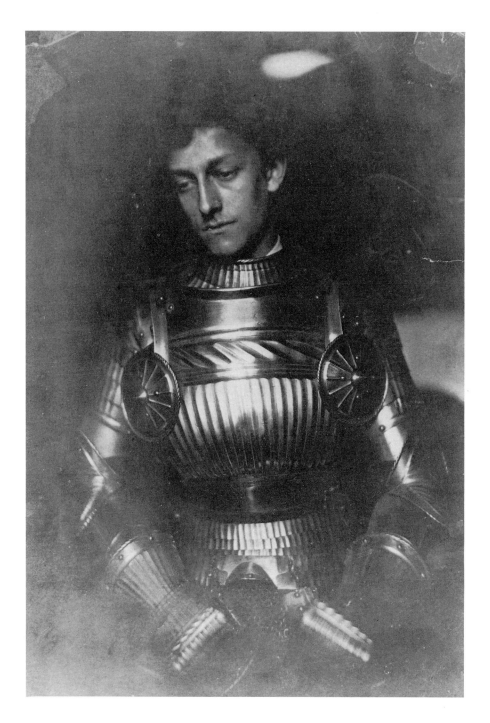

106. *Johnston Forbes-Robertson in armour, Heatherley's, 1870*

CHAPTER FOUR

The Ignorant Eye:
Photography and the Future

———

One of Butler's *Unprofessional Sermons* conveys the sheer unscrupulous pleasure of the photographic hunt. On the text of 'Lead us not into temptation' he describes temptation triumphant:

I have my camera in my hand and though the sea is rough the sun is brilliant. I see the archdeacon [the popular preacher, Archdeacon Farrar] come on board at Calais and seat himself upon the upper deck, looking as though he had just stepped out of a band-box. Can I be expected to resist the temptation of snapping him?[1]

Temptation increases as the face of the Archdeacon (we recognize one of Butler's target titles) grows 'saintlier and saintlier' with seasickness:

I am an excellent sailor myself, but he is not, and when I see him there, his eyes closed and his head thrown back, like a sleeping St. Joseph in a shovel hat, with a basin beside him, can I expect to be saved from snapping him by such a formula as 'Deliver us from evil'?

An Old Testament parallel (and Butler's comic use of typology is significant for much of his photography) gives the *coup-de-grâce*:

Is it in a photographer's nature to do so? When David found himself in a cave with Saul he cut off one of Saul's coat-tails; if he had had a camera and there had been enough light he would have photographed him; but would it have been in flesh and blood for him neither to cut off his coat-tail nor to snap him?[2]

Both the Biblical context and the placing of the phrase 'in flesh and blood' suggest the savagery of the medium; Strindberg, a fellow painter, photographer and naturalist, called his camera a 'revolver' with which he could 'shoot' his subject. Butler's 'Sermon' concludes: 'There is a photographer in every bush, going about like a roaring lion seeking whom he may devour.' 'Wild eyesight' may be on the loose.

Butler stalked bigger game as well, and accompanied his photographs with Homeric passages, nothing daunted by charges of 'vulgarizing the classics' in the 'low' media of translation and photography – and his title, 'Snapshotting a Bishop', captures the note of aggression:

205

I must some day write about how I hunted the late Bishop of Carlisle with my camera, hoping to shoot him when he was sea-sick crossing from Calais to Dover, and how St. Somebody protected him and said I might shoot him when he was well, but not when he was sea-sick. I should like to do it in the manner of the *Odyssey*:

... And the steward went round and laid them all on the sofas and benches and he set a beautiful basin by each, variegated and adorned with flowers, but it contained no water for washing the hands, and Neptune sent great waves that washed over the eyelet-holes of the cabin. But when it was not the middle of the passage and a great roaring arose as of beasts in the Zoological Gardens, and they promised hecatombs to Neptune if he would still the raging of the waves ...

At any rate I shot him and have him in my snap-shot book, but he was not sea-sick.[3]

As every hunter knows, the biggest one was the one that got away.

For Butler the imagery of the hunt signalled still bigger photographic game than bishops: the possibility at last of the death of the 'Grand Style', of 'High Art', and of academic values. The arguments by which photography painfully claimed a place next to painting in England were beside the point, for they all required muffling or concealing photography's salient features. Photography of its nature knocked the grand style off its pedestal, by doing what it could do better (the detailed imitation of nature), by stripping out pretence, and by pushing art to do something else altogether. Photography resolved the conflict between 'studies' and 'out of one's own head' that dogged Butler's painting: for through photographic reproduction one gets more accurate detail than the most gifted painter could ever hope to achieve. Fear runs through the whole nineteenth-century response by painters to the new medium, which indeed put engravers and miniaturists out of business. While the fierce debates that raged over the status of photography – was it art or mere mechanical reproduction? – circled round the artists' denial that photography could ever come near painting, and the photographers' rejoinder that an intelligent eye stood behind the hand that manipulates the machine and planned a 'painting' in advance just as a painter would, Butler positively revelled in the vulgarity and the impromptu of the medium. Photography not only delivered accuracy of detail, it delivered it quickly: the contrast between the speed of eye and brain and the tedium of reproduction had always plagued Butler. For all its accuracy and detail, photography was utterly open to the winds of chance and instantly alert to unexpected, spontaneous, ephemeral apparitions and epiphanies. At the same time, and perhaps most significantly, it resolved the tension between reduction, or stripping down, and hyperrealism in

Butler's thought and practice: in photography, one could reduce through verism itself. Because photography was quick, ephemeral, low and above all cheap, any use of the photographic medium reduced pretensions to rubble. It was vulgar by definition; it automatically lowered, automatically swept away value.[4] Photography was like life, in so far as 'Dutch boors' predominate in life; but more, it was a satirist's medium that preferred and favoured the grotesque, the unusual, the 'sport of nature'. Warts are distinctly 'on'. The ways in which it was not like life were as welcome and natural to Butler as the ways in which it was. The view through the 'peephole' of a box in which perspectival optics created an illusion was the viewpoint of the Sacro Monte chapels; the camera has a theatrical quality, as Barthes has pointed out.[5] This is linked at a fundamental, perhaps even unconscious level with his obsessive viewing through a constricted viewpoint of successive interiors which open out into an imaginary landscape, itself intricately 'mapped'.[6] At the same time, with the camera he could penetrate behind and destroy the privileged and restricted view of the interior of the chapel, as he had done with 'the old Adam and Eve'. Like caricature and cartoon the photograph was black and white. Like the earlier popular prints of Hogarth, and the sporting prints that Butler thought suited the genius of British art (unavoidably industrial and technological), it was a triumph of commercial invention, cheap and easy to reproduce on a mass scale. The very language it generated was in line with the comic genius of the English language – 'snapshotting', terse, brief, pungent, and disrespectful (as Swift wrote of the 'mob' that English made of *mobile vulgus*). Above all, it pushed art to return to the primitive and abandon the mastery of mere imitation. Thus the ambiguity of photography's position made it ideal for the 'hunt': since the opinion that it was not an art predominated, Butler could use it to bash 'art' with; and at the same time, in so far as it conformed to what he wanted of art, he could promote his alternative vision through it.

Butler's photography, although virtually unknown, represents much of the development of style and technique in the new art between 1865 and the turn of the century. His attitudes and values in painting intersected at an important point with what were considered to be photographic virtues: the sobriety and Rembrandtesque realism aimed at by some of his own painted portraits was widely claimed as attainable by photography, and was carried out in portraits such as those by David Octavius Hill in the 1840s and '50s, praised by Lady Eastlake as 'small, broadly treated Rembrandt-like studies . . . which first cast the glamour of photography upon us.'[7] Photography was often compared to 'Dutch realism', and Teniers's 'Dutch boors', uncomfortable in 'High Art', were permitted to come into their own in the implicitly (and explicitly) vulgar medium of photography. Butler contributed to the leading genres of Victorian photography, especially street scenes, portraits, and architecture, both at home and in more exotic settings, and he is a particularly interesting exponent of the transition to naturalism, even before the technology of the instantaneous snapshot was fully available. Yet at the same time all of his photography arises out of his own special concerns and can only be understood against the background of his struggles to paint and to establish a personal art history – a distinctive version of the Renaissance which could serve the development of an English art and art history, exemplary 'Lives of the Artists', a genealogy for his own art, and a way of seeing. He succeeds in establishing a distinctive character of his own in photography, as in everything he touched; his major themes are drawn together. It could even be said that in photography he at last found his true medium as a visual artist.

Technology touched his imagination: there are few better essays on it than the opening of Chapter 5 in *Alps and Sanctuaries*, which leads into the dream of the Renaissance quoted above. 'Our inventions increase in geometrical ratio', he begins, imagining how after aeons someone invented a bridge by venturing to cross a pine log accidentally fallen across a chasm, and a second genius ventured to move it into a more useful position – 'This man was the inventor of bridges – his family repudiated him and he came to a bad end.' Yet now, only fifty years after the proliferation of carriage roads,

we are already in the age of tunnelling and railroads . . . What will come next we know not, but it should come within twenty years, and will probably have something to do with electricity . . . It follows by an easy process of reasoning that, after another couple of hundred years or so, great sweeping changes should be made several times in an hour, or indeed in a second, or fraction of a second, till they pass unnoticed as the revolutions we undergo in the embryonic stages, or are felt simply as vibrations.[8]

On a practical level, he was quick to adopt technological advances: in 1885 he acquired a typewriter and dilated on its joys.

Still more, it is in a distinctive marriage of text and photography that he creates the works he had striven for in vain. The 'ignorant eye' finds its own vantage-point.

Jones tells us that Butler took up photography in 1888. But this is highly misleading, as there are extant photographs by Butler from 1866. It seems that Jones was referring only to Butler's acquisition of a camera lucida, in 1882, to help him with his painting. Butler wrote to Miss Savage:

I was nearly drowned out at Verona during the inundations, but have had no other mishaps. When will you come and see me? I am not going to write for some time: I have got a painting fit on. I have got a new toy called a Camera lucida, which does all the drawing for me, and I am so pleased with it that I am wanting to use it continually.[9]

Like many another artist, he became disillusioned with it on realizing how much it distorted perspective, and gave it up after about a year; as his 1901 note indicates: 'As for the Camera lucida – what a lot of time I wasted over it, to be sure!' He neither took up photography at that late date, nor did he give it up then.

His major activity as a photographer is related to his painting and to his writing: he often photographed the same subjects as he sketched and painted, both as an *aide mémoire* and because the subject appealed to him; but it seems to have been intensified by his plans for writing *Ex Voto*. To that extent Jones's date is a significant one. Most of the extant negatives (about 3000) are dated between 1889 and 1900.[10] *Ex Voto* was illustrated with his photographs of the chapels and other material relating to the sites of his art-historical research, as were the related art-historical articles. His next major book, *Authoress*, used his travels to classical lands, with photographs, as a basis for his argument, and this is closely linked to his translations of Homer, which were also accompanied by photographs; in both cases the photographs are an integral part of a satiric exercise. In short, after *Alps and Sanctuaries* his books were illustrated with his own photographs rather than with his drawings. Behind *Alps* lies a bank of photographs of Italy from the sites described in the book. Behind *Authoress* and the Homeric translations lies a far more extensive photographic record than he published: photographs from Trapani and from major classical sites in Italy, Sicily, Greece, and Asia Minor including Roman ruins, Paestum, Pompeii, the temples at Segesta and Selinunte, Athens, Mycenae, and the Troad.

His photographs were not taken simply as illustrations to or evidence for the arguments of his literary and art-historical works. They cover a range of subjects and styles that show he was well aware of the development of photography both as an art and as a science in the latter half of the nineteenth century, and that he was a major practitioner of it. Moreover, his grasp of the significance of photography as an art form plays an important role in his arguments and in his style. Finally, photography permitted him to surmount the contradictions and limitations of painting theory and practice in his time. His art-historical explorations of the nature of the gothic in the intermingling of Flemish and Italian in the Alpine valleys led him to a form of the modern grotesque. Ruskin had seen the possibility of such a form; but he situated 'the dawn of a new era of art', in a remarkable lapse of the 'prophetic' imagination, in Watts and Rossetti, and in the direct imitation and revival of medieval illumination.[11] Ruskin changed his mind more than once about photography, but was unable to make the mental leap into the new technology that Butler took as the clue to the modern grotesque. The values attached to 'Tabachetti' enter a new world. 'Low life' takes on fresh vigour in what was still felt to be a vulgar medium, even, perhaps especially, by those who made most (often surreptitious) use of it, the painters. If in the end Butler's most characteristic genre was a new one, intricately linked with his writing, it was through the conjunction of his art criticism of the Renaissance with photography that he invented it. His photography can only be understood in the light of his whole trajectory as an artist.

His earliest acquaintance with photography was simply as a record; just before he set sail for New Zealand he wrote to his sister that he would visit the photographers 'Maull and Polybank' (archetypal names for a new breed just joining the satirists' rollcall, the photographic mountebanks).[12] On several occasions later he sends members of his family to be photographed.

His first acquaintance with photography as an art goes back to his days at art school, as we have seen. Many of Heatherley's students practiced photography. The impetus was given by D. W. Wynfield's series, *Portraits of Royal Academicians in Fancy Dress*.[13] Several of these are very familiar: the profile of John Everett Millais as jester, and Holman Hunt as Henry VIII. Leighton, with downcast eyes, and G. F. Watts, in a rich shining fabric, are there too, with a thin, fine John F. Hodgson in a ruff, and a dashing Henry Phillips decked out in lace, chain, and embroidery. Perhaps the most characteristic is the wonderfully atmospheric William Frederick Yeames, with its intense feeling, soft focus, balance of lights and darks, and props of fine embroidery. Pensive, intense, and inward is the dominant note, beautifully carried out in sepia. Clearly these photographs, with their note of artistic swanking, high spirits, and hint of self-parody affected Butler as well as Julia Cameron. One very fine photograph Butler took at that time, clearly in Wynfield's manner, is extant: of Johnston Forbes-Robertson, later the famous Shakespearean actor, then Butler's fellow art student (illus. 106). He was already celebrated for his face, however, and sat as a model to more than one painter. The photograph displays a Pre-Raphaelite young man, glamorously dressed in Heatherley's suit of armour, replete with fine highlights. The harmonious tonalities give an inward yet striking impression of unity. Butler has caught just the note of Wynfield's series, with the help of Forbes-Robertson's effective posing. The young aspirant – if 'fancy dress' is all that's wanted – is elevated into the ranks of the Royal Academicians by Butler's photographic art.

Forbes-Robertson in his memoirs gives a vivid account of Butler as photographer:

> I remember his having a mind one day to take a photograph of me in a suit of armour Heatherly had in his back room. Thither some of us adjourned [from the pub] to assist in the proceedings. There was much ado to get the armour on me, as most of them insisted that the gorget should come over the breastplate, which Butler and I knew was wrong. Such a fuss there was, with much gesticulation and vain chattering, Butler meanwhile calm and smiling amid the storm. Slowly he got a hearing, and with great deliberation and softly smiling all the while, he gave them a lecture, full of biting sarcasm, proving that he knew more about armour and the proper wearing of it than all of them put together. They were set down as naught, and, buckling me up correctly, he at last took the photograph.[14]

Knowing Butler's use of Heatherley's kit of studio props in his painting, and J. B. Yeats's account of his waggish spirits, not to mention the bibulous setting in which the idea was broached, we can imagine that a certain humour attached to this; yet the photograph gives the sitter his full meed of aesthetic value, and is prophetic of his later career. Forbes-Robertson always claimed that he was a painter at heart, and complained that he had only been pushed onto the stage, first in amateur theatricals, because he looked well in costume. Butler's insight into character is at work here, as well as his undeniable skill as a photographer, and his awareness of the style of the day. His command of the style underlines the fact that his refusal of Aestheticism in later years was deliberate and programmatic. Even here we have another depiction of Mr Heatherley's – where the would-be artist is half-buried in the paraphernalia of the studio. Not only the suit of armour, but the aesthetic style itself is a piece of paraphernalia that must be escaped and left behind. Forbes-Robertson included the photograph in his memoirs as 'J. F.-R. at seventeen' (which allows us to date the photograph to 1870), and among the later posed paintings and the photographs of him got up as Macbeth, Othello, and Caesar it stands out from the theatrical flummery as capturing the spirit of a young Hamlet playing the ghost of his father.[15]

In another photograph of still earlier, his first extant photograph, *Mrs Bassatt* in 1866 or 7 (illus. 117), printed later from an early negative, Butler produced a fine rural scene, in which Mrs Bassatt's setting – her sharply delineated ivy-covered cottage – is as important as she.[16] Indeed, we see already a characteristic that was to come to the fore in the later photographs: the dislike of 'pose', the stress on naturalness, and on capturing character at work. The knitting woman is not looking at the camera, but concentrating on her work. There were many photographers of 'characters' emblematic of their occupation, for example, Frank Meadow Sutcliffe's *Retired from the Sea*, but they, like the old salt, whose occupation is stressed in the narrative title, definitely posed for their portraits.[17]

The problem of 'pose' was most intense in street scenes, or any activity which the photographer wished to capture. The best-known Victorian scenes of street life, for example John Thomson's *Street Life in London* (published in 12 monthly instalments 1877–8) are, in fact, carefully posed: the photographer approached people in the street, arranged his group as he wished, and exposed his picture for as long as he needed.[18] This was a technical necessity, and photographers described their techniques in the growing literature on the subject. Sutcliffe 'refused to pose people. He set up his camera in front of the activity he had decided to photograph and when the grouping was to his liking he asked those in the picture to keep still whilst he made the exposure.'[19] Thomson's directive method and Sutcliffe's less obtrusive procedure seem to have been influenced also by notions of dramatic pose derived from the stage and from book illustration; illustration of the novel, especially Dickens, played a role. Butler's sense that illustration was the only branch of art that was not decadent in his period was a strong argument in favour of photography. A certain deliberate dramatic element, the frozen moment of sculpture was still valued. Pictures in which attention is drawn not to the dramatic posed gesture, but to the spontaneity of the action (even where the picture is still in fact posed, for technical reasons), are transitional to naturalism. Lyddell Sawyer's photographs, for example, are said to be 'transitional in content and treatment between the contrived scene and naturalism', as in *Waiting for the Boats* (1889).[20] Butler did comparable photographs, for example, his studies of women on the quays (illus. 139), with the boats in the background, where a group is engaged in a static action – a patient group at Boulogne waiting for the ship; a grim group of *Three women on Greenwich Pier*; a group implying waiting in motion, *Crossing from Newhaven to Dieppe*, showing three women and a man wedged in under rugs among their bulky luggage on deck, the vast woman in the centre slumped down fast asleep; his many studies of sleeping groups and individuals take advantage of their uncontrived immobility, and achieve a high degree of artlessness and spontaneity (illus. 154, 156, 158).

These extend – even in these relatively simple examples – to a range of meditative or contemplative poses in which the subjects are still and unmoving, wrapped in their own concerns. In others, they are so deeply engaged in their work that they are virtually transfixed within it: spinning, washing, drawing water (illus. 120), hanging clothes, mending nets, sitting by wares in the marketplace (illus. 123), singing or playing an instrument. This was not uncommon in scenes of peasant life (in painting, for example, Millet's *Peasant*), and some of Butler's photographs are rural, showing a solitary man or woman or small group in the fields; the most successful examples in English photography were probably P. H. Emerson's studies of Norfolk working lives, in which the human figures are embedded in the landscape and rhythms of their activities as in, among many examples, *Ricking the Reed* and *The Sedge Harvest*; but all sense of individual character is deliberately suspended in common labour, observed at a distance.[21]

The painting of such scenes, and the quality of absorption, was familiar in genre painting. But to catch this absorption in action in a photograph, and more especially in a busy urban scene, was novel and difficult. Some of Butler's photographs are posed, but many of them capture his subjects' quality of absorption in action, unaware of the camera. In the midst of a busy Italian market-place a girl leans over to fasten her garter; everyone else, intent on his own work, is unaware both of her and of the photographer (illus. 121). The most effective actions are those that require the subject to maintain one position, yet convey the sense that work is being carried out. In a photograph of a knife-grinder (illus. 122), for example, the man is still as he concentrates on his work; but the wheel can be seen to be in a blur of spinning. Moreover, many of his photographs of urban scenes are in Italy, in places he knew well and spent time in, like Varallo and Trapani, and where he had won people's confidence; his photographs benefit from this quality of implicit trust, for he was not, like Thomson, a sociological chronicler from the outside, nor a manipulator of unwilling actors, but a frequent visitor and friend. Photography was his idiosyncratic but tolerable deformation, and like *The Funny Boy of Varallo*, one of his recurrent subjects, he had his place in the order of things. The connection between this technique and his stress on the communal presence in the minor masters of Varallo is clear: the 'anonymous craftsman' – of whom the photographer is the most obvious modern equivalent – is, in his place, known to all.

It is probably a mistake to see this mode of rendering action merely as a transition to naturalism, as the photographic literature does. Rather it is related to the quality of absorption in genre painting generally from the eighteenth century, as described by Michael Fried. Photographers were perfectly aware that their work would be 'read' as genre painting, and some courted the comparison. In Butler's work, this quality of absorption is linked with a suggestion of intense, heightened activity transfixed in immobility; sometimes it is linked with a sense of passivity, or suffering. There is a powerful link with his painting, *Family Prayers*. In general, the dramatic absorption characteristic of painted genre subjects is rendered more poignant by the technical *tour-de-force* required to capture the brief photographic moment of stasis in action.

A very considerable number of Butler's most striking photographs deal with the abnormal or grotesque, usually treated in a comic vein. His immersion in the grotesque realism of the Sacro Monte statuary is echoed here, as he finds his own note. We find blind subjects (who like sleeping subjects would not remark the camera), deaf-mutes, cretins, the crippled, the lame, and less obviously disabled (illus. 127, 129, 132, 133, 136). One of his finest subjects is the *Blind Man reading the Bible* (illus. 107), a contradiction in terms which sums up the spiritual state of the age. It contains the further irony of displaying to the sighted viewer not the words of the Bible but those of the bills posted behind the blind man advertising wanted criminals. A further sign held by the blind man shows he is deaf and dumb as well. It is in these studies of the viewless Bible contrasted to the sharply readable 'page' of urban hoarding behind the blind man that Butler finally executes a successful version of his 'Advertising painting'. The man and his readers are engrossed by a new

107. *Blind Man reading the Bible near Greenwich*, 1892

text of ignorance, the opposite to the text that procured salvation for the old woman reading the Bible in Maes's painting. 'Absorption' itself is ironized. The new medium is capable of the layered inset graphic complexity of the Dutch interior views of churches by Pieter Saenredam and the incorporation of detailed inscription in Dutch painting in general.[22] This form of unity of word and image is another way in which Butler's art is 'Northern'. Moreover, it is a special case of that grotesque whose quality is to render the animate inanimate, the inanimate animate which we noticed in Butler's play with 'the old Adam and Eve' and the relations of hyperreal statuary to humans in general. The old blind man is written over with the hieroglyphs of incomprehension; he is turned into a text whose meaning is the opposite of what he gropes for, and it is that text that lives for the photographic onlooker. The capacity to render animate inanimate and vice versa has been seen by Sontag as one of the characteristics of photography, one of its 'perennial successes'.[23] She fails to identify this as grotesque, but perceives its relation to the 'dissociation' of seeing from other perceptual functions. Butler catches here – and his whole photographic *oeuvre* takes place at this moment in the history of photography – the moment of reduction that is part of what Moholy-Nagy called the 'hygiene of the optical', a moment in the movement towards the ignorant eye which he enforces and forwards, not in simple affirmation, but in the complex and ferocious irony sometimes bordering on terror which the mind trained up on the literary and the painterly feels as it deliberately sheds its carefully nurtured associations of intellectual and moral value. That special aesthetic *frisson* which the unhallowed comparison of Tabachetti and Raphael inspired in the viewer being trained to attain the ignorant eye is carried to the next stage. A variant on this photograph, *Blind Man with Children, Greenwich* (illus. 108), showing the blind man reading in the company of children who stare straight ahead, suggests the Lamarckist transmission of the acquired ignorant eye to the next, unconscious generation.

Often his most bizarre or grotesque characters reappear, as with 'the funny boy' of Varallo, exerting a continuing fascination. The social gradations are negated; the substantial, respectable matron, *Mrs Negri*, with a pronounced squint is their equal in deformity (illus. 134). Temporary disabilities also are pinpointed yet accommodated, as in the brilliant, Dutch portrait of *Old Mrs Kaufmann, Basle* (illus. 135), whose arm in a black sling at first is appreciated simply as part of the tonal

108. *Blind Man with Children, Greenwich,* 1892

palette of the photograph, and then stands out as an anomalous detail in a familiar composition. There is an arresting, disturbing Arbus-like quality about many of these photographs, which represents Butler's interest in the 'sports of nature' or what Bacon called 'aberrations'. These are his version of 'the goitred man', and again an aspect of his adherence to 'Northern' art.

Yet often, as at Gaudenzio's chapels, taken in context Butler's grotesques represent one of the things he valued about Italian society, the naturalness with which the range of humanity was accepted. A photograph by Thomson, *'Caney' the Clown*, in *Street Life in London*, in which an individualized, slightly grotesque character is seen in profile on a very low stool re-caning a chair seat, offers a parallel to some of Butler's natural grotesques, but he is artfully posed and distanced: the caner is counterbalanced by a woman watering plants inside the window behind him.[24] There is often a kind of cheerfulness and humour which appears as part of the individuals' life, not simply as the photographer's attitude towards them. Thomson again offers a close parallel, with a photograph like The 'Wall Worker', which depicts working men absorbed in the pleasure of not working, as three men occupy a bench outside a pub, smoking pipes and holding mugs.[25] This represents a relatively subtle solution to the technical problem of photographing action with a slow camera. Eugène Atget's series of Paris street life, or petits métiers, in the last two years of the nineteenth century, also offers parallels, for example, his Joueur d'Orgue, capturing his street musicians in a moment of joy.[26]

Butler was able to perceive the same quality he found most fully embodied in Italy in certain English scenes, especially at the seaside. Seaside pictures were identified as a genre at about this time, as bathing became popular. One of the most deservedly famous photographs in this genre, and which inspired many imitations, was Sutcliffe's Water Rats (1885), showing a group of mainly naked boys playing with a rowboat at low tide.[27] Paul Martin, labelled as 'probably the most able photographer' in the new genre of the 1890s of 'street characters and incidents of street life', as the exhibition catalogues called it, took a number of photographs while on holiday at Cromer and Yarmouth.[28] Butler's photographs at Brighton and Clacton and the river ports – the Greenwich of Blind Man with Children, the rakish young woman with baby on a bench Nr Limehouse Pier – have a verve and jauntiness of their own, and catch the sense of a society in which all are unconsciously grotesque and enjoying themselves and others. In many ways these are not so much 'seaside' photographs, however, as an extension of his urban street-life photographs, carrying out the themes of his Ramblings in Cheapside. Seen in this light, Butler emerges as a photographer of urban life, in which all experience is fragmented, yet showing unexpected comic symmetries and concealed threads of association. One of his best in this mode is another of his subterranean self-portraits – Butler and a sea of city look-alikes in bowlers perched back to back on deck on a day-trip (illus. 137). Even the reduced, sober dignity of his painted portraits is mocked and doffed. Ramblings in Cheapside begins and ends with an unconsummated encounter with a turtle in a shop window – unconsummated, in that only eating turtles could truly unite him with them. In the civilized state, lack of money prevented him from the consummations celebrated up and down the 'food chain' of nature. Other passages show his fascination with the Hogarthian crowd scenes and bizarre, unexpected incidents of the street:

Another curious sight I saw this morning. I was going to the British Museum and saw a crowd outside the corner house of the street going from Gt. Russell Street to Russell Square. It was a curious shaped crowd & a curiously behaving crowd. I cd see in the distance that it was not a fight, nor a fire, nor a man being taken up & I kept thinking to myself what an *odd* behaving crowd it was – all the time I drew nearer. The people walked up to the area, looked down – talked a little and went on. When I came up I found that two horses had found their way into the area. One had shied, swerved from the road and falling against the iron railing had knocked it down & tumbled down the area. The other was blind & went where its mate went, and there they were. They said one was hurt but the other not. The area was so narrow that there was no room for them to turn round so how they are to be got out I know not.[29]

The 'humour of horses' appealed to him almost as much as the 'Humour of Homer', and one of his shipboard photographs shows a boxed horse looking alarmed and out of place, as the two who had tumbled into the area might have done (illus. 142). There are a number of 'modern bestiary' photographs of animals or humans likened to animals – a serious theme in post-Darwinian literature –, for example, *Man with monkey, Varallo* (illus. 125), *Turk with goat, Trapani, Man shaving poodle, Naples*, and not least *Marketing the turkey, Piazza S. Carlo, Varallo*, in which the shape of the turkey matches the rump of the woman sitting, back to us, next to the turkey.

His old habit of the 'imaginary portrait' in which a passer-by or a transient instant is identified comes into its own in these settings of urban anonymity, especially in relation to the new technologies of travel, the railways, the steamers that used to ply from London to Clacton, as when one day, travelling with his camera, he saw the Wife of Bath, Chaucer's outspoken and downright profane woman, in a class with the Nurse in *Romeo and Juliet* or indeed with 'The Grandmother of the Virgin', that '*suocera tremenda*' – or Gertie McDowell as Nausicaa. The identification of individuals is here embedded in the larger parallel between the pilgrims of the past and the tourists of today, and suggests in each case the germ of a modern 'tale'. His description of how he spotted and snapped 'The Wife of Bath' on board the *Lord of the Isles* going on a day-trip to Clacton-on-Sea gives a sense of the literary allusions or games of identification that often lay behind his photographs, and how much he enjoyed capturing the 'detective' process itself:

There are Canterbury Pilgrims every Sunday in summer, who start from close to the old Tabard, only they go by the South-Eastern Railway and come back the same day for five shillings. If they do not go to Canterbury they go by the *Clacton Belle* to Clacton-on-Sea. . . . Why, I have seen the Wife of Bath on the *Lord of the Isles*

109. *The Wife of Bath*

myself. She was eating her luncheon off an *Ally Sloper's Half-Holiday*, which was spread out upon her knees. Whether it was I who had had too much beer or she I cannot tell, God knoweth; and whether or no I was caught up into Paradise, again I cannot tell; but I certainly did hear unspeakable words which it is not lawful for a man to utter, and that not above fourteen years ago but the very last Sunday that ever was. The Wife of Bath heard them too, but she never turned a hair. Luckily, I had my detective camera with me, so I snapped her there and then. She put her hand up to her mouth at that very moment and rather spoiled herself, but not much.[30]

Three photographs identified by Jones as 'The Wife of Bath' are extant; all three show imposing women on shipboard, but only one answers fully to Butler's description. (The other two are of the same dark, elaborately bonneted woman, in one ill-tempered, in the other asleep.) *The Wife of Bath* (illus. 109) shows a once fine figure of a woman wearing an extraordinary piece of headgear shaped like a mitre, a narrow band of veiling across her forehead, a bow in a light shade perched on top with long streamers coming down over her shoulders to her waist, and with a bottle beside her and a bowl beyond it, a basin with a spoon on her other side, a picnic basket on the floor before her, and a hand up to her mouth.[31]

A number of Butler's photographs have literary titles of this kind: for example, *Shylock* (illus. 145), and the Odyssean ones we have already mentioned, such as Odysseus' palace (*Courtyard, Selinunte*), *Laertes' Villa* and *Eumaeus' Leggings*, and the frequent *Men with Pigs*. The association of pigs and men had, of course, Homeric connotations for Butler, with the Circe episode, and with the small-farming of Laertes and Eumaeus. Women washing clothes in streams (for one among many, the *Women washing at Pantelleria*) is also an Odyssean subject, one which Bérard waxed lyrical over as a sign of the permanent, unchanging civilization of the Mediterranean. Biblical iconography was always a resource for Butler, as in his photograph of *The Flight from Egypt*, showing a man on a donkey sheltering himself and a baby under an umbrella in a desert of sun; it is both a comic version of Gaudenzio's *Flight* and an allusion to the primitive Lombard lineage of the theme (in which Joseph's painstaking care is stressed) back through Foppa to folk experience.

Other descriptions are related directly to art. Raphael himself, and his model, make an appearance:

At Modena I had my hair cut by a young man whom I perceived to be Raffaelle. The model who sat to him for his celebrated Madonnas is first lady in a confectionery establishment at Montreal. She has a little motherly pimple on the left side of her nose that is misleading at first, but on examination she is readily recognised; probably Raffaelle's model had the pimple too, but Raffaelle left it out – as he would.[32]

Michelangelo, who was kept down in *Ex Voto*, makes a louche appearance in *Ramblings in Cheapside*; there is no photograph with his name on it, but he offers a number of poses of a kind that attracted Butler's photographic pounce. The steamer from London to Clacton was again his hunting ground:

Michael Angelo is a commissionaire; I saw him on board the Glen Rosa, which used to run every day from London to Clacton-on-Sea and back. It gave me quite a turn when I saw him coming down the stairs from the upper deck, with his bronzed face, flattened nose, and with the familiar bar upon his forehead. I never liked Michael Angelo, and never shall, but I am afraid of him, and was near trying to hide when I saw him coming towards me. He had not got his commissionaire's uniform on, and I did not know he was one till I met him a month or so later in the Strand. When we got to Blackwall the music struck up and people began to dance. I never saw a man dance so much in my life. He did not miss a dance all the way to Clacton, nor all the way back again, and when not dancing he was flirting and cracking jokes. I could hardly believe my eyes when I reflected that this man had painted the famous 'Last Judgment', and has made all those statues.[33]

In the context of photography the great names of 'High Art' take on a low-life vitality: this is caricature, but like any good caricature it is also insight into character – the vigour that Lomazzo had found in the artist born under Saturn is expressed in the terms of another medium. It is also a comment on the sources of art – the street is not remote from them. Raphael and Gaudenzio found their models on the street; Michelangelo may be among the 'Group going to Clacton'. Not one but two Beethovens, we recall, were staying at the same inn. Moreover, Butler's 'instant identities' mingle fictional and real characters at will – he sees both Shylock and Shakespeare; they mingle epochs and nationalities – Dante is cheek by jowl not only with Beatrice but with Aeschylus. Photography is urban and levelling and its effect is universal: the great men of the past are turned into so many *cartes-de-visite*, the photographic calling cards popular among Butler's contemporaries.[34] The aura of the past is dispelled as Michelangelo and Raphael become 'sure cards' – the prominent queens-for-a-day sought by collectors. In a film of our own day, 'Michel-ange' and 'Ulysse' return from their ten-year travels with a bag of postcard views.[35]

Butler usually recognized fictional characters from the past, but occasionally his photographs represent contemporary literature: we are not surprised, given his praise for periodical illustration, to find Dickensian illustrations, three photographs of 'The Little Nipper', an allusion to *Nicholas Nickleby*, to the family of the Kenwigses who fawn on their 'great' relative the water-rate collector, in the hope that he will leave them (and all the little Kenwigses) something. Butler's 'Little Nipper,' a jolly babe of about eight months old, is wearing a most fabulous lace cap or bonnet with ruchings and a sort of sunburst-halo around it; such indeed as Phiz's illustration *Emotion of Mr Kenwigs on Hearing the Family News from Nicholas* shows. Butler's *The Little Nipper* sequence displays him with his cap; laughing; and, finally, without his cap – a sad come-down.

Recognition in these photographs engages with Butler's theme of the anonymous artist. The continuity between life and art that he prized was effaced by the 'aura' of reputation (and the 'chicane' that often produces it). If Butler started in photography with a portrait of Forbes-Robertson that vaulted him falsely through fancy-dress and sepia tones into the

Royal Academy – a piece of institutional comedy – he went on to perform instant transformations of the 'nobodies' on the Clacton steamer into the great men of history and art whose names are uttered in reverential tones.

Thus where Walter Benjamin is ambivalent about the loss of 'aura' through mechanical reproduction, in what has become one of the most influential essays on new media in this century ('The Work of Art in the Age of Mechanical Reproduction'), and makes there and in his 'Short History of Photography' the surely specious argument that 'aura' is maintained in early photography by the slowness of the take (as it is sometimes said to be maintained in Julia Cameron by 'soft focus'),[36] Samuel Butler welcomed the loss of aura and greeted photography as one of its major instruments. Benjamin's argument is itself a reminiscence of the early history of photography, in which the wishful hope that photography could be 'like' painting still lingered. As we have seen, a meditation on aura, its nature and sources, and an attack on its current manifestations, is a constant theme throughout Butler's *oeuvre* in every medium. The loss of aura signified a positive gain in understanding. If at first his attack on it was based on the sense that art was in decline and aura was currently founded on false principles and a vitiated taste, Butler elaborated this local analysis into a general method. Only the loss of aura could strip off the distorting interpretations superadded by culture (in any time and place) which prevent one getting to the bottom of 'what one likes and dislikes'. The camera eye becomes an aid that is more than technical, precisely because it is wholly ignorant.

Butler's satires on 'aura', of course, depend on culture: for the more the photographer and the viewer know about the Wife of Bath, Michelangelo, and the Kenwigses, the better the joke works – and finally, only those subjected to the falsehoods of culture can respond by the appropriate surprise, shock at the impermissible (which Freud, another eminent late Victorian, thought was the essence of the joke), and liberation from stock responses. The camera produces another form of irony in the contrast between the overtrained eye of the artist behind the lens and the unabashed ignorance of his new medium. A new meditation begins as the overtrained eye learns how to become ignorant. In the hybrid, arbitrary, and random nature of the photographic gallery of low-life heroes and rogues that emerges (random at least for those who have not followed Butler's trains of thought), we see a levelling of history and art, of epochal and generic conceptions, and space made for the recognition of the anonymous seed of the future flung up by biological chance.

The ephemeral nature of the identifications is also a source of pleasure, as Lawrence praised the ephemeral quality of Etruscan art in contrast to Roman marmoreality: all art should be made of bread. *Sic transit.*

Many of Butler's photographs, like his drawings, cluster round the course of his numerous journeys, across the Channel to Boulogne or Dinant, through Paris, and the passes of Switzerland to his alps and sanctuaries in Italy. Again, he travelled these routes many times over, and knew them well. Some of his best photographs are taken on shipboard: the *Stoker* (illus. 140), with its brilliant assemblage of stripes and the self-conscious allure of the averted profile, the *Fruitseller* (illus. 141), with its precise balance of light and dark on the cross-channel ferries, *Turk and sheep on board Steamer between Palermo and Trapani* (illus. 143). Some of his best animal pictures were taken in these unlikely circumstances: the comic *Boxed Horse*, the brilliant white *Parrot on the quay, Paris*, a 'rarer bird' than Flaubert's parrot.

On his journeys architectural subjects become as important as people. He photographed as he drew townscapes of houses, churches, castles, cathedrals, classical ruins. Sequences of what we might now regard as tourist photographs of foreign cities and major sites began to be available commercially from the 1850s on; the most interesting of these run-of-the-mill photographs (which today would appear as picture postcards) are of exotic places, especially Egypt, India, and the Levant. At the end of the century Atget's architectural photos of Paris, and especially the exquisite *Shop Signs* series, have a formal aestheticism alien to Butler, though as ingrained in Parisian life as Butler's careless ease is in Italian street life. Among the best of Butler's photographs are those that set human subjects off against architecture, as do the chapels of Varallo, or *Mycenae, Tomb of Atreus with Ladies* (illus. 163), in which the familiar yet portentous triangle of the entrance to the beehive tomb of the doom-laden founder of the line of Agamemnon is echoed in the reverse triangles of the ladies' parasols; even without the mythological and literary reference the visual comedy is irresistible. In general, the visual symmetry of the sublime and the ridiculous yields some of his best comic effects. His play with geometries, often in an architectural context, is a last, comic reminiscence of his one-time interest in Ruskin's *Elements of Drawing*.

110. *Jones at Wassen*, 1895

Some of Butler's photographs *en route* are closely allied with his art-historical concerns. His interest in ecclesiastical architecture was scarcely that of a mere passer-by, or a photographer in search of a subject. His many photographs of this kind – one of the largest categories of his work – perhaps had as their starting-point the series of churches his drawing master Vandyck Browne had carried out for his grandfather. If Butler's excellent photograph of the west front of the Cathedral at Pisa, a centrepiece of Lombard architectural achievement in one of Lindsay's most persuasive and heartfelt passages, could have been taken by many another traveller, his *Wayside Oratory at Dinant* (illus. 173) would not have been, nor his fine *Church Porch at Meien* (illus. 175), where the shadow of the porch forms another interior enclosed by light. Some photographs are on the sites of his paintings, such as his several views of Wassen – one virtually identical with his painting of the Church at Wassen, with its almost cubist treatment, another adding a figure (illus. 110). As in his sketches and paintings (for example, *The Washing-place at Varallo* and *Church Porch at Rossura*, in *Alps*), he was interested in the involutions of space, the interior glimpsed through the porch, the interrelations between exterior and interior (illus. 1, 35); his concerns are very close to those of Frederick Evans in classic photographs such as *The Sea of Steps* and *Lincoln, Stairs in S. W. Turret* (1898).[37] There is a large group of photographs of Sicilian church architecture as well, ranging from *The Porch of the Mother Church at Erice*, with its detailed study of the porch, to the *Church of Madonna di Trapani* (illus. 171), with its delicate treatment of the tower and two-storeyed cloister below, and a variety of the extraordinarily tiny village churches such as the *Church at Pantelleria*. A photograph of the *Monastery at Mt Lycabettus, Athens* (illus. 169), shows a staircase leading up, through unlike arches, into space, in which the subject, while still recognizable, dissolves into a tonal study of light and shadow.

There is a range of portraits of priests and nuns, sometimes within the church, more often caught eerily outside it – nuns on shipboard with flying white coifs (illus. 160); priests on picnic; a jovial Sicilian *bon viveur* (illus. 159); a dapper priest with ladies at the Gobelins, looking upward, with a Renoiresque sensuousness, from under sun-dappled parasols, in rapt surprise – 'with a wild surmise' (illus. 164). This is one of his most unusual and successful shots of absorption – here, in an unknown object. Absorption is caught pure, in the abstract; and this is also a source of humour. There is, surely, an ironic reminiscence of the terrible wonder with which '*Il Vecchietto*' gazed upward at the crucified Lord.

The weight of his photography tells most, of course, in the photographs associated with the Sacro Monte, both those incorporated in *Ex Voto* and those parallel to or augmenting the drawings of *Alps and Sanctuaries*, and the photographs of associated works like the sanctuaries and chapels at Crea and Montrigone: the ecclesiastical interiors of the chapels, the photographs of works of art by Gaudenzio, Tabachetti, D'Enrico and others. Taking these together with the photographs of the sites, visitors, and townspeople, we have a formidable series representing 'the world of the Sacro Monte'. By any standard these are invaluable photographic records of artists and of a form of art too little known and studied. Gaudenzio in particular is an artist of the first rank. At quite another level, the works *in situ* are extraordinarily well-suited to the photographic medium, for reasons we have already suggested: their theatricality, their populist literalism, their unashamed grotesque. In them Butler located a style that through a long process of interpretation of his own values and experiences in art suggested and required the new medium. There is, then, the rare marriage of style, subject, and medium in these photographs that marks the best photographers.

Around the photographs of the works of art cluster the many photographs of the people on the Sacro Monte and of the town of Varallo and its citizens. The variety of people and activities on the Sacro Monte is legion – the *Lame Boy* (illus. 150), the *Picnickers*, the *Child having her hair dressed on Sacro Monte*, and the *Women looking into chapel* (illus. 51). There are comparable pictures from other Sacri Monti, for example the *Old Beggar at S Eusebio chapel* (illus. 151), at Crea, where the pastoral landscape is given its liberty, with the ruinous textures of the shaggy old man blending into the old stone and wild vegetation. Some of the photographs of the town are primarily architectural, like the handsome *Steps of S Gaudenzio* (illus. 165), some primarily of people, but nearly all integrate the inhabitants and their surroundings. The pungency of Butler's Varallo photographs contrasts with the idealized description of the townspeople given by the Revd King:

We had now been long accustomed to their striking types of face and charming varieties of costume; but when we first saw them assembled here in crowds on a brilliant day, we were wonderfully struck; for there was something so Grecian in the contours of their finely-chiselled features, and in their picturesque dresses, that we felt as if suddenly introduced into a land of romance. Even the old women were extremely fine-looking, retaining the traces of their early beauty, to which was added the dignity of age; and in carriage and manner suggested to us at the time the idea of well-born dames, who for some freak or other had gone to market with their own produce.[38]

How fond Butler was of the people of Varallo we know: and so he refused the condescension of romanticizing them in the manner of those marine artists who touching at exotic Pacific shores (such as New Zealand) had dressed the Polynesian natives in Grecian costume and sold the portraits of the 'noble savage' far and wide in Europe. Instead, Butler gives us the homely, grotesque figures already named, like *The Funny Boy* and his brother, the cripple, and their friends; and other characteristic pictures like *Sleeping pigs in piazza Gaudenzio Ferrari, Varallo* (illus. 153), the spacious piazza opposite the cloisters of S Maria delle Grazie where the artist had his home; the linking of the artist's name with the common life of the town undoubtedly pleased the photographer.

As we look at this assemblage of photographs of the world of the Sacro Monte we become acutely aware of a Butlerian style of seeing. It is quite different from the Renaissance mode of seeing which is partially at least conserved in Italian catalogues and books of Gaudenzio's and his colleagues' work, with their stress on the relation to fresco painting – a 'higher' art – of the time, on graceful and coherent groupings of figures selected from among the crowded scenes of the chapels such as the weeping mothers in the 'Crucifixion' Chapel, or the procession of the Magi, or on individual details displaying consummate painterly skill, like the man in the superb white fur hat worthy to be set beside the plump polygonal hat of the warrior in Paolo Uccello's *The Battle of San Romano*, which Lorenzo de' Medici hung in his bedroom. Butler's photographs look away both from the Quattrocento mode and from the fixed perspectives of the chapels, and create a parallel between the characters of the chapels – Il Vecchietto, the goitred man, the man bending over his sandal, the bad thieves – and the people of the town – the funny boy, the cripple, the men with pigs, the girl doing up her garter in the busy marketplace.

Taking the photographs in conjunction with their accompanying texts creates a further range of effects: as we have seen in the cases of the *Old Adam and Eve* and the *St Joachim*, we are given a dazzling comic ambiguity in which the assumptions of the viewer still in charge of the narrative of the Birth of the Virgin and its iconography are challenged and overturned. Butler's procedure depends on a modern viewer whose command of these narrative and pictorial conventions is less than assured. Photography supports and enforces ambiguity through ignorance – its own and the viewer's. Butler's photograph of the statue of St Joachim pinpoints this precisely: the viewer of the photograph cannot resolve the question posed by the text – whether it is the father of the Virgin or her grandmother. Part of the power of this photograph is that the viewer looks to it confidently to resolve a matter of simple fact – is it a man or a woman? – and finds it cannot do so.

Thus Butler suggests a world of naturalism exploiting the photograph's innate tendency towards the grotesque and its historical tendency towards deflation and comedy (of which Butler is one of the best examples) and opens a newer world of bedazzling ambiguity, free speculation, and new creation from a perspective of ignorance. The Hogarthian intention of 'lifting the skirts of nature' is still there but the outcome has become less predictable. A game of relationships and

111. *Samuel Butler sitting on stile near Abbey Wood, 1891*

identities is still being played, but it is loosed from its moorings. The biblical and classical education that Butler was certain closed the eyes is jettisoned. New definitions are needed of what is 'seen' and 'unseen'. With the photograph the eye of the viewer is ignorant and open.

Yet photography confers one more advantage. Behind *The 'Life of Jesus' in photographs* – the very title presents a paradox and an irony – lies the passion of Butler's conscious abandonment of the faith that informed these works of art; only photography could render them as they appear to the modern. Emptied of inward conviction, it delivers a comedy of the hyperreal in which humans and statues like automata mingle indistinguishably. Yet the inability of the camera to distinguish between the real and the hyperreal restores the spirit of the original. Devoid of the faith that made primitive hyperrealism a visualisation of a supernatural world mapped onto this world, the photographer uses the ignorance of the camera eye to restore their unity. The camera sees the 'New Jerusalem' plain: a grotesque but authentic work of art.

229

112. Samuel Butler, the 'Falstaff', at Gad's Hill, 1893

In the genre of the self-portrait Butler's photographs are directly comparable to those of his contemporaries, and indeed to a major thread in the history of photography. Photographers, as deprecating about their right to appear as subjects as they were doubtful about the claims of photography to be 'art', tended to pose in disguise as their own habitual subjects, to render themselves 'other'. So Roger Fenton, famous for his photographs of the Crimean battlefields, photographed himself in uniform. Oscar Rejlander photographed himself in one disguise introducing himself in another (*Rejlander the Artist introduces Rejlander the Volunteer*). Often this required becoming an 'exotic': Gaspar-Félix Nadar photographed himself in Indian costume, a very occidental Francis Frith posed pensively in Turkish summer costume; Toulouse-Lautrec photographed himself in Japanese costume with his eyes crossed.[39] At the very least the photographer grafted himself onto a grander object or onto his own equipment. There was a clearly a strong element of humour in this flaunting of disguises, this masquerade for the

113. Samuel Butler atop Staffel Kulm, 1894

humble photographer, in an imaginary 'Royal Photographic Academy in Fancy Dress'. (We recall the long debates in the Academy about the propriety of admitting photographers as 'associates'.) 'The experience of otherness could generally be reduced to a limited imaginary effect or, at best, to a studied rhetoric of exoticism.'[40] Even Dada fantasy only took this already established tradition a step further. René Magritte's photographs of the casual clowning of himself and friends (*les extra-terrestres*), often *en route*, often seen from behind (for example, Magritte from behind facing his shadow on the sand: *L'Eminence grise*), extend it in the direction of surrealism.[41] This chimes with Butler's habitual eirenic pose. He photographed himself, with friends, and his friends on their own: his 'doublets' with Alfred – one snapshot of each in the same pose, forming a sub-genre of comic portraiture – at a favourite pub, the Falstaff at Gad's Hill (the allusion to Falstaff and his company of rogues at the site of one of Falstaff's tallest stories is an unmistakable part of Butler's technique); genially out of place in grand alpine land-

114. Samuel Butler on an avalanche, 1894

scapes (illus. 113); perched on a stile (illus. 111); and similarly with Jones, dwarfed like Ulysses himself in Polyphemus' cave (illus. 104). His *Alfred on top of the Arc de Triomphe* is another study in the humorous relations of architectural shapes, with the cocky Alfred triumphing over the Arc, his umbrella echoing in reverse the shape of the spanking new industrial triumph, the Eiffel Tower. His *Gogin and blocks of ice on the quay, Boulogne* (illus. 138) approaches the surreal note of Magritte. He photographed himself on steamer back to back with other unidentified bowler hats, and as part of Italian family portraits. He is seen in *Samuel Butler's Bodyguard* with four stalwart, fierce-looking Turks in uniform. He photographed his friends mingling with the statuary, the new medium carrying the confounding of the real with the hyperreal one step further, permitting a Gulliverian effect of disorientation in which the statue overtops the humans as in the gigantic *St Christopher, Castiglione d'Olona* (illus. 174), or again is much smaller, as in the tiny Virgin Mary climbing the steps of the temple towards the life-sized priest who looms behind the seated human visitors (illus. 61). Most striking is his double portrait of the artist as an unknown: himself with Stefano Scotto, the Renaissance sculptor, Gaudenzio's master in Milan, seen in a statue by his pupil (illus. 57). Nearby in the same chapel is a statue identified as Leonardo; but it is Scotto he chooses as his counterpart. The grotesque element of hyperrealism now serves self-identification: there is an uncanny resemblance between the statue and the man, and one is hard put to say which is real, which the work of art. The game of disguises is again in evidence: but here it intersects with a literary form of it, the theme of Pygmalion, the story of the creator with his creation, proof of creative power given in the coming to life of the created object, a subject that exercised other Victorians like Robert Browning. It is an accolade to Scotto's art, for he successfully confounded reality with sculpture – and an ironic commentary on it; it confers artistic status on Butler by the resemblance, and on Scotto too – perhaps Butler had recreated Scotto, if only in *Ex Voto*, if only in a photo? Yet both artists, and the artist in general, are cut down to size: unprepossessing, stiff, wooden, comic little men, whose works are lost or unknown. The resemblance between the two is uncanny, though one is painted terracotta, the other flesh: the problem of 'realism' is dissolved in the higher artifice of photographic technique. All photography is hyperreal. Lawrence complained that after the long search for one's identity at the end of it one found oneself as a kodak snap – the lion pounced and found only a kodak snap between his paws. For Butler, however, photography and new technologies generally threw up a new form of anonymous, unsung craftsman typified by his friend and neighbour Emery Walker – a founder of modern typography both for art presses and for ordinary book-printing, an associate of William Morris at the Kelmscott Press, and the producer of an immense quantity of photogravure, whose work has only barely been saved from destruction in recent years. To find a kodak snap at the end of the long search for identity which paired him with a Scotto or a Walker was an appropriate fate for the 'artist', itself a role inflated by romanticism and overdue for dismissal.

Butler's nearest parallel as writer and photographer is Emile Zola, whose contribution as theorist and exponent of naturalism is similarly undergirded by his excursions into evolutionary theory. Zola's photographs include a range of his own family life (many portraits of his wife and children) that was closed to Butler (except at a remove in his numerous photographs of the families of his Italian friends, his usually

115. Emile Zola, *Un enterrement, Cristal Palace*, 1898

116. Emile Zola, *Environs du Cristal Palace*, 1898

separate 'doublets' with his male companions, and a number of photographs of an old man or woman with a young child). But Zola like Butler is at his best in cityscapes of Paris and London; the London photographs single out the Crystal Palace and railways, as in Paris he singled out other expressions of modern technology such as the Eiffel Tower and nonce-constructions for expositions. He contrasted in a series of photographs the sleek modern forms of the Crystal Palace with its dingy surroundings, the tiny crowded houses and the 'Lower Level Station'.[42] The glossy and elegant Palace is matched by the glossy funereal horses, catching the contrast between the organic of the horses (and of the body carefully hidden in the handsome hearse) and the inorganic of the new architecture, summing up the macabre finish of technology in *Un Enterrement*, a burial (illus. 115). The humour of the feeding horses pulling the dog-cake wagon (illus. 116), which is literally the vehicle of the density of mobile advertisement, the graphic commercialism that Butler tellingly used as the backdrop for *The Blind Man reading the Bible, Greenwich*, similarly turns on the happy inability of the animals to read the messages they bear. His auto-portraits like Butler's join the line of self-deprecating photographers witty at their own expense: Zola the cyclist is at the front of the long queue of dada and surreal cycles that wheel through the early years of the twentieth century, in literature as in photography, from Jarry to Beckett.

Butler too took pleasure in the Crystal Palace, casting it, if somewhat more ironically, as a modern Sacro Monte, with music to match. Describing a day's outing at the Sacro Monte at Varese he remarked:

The processions were best at the last part of the ascent: there were pilgrims, all decked out with coloured feathers, and priests and banners and music and crimson and gold and white and glittering brass against the cloudless blue sky. . . . It was as though the clergymen at Ladywell had given out that instead of having service as usual, the congregation would go in procession to the Crystal Palace with all their traps, and that the band had been practising 'Wait till the clouds roll by' for some time, and on Sunday, as a great treat, they should have it.[43]

Zola's fascination with the Crystal Palace and its contrast with the old streets around it bespeaks the clash of Victorian and early modern architectural and artistic values so well expressed by Ruskin, whose dislike of the building is legendary. From his window at Herne Hill he found that the Crystal Palace obstructed his view of the Norwood hills, and he compared it to a giant cucumber frame stuck between two chimneys. In *The Stones of Venice* he remarked drily that it was 'neither a palace nor of crystal'. His pamphlet on its reopening at its new location in Sydenham was no more favourable. It seemed to sum up everything that was cold, abstract, lifeless. 'With the Crystal Palace, the machine literally became the building', a modern critic has written.[44] It was a triumph for 'the railway architects' and the principle of 'industrial ornament' as a by-product of construction itself, rather than of the individual labour of ornament that Ruskin valued. What comes through his discussion most powerfully is the sense that the building is 'unreadable', a blank page. His metaphors of blankness, of whiteness dominate the pamphlet and link Ruskin's dislike of the gothic restoration work being carried out by Viollet-le-Duc inserting its 'white accuracies of novelty' in the cathedral gables of Normandy, his dislike of the new arcades and boulevards of Paris, the 'whitened city', and his dislike of the loss of ornamentation in the 'whitewashed cottages' of the Norman countryside, to the central image of whiteness that haunts him, the Crystal Palace. This public amnesia, the mnemonic blankness spreading over the monuments of the past, was a threat to all significance.[45]

It was this erasure, this blank that Butler moved towards, as we have seen: in his refusal of the self-deceptive gestures of Victorian Hellenism in favour of forms of primitivism, his refusal of the fine writing, the 'purple passages' of Ruskin's and Pater's art criticism, in his refusal of 'the grand style' of Gladstone's Homer in favour of the colloquial and domestic voice of the Authoress, and his refusal of the Academy painting for the bare, momentary photograph. The turning-point of Butler's career as a painter, his 'Advertisement painting', is also a blank overwritten by ephemeral urban 'messages', an ironization of the Victorian theory of 'speaking architecture' expressed by Ruskin. This painting could be carried out only in his photography and in a new graphics yet to come. He had painfully evolved a new consciousness.

Yet, finally, Butler's achieved 'whiteness' is the top layer of a complex palimpsest of scriptures. His form is after all the map, like the photograph an item of apparent sobriety, technical expertise, constrained by factual knowledge, and dedicated to practical application, but leading from the known to the unknown, opening new worlds: a fantasy map, a map of utopia spelt backwards. His three great fantasy maps – of Erewhon in the Rangitata Valley of New Zealand, of the 'New Jerusalem' on the foothills of the Alps at Varallo, and of the voyage of Ulysses round Trapani – all have the same quality – invention flaunting its restraint. One is a map of the classical past as we now see it, one is a map of the Renaissance as a human community of the spirit, one is a map of the future in which the hard-won present is already a museum. These imaginary countries are permanently let in to the map of the world. Nowhere spelt backwards is a place, a topographical and linguistic presence. In German it is Ergindwon; in French, Italian, and Spanish it is Erewhon; and in Greek it is Aipotu. Butler's maps will take you there.

If in photography Butler was finally enabled to complete his ill-fated 'Advertisement painting', he executed it again in an invented form which is poised between literature, drawing, and imaginary photography. In Chapter XXIV of *Alps and Sanctuaries* he describes the culmination of his trip, his last visit to a Sacro Monte, that of Locarno, before climbing into the high Alps again for the return home. He was attracted by 'the approaching fêtes in honour of the fourth centenary of the apparition of the Virgin Mary to Fra Bartolomeo da Ivrea, who founded the sanctuary in consequence'. A festival programme of two days offered the carrying of the sacred image of the Virgin from the sanctuary to another church, 'illuminations, fireworks, balloons' in the evening; and the next day, Sunday, 'a grand procession' would convey the Holy Image to a temple in the market-place. The image would be crowned by the Patriarch of Alexandria, carried round the town, and returned. The climax would come in the evening:

At eight o'clock there were to be fireworks near the port; a grand illumination of a triumphal arch, an illumination of the sanctuary and chapels with Bengal lights, and an artificial apparition of the Madonna (*Apparizione artificiale della Beata Vergine col Bambino*) above the church upon the Sacro Monte.[46]

The next day the Holy Image was to be carried back to its normal resting-place at the sanctuary. 'We wanted to see all this, but it was the artificial apparition of the Madonna that most attracted us.'

Butler's illustrations give a sense of the distances which had to be traversed to the sanctuary high above the town (nowadays there is a convenient tram to the sanctuary, and a ski lift beyond it), and he locates the points from which they were drawn precisely: from the wooden bridge which crosses the stream just before entering upon the sacred precincts, the church and chapels and road arrange themselves as in his first drawing (illus. 44). One proceeds then to the second view:

On the way up, keeping to the steeper and abrupter route, one catches sight of the monks' garden – a little paradise with vines, beehives, onions, lettuces, cabbages, marigolds to colour the *risotto* with, and a little plot of great luxuriant tobacco plants.[47]

The second view is 'the best view of the sanctuary from above' (illus. 43). Only then does he describe the sanctuary. The whole chapter is a play with what can be depicted in various media, and what eludes them.

The next day the Patriarch arrives by water, to light music. As at Piora, as in all Butler's visionary passages, music plays a vital role, as he contrasts the popular music to the more portentous musical overtures that would be expected by, say, the Bishop of London:

The music of Locarno was on the quay playing a selection, not from 'Madame Angot' itself, but from something very like it – light, gay, sparkling opera bouffe – to welcome him.[48]

This 'opera bouffe' of the sacred is a negative musical example, as Handel in the Piora passage was an affirmative one.

The picture accordingly darkens:

One thing made an impression upon me which haunted me all the time. On every important space there were advertisements of the programme . . . but hardly, if at all less noticeable, were two others which rose up irrepressible upon every prominent space, searching all places with a subtle penetrative power against which precautions were powerless. These advertisements were not in Italian but in English, nevertheless they were neither of them English – but both, I believe, American. The one was that of the Richmond Gem cigarette, with the large illustration representing a man in a hat smoking, so familiar to us here in London. The other was that of Wheeler & Wilson's sewing machines.[49]

These figures take on a life of their own, like the diabolic apparition of the pair of servants in *The Turn of the Screw*: as the Patriarch drove off 'the man in the hat smoking the Richmond Gem cigarette leered at him, and the woman working Wheeler & Wilson's sewing machine sewed at him'.

These grotesque figures haunt the festivities, and come to full power first on the Saturday evening, then on the Sunday evening, as the crowds gather in the market-place to experience the founder's vision. The scene is an extraordinary chiaroscuro, ideally suited to the camera yet beyond its scope then or now:

During the illuminations the unwonted light threw its glare upon the effigies of saints and angels, but it illumined also the man in the black felt hat and the woman with the sewing machine; even during the artificial apparition of the Virgin Mary herself upon the hill behind the town, the more they left off fireworks the more clearly the man in the hat came out upon the walls round the market-place, and the bland imperturbable woman working at her sewing machine. I thought to myself that when the man with the hat appeared in the piazza the Madonna would ere long cease to appear on the hill.[50]

The new dark mythic shapes down in the market-place threaten the old figure of light over the sanctuary, but both are momentarily equal and present. The apparition of the Madonna does indeed take place:

the church of the Madonna was unilluminated and all in darkness, when on a sudden it sprang out into a blaze, and a great transparency of the Virgin and child was lit up from behind. Then the people said, 'Oh bel!'

For one moment the two sets of lights and darks are in place. The 'Advertising painting' is completed, not in London, but in Locarno, as north and south are poised, equal and opposite, and the illusionistic Madonna faces the cut-outs of industrial power.

But the apparition is a disappointment, not well managed (the 'Crystal Palace people' would have done better, Butler comments); and its successor is already in possession. Looking back on Butler's description of his 'Advertisement painting', *The last days of Carey Street*, we recall that the 'Messiah' was the central advertisement, between 'Nabob Pickles' and 'Three millions of money', and the 'Messiah' was much smaller than 'Mr. Sims Reeves, and Signor Foli'. The mini-Messiah is now joined by an extinguished Madonna among the cloudy trophies of a new pantheon.

This nocturne is preceded and followed by another:

Later on, passing through the town alone, when the people had gone to rest, I saw many of them lying on the pavement under the arches fast asleep. A brilliant moon illuminated the market-place; there was a pleasant sound of falling water from the fountain; the lake was bathed in splendour, save where it took the reflection of the mountains – so peaceful and quiet was the night that there was hardly a rustle in the leaves of the aspens. But whether in moonlight or in shadow, the busy persistent vibrations that rise in Anglo-Saxon brains were radiating from every wall, and the man in the black felt hat and the bland lady with the sewing machine were there – lying in wait, as a cat over a mouse's hole, to insinuate themselves into the hearts of the people so soon as they should wake.[51]

This grotesque black-on-black calls on mixed media (and on the inadequacies of each of them) for its effect. Parts of it are recognizable as a paintable subject, especially the moonlit lake with the reflections of the mountains, perhaps the marketplace – we recall Gaudenzio's fresco painted by moonlight, or Rembrandt's dark canvases lit by a flare or a gleam. But it is unpaintable not because of the lighting conditions, but because an alien iconography has intruded onto the scene, the iconography Butler had tried in vain to capture in the scene of urban destruction in London overwritten by the new graffiti. The 'busy persistent vibrations' are beyond the reach of any pictorial medium. Strangely enough, the scene held a special interest for Victorian photographers and their literary advocates. Despite the frequent references to photography as 'painting with the sun' or 'sun sculpture', there was much experiment with other forms of light – light, the great 'magician', as Lady Eastlake said. Edgar Allan Poe – who would have appreciated this grotesque scene – wrote excitedly in 'The Daguerrotype' as early as 1840:

The results of the invention cannot, even remotely, be seen . . . [A] correct lunar chart will at once accomplished, since the rays of this luminary are found to be appreciated by the plate.

These eerie scenes are a vision of hell, like Gaudenzio's 'grey' *Christ Descending into Hell*, drawing on the Lombard tones of Foppa and Sodoma. They are entirely visualizable, yet unrenderable as a whole. They require the vast theatre of the marketplace with the Sanctuary on high whose distance Butler's drawings have conveyed; having ascended and descended, and now standing within it, with Butler, we experience the two levels as well as the two sets of inverse chiaroscuro. The 'descent' from the sanctuary to the marketplace into the imaginary landscape of photography is another example of Butler's ironized sublime. But from what vantage point could he snap the nether and the upper apparitions at once, capture 'Saul's coat-tail'? Now this prophetic union of media in a pictorial narrative appears immediately cinematic.

These are, finally, comic and satiric nocturnes, but with great power, like Hogarth's Midnight Conversations. They sum up the search for the Sacro Monte; and the search for a form and a medium; and the theme of the decline of art. The art of the north and the south meet again, both in a state of degradation. This is at once a horrific nightmare of the future – and a vision of a new primitive epoch in which a new popular art will flourish. These scenes are still 'sublime', even apocalyptic, reminding us of 'the burnished man' who stood at the threshold of the vision of the pagan Renaissance; yet finally they suggest a humorous equation between the 'old Adam and Eve' and the new Cigarette Man and Sewing-machine Lady. A new culture, a new art is born of this grotesque coupling. Butler had long ago foreseen the pleasure his countrymen would take in the miraculous 'coupling of two locomotives', a technological Virgin Birth. As 'resurrection' had given way to its secular version in the 'Renaissance', so now a new age reared up: the age of mechanical 'Reproduction'.

Butler had a long view: in 1870 in *Erewhon* he had already consigned the society of the machine to a museum of what is banned in utopia, and he wrote of the phenomenon of the museum as *merzbau*:

When a thing is old, broken, and useless we throw it on the dust-heap, but when it is sufficiently old, sufficiently broken, and sufficiently useless we give money for it, put it into a museum, and read papers over it which people come long distances to hear. By-and-by, when the whirligig of time has brought on another revenge, the museum itself becomes a dust-heap, and remains so till after long ages it is re-discovered, and valued as belonging to a neo-rubbish age – containing, perhaps, traces of a still older paleo-rubbish civilisation.[52]

It was unnecessary, he thought, indeed mistaken, to 'catch the tone of a vanished society' to understand Rembrandt or Giovanni Bellini (or Shakespeare) – 'the folds do not thicken around these men', they speak more clearly now than to their contemporaries.[53] As for himself, the old satirist would have taken considerable pleasure in the comedy of finding his snap-shots, quite unvarnished, hanging in the paleo-rubbish museum of our time.

117. *Mrs Bassatt, Langar,* 1866 or 7

118. *Alfred Cathie on station,* 1893

119. *Jones giving child a penny*, 1893

120. *Girl drawing water, Montreuil, 1893*

121. *Novara market-place, girl and garter*, 1891

122. *Knifegrinder, Bellinzona,* 1895

123. *Old Woman, Novara market-place,* 1892

124. *Brighton Parade*

125. *Man with Monkey, Varallo,* 1891

126. *Old Woman, Novara market-place,* 1892

127. *The Funny Boy, Varallo,* 1892

128. *The Funny Boy, Varallo,* 1892

129. *The Funny Boy and his brother The Cripple, Varallo,* 1892

130. *The Funny Boy, Varallo, 1892*

131. *The Funny Boy and his friends, Varallo,* 1891

132. *The Blind Fiddler and his Mate*, 1893

133. *Cretin at Colico*, 1891

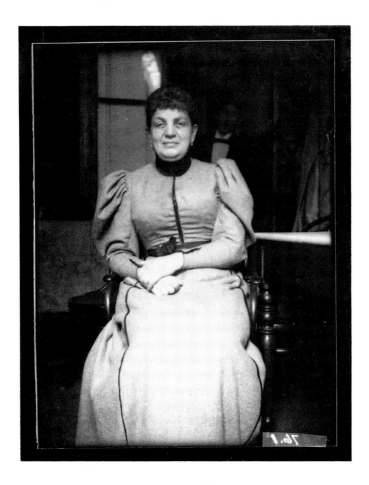

134. *Mrs Negri, Casale*, 1892

135. *Old Mrs Kaufmann, Basle*, 1895

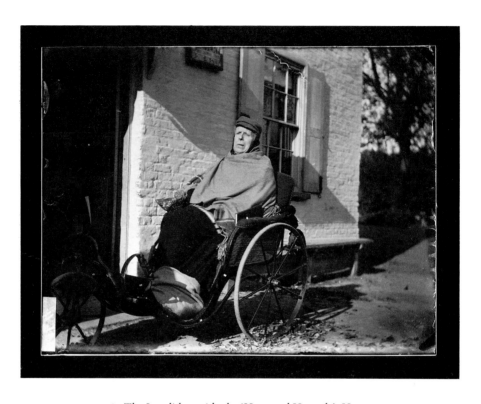

136. *The Invalid outside the 'Hare and Hounds', Harrow*

137. On Board Steamer, near Greenwich, 1891

138. *Gogin and blocks of ice on the quay, Boulogne*, 1891

139. *Boulogne Quay*, 1891

140. *Stoker on Steamer crossing Channel,* 1892

141. *Fruitseller on Steamer, Calais*, 1893

142. *Boxed Horse on Steamer going to Boulogne*, 1892

143. *Turk and sheep on board Steamer between Palermo and Trapani,* 1892
144. *Turk on board Steamer between Palermo and Trapani,* 1892

145. *Shylock, Smyrnah,* 1895

146. An old Turk smoking his hookah, Smyrnah, 1895

147. Girl at fountain, Trapani, 1893

148. *Professor Romano at Cefalu, 1892*

149. *Mr and Mrs Marchini*, 1891

150. *The Lame Boy, Sacro Monte,* 1891

151. *Old Beggar at S Eusebio Chapel, Crea, 1892*

152. *Boy and Basket, Chiavenna,* 1895
153. *Sleeping pigs in piazza Gaudenzio Ferrari,* Varallo, 1889

154. *Sleeping men, Trapani,* 1894

155. *Men sleeping,* 1892

156. *Man sleeping, Paris,* 1891

157. *Man sleeping, Trapani,* 1894

158. *Boy sleeping, Trapani,* 1893

159. *Padre Grazie, Catalafimi (Sicily)*, 1895

160. *Nuns on Steamer,* 1895

161. *Carrying the Madonna, Civiasco,* 1889

162. *Old priest*, 1894

163. *Mycenae, Tomb of Atreus with Ladies, 1895*

164. *Priest and group looking up, the Gobelins*, 1892

165. Steps of S Gaudenzio, Varallo, 1892

166. Chiavenna, c. 1895

167. *Dionysus' Ear, Syracuse,* 1893

168. *The Washing-place, Varallo,* 1892

169. *Monastery on Mt Lycabettus, Athens,* 1895

170. *Church at Bormio through an opening*, 1891

171. *Church of Madonna di Trapani*, 1891

172. *Dinant*, 1891

173. *Wayside Oratory at Dinant*, 1893

174. *'St Christopher', Castiglione d'Olona, 1892*

175. *Church Porch at Meien,* 1895

176. *The Count, Erice,* 1893

Exhibitions of Butler's work

The following is a list of exhibitions since 1902 which have included art works by Butler. There may well have been others. For catalogues and handlists, see the Bibliography.

1912 – The British Museum in its Summer Exhibition showed two of the watercolour drawings given to the Museum in that year.

1923 – An exhibition of 'Hill and Mountain Landscapes' held at the Fitzwilliam Museum, Cambridge, included seventeen of Butler's paintings and drawings, all relating to *Alps and Sanctuaries*.

1933 – The Robert McDougall Art Gallery *Self-portrait* (1873) by Butler was shown in 'New Zealand Art: A Centennial Exhibition' at the Robert McDougall Art Gallery, Christchurch, New Zealand.

1935 – A large travelling exhibition of British art, the British Empire Loan Collection, drawn from the Tate Gallery holdings, was sent round the Empire, under the auspices of the Empire Art Loan Collections Society. It went to Australia and New Zealand, including Christchurch, Dunedin, Auckland, and Wanganui; in Melbourne it was visited by 100,000 people in four weeks. It was an impressive collection of 74 paintings including works by Turner, Constable, C. R. Leslie, Reynolds, John Crome, and Gainsborough. One painting of Butler's was shown, *Mr Heatherley's Holiday: An Incident in Studio Life*, part of the Tate's holdings since 1911.

1940 – The Robert McDougall Art Gallery *Self-portrait* (1873) was shown at an exhibition of 'New Zealand Art', with a note stressing Butler's links with the South Island.

1946 – An exhibition took place 20 February – 25 March on the occasion of the gift to the Chapin Library, Williams College, Williamstown, Massachusetts, of Butler works belonging to Carroll A. Wilson. An alumnus of the college, and a notable book-collector, Wilson intended the gift to enhance the educational value of the library of the liberal arts college by placing within it 'some one author complete'. The collection included not only every edition published in Butler's lifetime, but a number of MSS, including his notebooks, and a selection of his works of art including four paintings and a number of drawings and sketches, and some photographs. The only painting exhibited on this occasion was the *Self-portrait* (1866).

1959 – A sizeable exhibition of 'Victorian Painting' was held at the Nottingham University Art Gallery 20 January – 15 February, in conjunction with a series of public lectures on 'The Victorian Age'. Paintings by 41 artists were shown, including one Butler work: *Family Prayers*.

1967 – An exhibition entitled 'The Life and Career of Samuel Butler' was held at the Chapin Library, Williams College, 20 February – 25 March. It included the painting of a *Girl's Head*, the Pinner farm landscape, the *Self-portrait* (1866), a small sketch-book of his drawings, and an album of Butler's snapshots (1889).

1972–An exhibition entitled 'Samuel Butler and his Contemporaries' was held at the Robert McDougall Art Gallery, Christchurch, 15–28 May. A number of his works now in New Zealand were shown, including *Self-portrait* (c. 1865) and *Self-portrait* (1873), *Portrait of an Unidentified Woman, Head of an Unidentified Girl, Old Fetter Lane, London* (watercolour), and the *Portrait of Thomas Cass*.

1986–An exhibition entitled 'Samuel Butler: A 150th Birthday Celebration' was held 4 December 1985 – 21 March 1986 at the Chapin Library, Williams College. It included all those previously shown in the 1967 exhibition except the Pinner farm landscape and, in addition, some sketches related to *Alps and Sanctuaries*.

Samuele Butler e la Valle Sesia was an exhibition held in the city library of Varallo in connection with the commemoration of the 500th anniversary of the founding of the Sacro Monte of Varallo. It included one of his oil paintings – the well in front of the sanctuary on the Sacro Monte (the painting belongs to the Museum of the Sacro Monte); the photograph of Butler with Stefano Scotto; together with correspondence in Italian with a number of his friends among the inhabitants of Varallo, and other memorabilia.

Notes

INTRODUCTION

1 – *The Notebooks of Samuel Butler*, ed. Henry Festing Jones (London, 1912; Hogarth Press reprint, 1985), p. 237.

2 – *Ibid.*, p. 20.

3 – *Ibid.*, p. 21.

4 – Lionel Stevenson, ed., *Victorian Fiction: A Guide to Research* (Cambridge, Mass., 1964), p. v.

5 – P. N. Furbank, *Samuel Butler (1835–1902)*, (Cambridge, 1948), p. 5.

6 – *The New Art History*, eds A. L. Rees and F. Borzello (London, 1986).

7 – 'Quis Desiderio . . .?', *Essays on Life, Art and Science* (London, 1904), p. 4.

CHAPTER ONE

1 – *Notebooks*, ed. Jones, p. 14.

2 – Butler wrote home in 1851: 'I get on very well with Mr. Brown[e]. I really think him a very clever little man in other respects besides drawing his conversation is always very sensible.' *The Family Letters of Samuel Butler 1841–1886*, ed. Arnold Silver (London, 1962), p. 45. Jones relates two further stories of Browne which show his humour. (Henry Festing Jones, *Samuel Butler: A Memoir* (London, 1919), I, p. 42.)

3 – The Clive House Museum at Shrewsbury has four of Browne's works. An exhibition was held at the Lower Nupend Gallery in Cradley, Worcestershire, and at the Federation of British Artists in London, 1977; see the catalogue, *Drawings and Watercolours of Henry Harris Lines 1800–1885 and P. Vandyck Browne 1801–1868*.

The excellence of the Moser Collection of Water-Colour Drawings, including works by artists such as David Cox, John Sell Cotman, and Peter de Wint, shows Shrewsbury's continuing link with the landscape tradition.

Butler's watercolours are not hung, though his *Self-portrait* is.

4 – An unpublished letter from Butler of 19 August 1898, in the possession of the School, shows that he went to considerable trouble to try to persuade the School to hang his watercolour drawing depicting one of the bedrooms. He argued for its historical rather than its aesthetic value: 'It is a slight and worthless drawing, but quite true and better than nothing.'

5 – Paget left the School in 1855 to become Rector of Kirstead, Norfolk. 'The Paget Scrapbook', later annotated by Butler, is now in the Library, the Schools, Shrewsbury.

6 – Hugh Honour, *Romanticism* (Harmondsworth, 1979), pp. 108–9.

7 – *Family Letters*, p. 66.

8 – *Ibid.*, pp. 88–9.

9 – John Pascoe, *Great Days in New Zealand Exploration* (Wellington, New Zealand, 1959), gives an account of Butler's role in the early exploration of the country.

10—Samuel Butler, *A First Year in Canterbury Settlement*, eds A. C. Brassington and P. B. Maling (Blackwood and Janet Paul: Auckland and Hamilton, 1964), pp. 45–6.

11—*A First Year*, p. 59.

12—*Ibid.*, pp. 60–1.

13—Butler, *Erewhon* [1872], (Harmondsworth, 1970), p. 53. The text is a reprint of the original edition; the cover design is interesting as part of the considerable history of the illustration of *Erewhon*, which has attracted the attention of a number of artists: Erewhon is represented by a detail from Jacopo Bellini's *St Jerome*, in the National Gallery, which registers not only Butler's admiration for the Bellinis, but his use of an Italian landscape in his description of the descent into the imaginary country.

14—Jones, I, 152.

15—*Family Letters*, p. 105. Letter to Mrs Philip Worsley, 19 Sept 1861.

16—*The Correspondence of Samuel Butler with his Sister May* (Berkeley and Los Angeles, 1962), p. 71. Butler wrote to his sister from Italy on 22 July 1878: 'So you are reading the Seven Lamps. It is so long since I did so that I have quite forgotten them, but I remember being very enthusiastic about them when I was at Cambridge – and I have no doubt (that) there is a great deal that is very true in them. I will look at them again when I get home, and see whether I still like them. The general impression however on my mind concerning Ruskin is one of decided dislike.'

17—John Ruskin, *Seven Lamps of Architecture*, rev. ed. (London, 1880), p. 4.

18—Other painters who worked at Heatherley's included Rossetti and Burne-Jones, who attended evening classes; John Everett Millais; Edward John Poynter; Frederic Leighton; Frank Reynolds; P. Macquard; J. T. Nettleship; Fred Barnard; H. H. Armistead; and Walter Sickert. Other writers who attended included Lewis Carroll (also an early photographer), who drew there in 1882; George Du Maurier (see his novel *Trilby*, 1894); and, in the 1920s, Evelyn Waugh. A pamphlet issued for the Centenary of the School in 1946 gives further information about painters who attended the school (Tate Gallery Library).

19—Graham Reynolds, *Painters of the Victorian Scene* (London, 1953), p. 100; Reynolds reproduces this painting.

20—Letter from the Principal, Gilmore Roberts, Tate Gallery Library. The passage begins: 'The School continues in a direct line from Heatherley and, whilst its teaching methods and curriculum have undergone some changes to meet changing needs, it follows the same pattern as it did in Heatherley's time.'

21—Jones, I, 123 (October 1865).

22—Sir Johnston Forbes-Robertson, *A Player under Three Reigns* (London, 1925), chap. 4, 'Art School Days', pp. 53–4.

23—*Ibid.*, p. 53.

24—J. B. Yeats, 'Recollections of Samuel Butler', in *Essays Irish and American* (Dublin, 1918), p. 9 and p. 13.

25—*Family Letters*, p. 70. Jones suggested that *Hand* and *Foot* were done later, at South Kensington. In any case, this was a staple of art education.

26—*Ibid.*, p. 71.

27—For a detailed account see Albert Boime, *The Academy and French Painting in the Nineteenth Century* (London, 1971). The experiences of a number of Victorian painters in French *ateliers*, including Leighton, Poynter, Du Maurier, and Whistler, have often been described.

28—Tate Gallery Library, Catalogue file: S. Butler.

29—Graham Reynolds, *Painters of the Victorian Scene*, p. 90.

30—*Letters between Samuel Butler and Miss E. M. A. Savage 1871–1885* (London, 1935), no. 100 (Butler's note, p. 134).

31—*Notebooks*, ed. Jones, p. 104. This is part of a longer note on 'Academicism'.

32–*Ibid.*, p. 158.

33–Christopher Neve, 'London Art School in Search of a Home – Heatherley's, I', *Country Life* (17 Aug 1978). For discussion of Wynfield's heads see chap. 4, p. 101.

34–*Family Letters*, p. 105.

35–Thomas Rowlandson, *The Microcosm of London* (1808–10). Francis Haskell and Nicholas Penny in *'The Most Beautiful Statues': The Taste for Antique Sculpture 1500–1900* (Ashmolean Museum, Oxford, 1981) point out that as it was realized that the Apollo Belvedere and the rest were Roman copies not Greek originals they fell from favour.

36–William Vaughan, *Romantic Art* (London, 1978), p. 68.

37–Neve, 'A question of survival – Heatherley's School of Art, II', *Country Life* (31 Aug 1978), pp. 570–1. For *Mrs Crompton with the Venus de Milo* and other photographs of the school interior in which artists, costumed artists' models, and statuary mingle, see also Jeremy Maas, *The Victorian Art World in Photographs* (London, 1984), pp. 35–6.

38–Neve, *Country Life*, Part I, p. 7.

39–Maas, *The Victorian Art World in Photographs*, p. 34 shows a photograph of Heatherley in the year of his retirement, standing on the steps to the Antique Room which Butler depicted in *Mr Heatherley's Holiday*.

40–Jones, I, 384.

41–*Ibid.*, I, 201–2.

42–On the relation between Burns's and Wordsworth's handling of the theme see E. S. Shaffer, 'The Hermeneutic Community in the *Biographia Literaria*', in *The Coleridge Connection*, eds Richard Gravil and Molly Lefebure (London, 1989).

43–Butler printed this ballad as an appendix to *Alps and Sanctuaries*.

44–*Letters (Butler/Savage)*, 16 Aug 1873 (No. 43). Butler edited out his own description of the painting for the memorial volume for Miss Savage which he prepared for the press in 1902, though pointing out that it 'was hung in the R.A. for 1874'.

45–Jones, I, 201.

46–See, for example, Pompeo Batoni's portrait of *Sir Gregory Page* (1768), now in the Manchester City Art Gallery.

47–*Letters (Butler/Savage)*, pp. 32–3.

48–*Samuel Butler's Notebooks: Selections*, eds Geoffrey Keynes and Brian Hill (London, 1951), p. 100. Compare his letter to his sister May of 15 March 1883: 'You asked me if I liked Rosetti's [*sic*] pictures; I dislike them extremely: in fact they have made me so angry that I cannot see any good in them at all, but there was a very beautiful Titian and a lovely Marco Basaiti in the same exhibition' (*Family Letters*, p. 217).

49–*Letters (Butler/Savage)*, p. 352.

50–*Notebooks*, eds Keynes and Hill, pp. 163–5. Butler disclaims any friendship with Oliver Madox Brown: 'I was supposed not to be so sorry as I ought to have been, the fact being that I hardly knew him at all beyond his calling on me sometimes and reading me his MSS. novels, which bored me very much. . . . I did not like either young Brown or his novels; besides as soon as I began to read any of my MSS. he used to go, and, indeed, this was the only way I had of getting rid of him.' Cf. Andrea Rose, *Pre-Raphaelite Portraits* (1981), p. 22.

51–*Notebooks*, eds Keynes and Hill, pp. 167–8.

52–John Dixon Hunt, *The Pre-Raphaelite Imagination* (London, 1968), p. 206. See Hunt's whole discussion of Beardsley's satires on Rossetti, chap. 5, 'The Soul's Beauty: The Pre-Raphaelite Image of Woman', pp. 203–9.

53–*Notebooks*, ed. Jones, p. 184.

54–Max Beerbohm, *Works* (London, 1895), p. 150.

55–*Notebooks*, ed. Jones, p. 184.

56–*Notebooks*, eds Keynes and Hill, p. 165.

57–*Ibid.*, p. 52.

58—*Ibid.*, p. 74.

59—*Letters (Butler/Savage)*, p. 149.

60—*Notebooks*, ed. Jones, p. 267.

61—*Ibid.*, p. 263. The allusion is to the section of Tennyson's poem to his dead friend Arthur Hallam, 'Ring out, wild bells'. Edmund Gurney was author of *The Power of Sound* and Secretary of the Society for Psychical Research.

62—Quoted in Jeremy Maas, *Victorian Painting* (London, 1969), p. 218.

63—*Ibid.*, p. 219.

64—Algernon Graves, *Royal Academy of Arts: A Complete Dictionary of Contributors and their work from its foundation in 1769 to 1904*. See also the annual catalogue *Exhibition of the Royal Academy of Arts* for 1869, 1871, 1874, and 1876, which gives lists of hangings by gallery.

65—Jones, I, 236.

66—*Ibid.*, p. 235. Miss Savage was, of course, well aware of Butler's avowed aversion to Goethe's novel *Wilhelm Meister*, in which the mysterious little girl 'Mignon' plays a leading role.

67—*Correspondence (Butler/May Butler)*, 29 March 1883, p. 103.

68—*Letters (Butler/Savage)*, p. 18.

69—*Family Letters*, p. 141.

70—*Notebooks*, ed. Jones, pp. 106–7.

71—*Ibid.*, eds Keynes and Hill, p. 181. This exhibition took place at Christie's in April 1887.

72—*Ibid.*

73—*Letters (Butler/Savage)*, p. 20. Note, however, that the point of this passage is that he dislikes Mrs Browning's *Aurora Leigh* even more.

74—Elizabeth K. Helsinger, *Ruskin and the Art of the Beholder* (Cambridge, Mass., 1982) points out that in Ruskin's description of La Riccia in *Modern Painters* I, 'word painting' becomes 'a painting in words' vying with particular paintings of the same scene by Turner, Claude, and Poussin (pp. 23–35).

75—*Further Extracts from the Note-Books of Samuel Butler*, ed. A. T. Bartholomew (London, 1934), p. 31.

76—*Correspondence (Butler/May Butler)*, 21 Aug 1879, p. 82. He was writing from Switzerland.

77—*Notebooks*, eds Keynes and Hill, p. 235.

78—Samuel Butler, *Notebooks*, I (1874–1883), ed. Hans-Peter Breuer (University Press of America, 1984), p. 199 [755]. This edition, still in progress, has the advantages of restoring Butler's text, giving the approximate dates he supplied, presenting the notes (numbered) in chronological order, and providing useful annotations. For the best description of the Notebooks as a whole, and the alterations made by successive editors in their selections, see Lee E. Holt, *PMLA* (Dec 1945); his review of Breuer's edition is in *The Samuel Butler Newsletter* (May, 1986). Jones's original selection still makes the best reading; Bartholomew added a number of 'Art Notes', and presented the material chronologically.

79—*Notebooks*, I. ed. Breuer, p. 283 [1274], and note p. 369. The letter, from Professors A. Legros (University College, London), W. B. Richmond (Oxford), and Sidney Colvin (Cambridge), appeared in the *Pall Mall Gazette*, 29 May 1879.

80—*Erewhon*, p. 130.

81—*The Works of William Hogarth*: Reproduced from the original engravings in permanent photographs and newly described with an essay on the Genius and Character of Hogarth by Charles Lamb, I (London, 1872), p. 7.

82—Hazlitt, 'On the Fine Arts' [1824], in *Hazlitt's Criticisms on Art* (London, 1843), p. 266. See also Hazlitt's 'An Inquiry, Whether the Fine Arts are promoted by Academies and Public

Institutions' (*Champion*, 28 Aug and 11 Sept 1814); and 'On Certain Inconsistencies in Sir Joshua Reynolds's Discourses', *Table-Talk, or Original Essays* (London, 1821): 'What, for instance, would have been the effect of persuading Hogarth or Rembrandt to place no dependence on their own genius . . . but to destroy both those great artists?' (p. 291).

83 – Ronald Paulson, *Book and Painting: Shakespeare, Milton and the Bible* (Knoxville, 1986), p. 23.

84 – *The Way of All Flesh*, ed. R. A. Streatfeild (London, 1903), pp. 96–8. The passages cut by Streatfeild are supplied in an appendix to the edition by James Cochrane, with an introduction by Richard Hoggart (Harmondsworth, 1966). Butler's MS has also been re-edited with the cuts restored by Daniel F. Howard and published under Butler's title: *Ernest Pontifex, or The Way of All Flesh* (London, 1965).

85 – *Ibid.*, p. 99.

86 – *The Way of All Flesh*, ed. Howard, p. 86.

87 – On absorption in genre painting as exemplified by Greuze see Michael Fried, *Absorption and Theatricality: Painting and Beholder in the Age of Diderot* (Berkeley, 1980), pp. 8–9. On 'harmonie' see Norman Bryson, *Word and Image* (Cambridge, 1981), pp. 115–20.

88 – *The Way of All Flesh*, ed. Streatfeild, p. 100.

89 – Samuel Butler's marginalia on a bound exhibition catalogue of Rembrandt's *Schilderijen*, 8–31 October 1898, Stedelijk Museum, Amsterdam.

90 – John Ruskin, *Modern Painters*, III, Part IV, p. 156, in *The Complete Works of John Ruskin*, eds E. T. Cook and Alexander Wedderburn (London, 1904), V. Ruskin often used Dolci as an example of false smoothness. Where he extended this to Dutch realism Butler parted company with him.

91 – Reynolds, p. 21. The paintings by James Hayllar and W. P. Frith are reproduced as Figs. 60 and 25.

92 – *Ibid.*, p. 89.

93 – James Ayres, *English Naive Painting, 1750–1900* (London, 1980), p. 26.

94 – Roger Cardinal, *Outsider Art* (London, 1972), pp. 58–9.

95 – *Ibid.*, p. 27.

96 – *Notebooks*, ed. Jones, pp. 97–9. *Notebooks*, I, ed. Breuer, p. 98 [239], gives the date: the note was written 1876–1880, and 'Edited [or rather rewritten] December 18, 1891'.

97 – For a series of notes relating to 'terseness' in the several arts see *Notebooks*, ed. Jones, pp. 100–102.

98 – Ruskin, 'Pre-Raphaelitism', *Pre-Raphaelitism*, ed. Sambrook, p. 100.

99 – *Notebooks*, I, ed. Breuer, p. 100 [242]. This note was written between 1876 and 1880.

100 – Aaron Scharf, *Art and Photography* (London, 1968) on 'photographic tone', pp. 58–61.

101 – *Letters (Butler/Savage)*, p. 115.

102 – *Notebooks*, ed. Jones, p. 106.

103 – *Letters (Butler/Savage)*, p. 142.

104 – *Ibid.*

105 – *Letters (Butler/Savage)*, p. 144.

106 – *Ibid.*, pp. 144–5.

107 – *Ibid.*, p. 147.

108 – *Letters (Butler/Savage)*, pp. 142–3: 'The Thames Ditton water colour I gave to Mrs. Danvers, some ten years later.'

109 – Advertising in the modern sense began and dramatically increased in the Victorian period, appearing on horse-drawn buses, advertising carts, and newspaper kiosks, and there were many complaints about the extensive bill-sticking. See Diana and Geoffrey Hindley, *Advertising in Victorian England, 1837–1901* (London, 1972), for examples.

110 – The unhappy tale is told in notes published in *Butleriana* (London, 1932). On attending Pauli's funeral in 1897 Butler became aware at last that he had not been Pauli's only benefactor.

111—*Letters (Butler/Savage)*, pp. 146–7.

112—E. H. Gombrich, 'The Cartoonist's Armoury', *Meditations on a Hobby-Horse* (London, 1963), p. 130.

113—One of his testimonials, from Richard Garnett of the British Museum, stresses *Alps and Sanctuaries*: 'Mr. Butler is an artist possessed of a technical experience which must be of great value to an instructor in the principles of Fine Art; he is also a subtle, independent, and original thinker. Should he obtain the appointment he seeks, he is the man of all men to inspire his pupils with fruitful ideas, which will carry them far beyond the mere routine of Art Study. The illustrations to his "Alps and Sanctuaries", and very many passages in the text, evince his remarkable faculty of suggestiveness, and power of expressing much in little with pen or pencil – a quality invaluable to a Professor whose opportunities of conveying instruction are necessarily limited and occasional.' Quoted in *Family Letters*, pp. 270–71, n.1. Other testimonials are at St John's College.

114—Correspondence with his father between 5 February 1886 and 10 March 1886 shows Butler's interest in the appointment, which his father shared, and his attempts to get the attribution published quickly (*Family Letters*, pp. 264–73).

115—Dominique Thiébaut, Conservateur au Département des Peintures, Musée du Louvre, writes in a letter to the author of 5 November 1987 of the attribution to Cariani: 'mais même au sein de notre département, tous ne sont pas convaincus.'

116—Francis Haskell, 'Compromises of a connoisseur', review of Ernest Samuels, *Bernard Berenson: The Making of a Legend*, and Colin Simpson, *The secret association of Bernard Berenson and Joseph Duveen*, in the *Times Literary Supplement* (5 June 1987), pp. 595–6.

117—J. A. Crowe and G. B. Cavalcaselle, *History of Painting in Northern Italy* (London, 1871), p. 134, quoted by Butler in 'Portraits of Gentile and Giovanni Bellini', *The Athenaeum* (20 Feb 1886), p. 151.

118—Rodolfo Pallucchini and Francesco Rossi, *Giovanni Cariani* (Bergamo, 1983), p. 26 and catalogue entry no. 64. They favour Giovanni rather than Gentile.

119—Butler's Letter 'To the Electors'. St John's College.

120—*Family Letters*, p. 271.

121—The five articles on art were 'L'Affaire Holbein-Rippel', 'A Sculptor and a Shrine' (in two parts), 'A Medieval Girl School', and 'Art in the Valley of Saas'. Although the Shrewsbury Edition reprinted Butler's illustrations, other editions of his essays omitted them, giving a misleading impression of his aims; in the popular *Essays on Life, Art and Science*, ed. R. A. Streatfeild (1908) the first of these is omitted, the second half of 'A Sculptor' included without illustration.

122—*Notebooks*, ed. Jones, p. 137.

CHAPTER TWO

1—Butler, *Alps and Sanctuaries*, p. 21. The first edition was published by David Bogue in 1881. References are to the second edition (1913), edited and introduced by R. A. Streatfeild. There is a paperback reprint, omitting Streatfeild's introduction (Alan Sutton, Gloucester, 1986).

2—By the time of writing *Erewhon* he had of course made further Italian trips, but the episode in which Higgs and Arowhena are picked up by an Italian ship captain is based on his sea journey from Livorno to Genoa in 1857. Claudio Vita-Finzi, 'Samuel Butler in Italy', *Italian Studies*, XVIII (1963), offers a useful if superficial overview of his various journeys. The best discussion is John F. Harris, 'Italy', *Samuel Butler, Author of Erewhon: The Man and his Work* (London, 1916), pp. 168–91. He first visited Varallo in 1871 (Jones, I, 145).

3—Fort, *Samuel Butler*, p. 1. He suggests this as one reason for Gallic interest in Butler.

4–Larbaud, Préface, *Erewhon*, p. 16. He also praised her for her excellent knowledge of French literature.

5–*Letters between Samuel Butler and Miss Savage* (2 Aug 1881), p. 255. The reference is to Wordsworth's 'Peter Bell', in which for Peter, before his conversion, 'A primrose by a river's brim / A yellow primrose was to him / And it was nothing more' (ll. 248–50). The reference turns up often in Butler, always directed against Wordsworthian pretensions; as he said: 'I never can see what there was to find fault with in that young man' (*Alps and Sanctuaries*, p. 143). Miss Savage uses the allusion to Wordsworth's much satirized poem to ironize her own emotion.

6–*Alps and Sanctuaries*, p. 140.

7–John Rosenberg, *The Darkening Glass: A Portrait of Ruskin's Genius* (New York, 1961), pp. 85–7 discusses the genre of *The Stones of Venice*, proposing this term; Helsinger attempts to overcome the opposition between the 'Romantic art critics' and the 'art historians', but finds Carlyle's *Past and Present* – another primarily literary example – the most fruitful comparison (*The Art of the Beholder*, chap. 5, 'History as Criticism').

8–D. H. Lawrence, *Twilight in Italy*, p. 134. See also Lawrence's letters of the time, and his article 'Christs in the Tirol', *Westminster Gazette* (27 March 1913).

9–Anthony Burgess, Introduction to *D. H. Lawrence and Italy* (London, 1987), a reprint of *Etruscan Places, Twilight in Italy*, and *Sea and Sardinia*.

10–Stephen Bann, 'A cycle in historical discourse: Barante, Thierry, Michelet', *The Clothing of Clio* (Cambridge, 1984), p. 53.

11–Frank Kermode, 'Botticelli Recovered', *Forms of Attention* (Chicago, 1985).

12–Helsinger, *Ruskin and the Art of the Beholder*, pp. 68–9.

13–Patricia Ball, *The Science of Aspects: The Changing Role of Fact in the Work of Coleridge, Ruskin and Hopkins* (London, 1971).

14–Felix Mendelssohn–Bartholdy, *Letters from Italy and Switzerland*, translated by Lady Wallace (London, 1862); letter from Venice, 16 Oct 1830. Butler's copy, inscribed 'from his affectionate sister May', contains his incredulous pencilled note on p. 357. (Butler Collection, St John's College.)

15–*Letters (Butler/Savage)*, 2 Aug. 1881, p. 255.

16–*Alps and Sanctuaries*, pp. 23–4. He suggests a similar test for the painter: 'The best test for a painter as to whether he likes painting his picture is to ask himself whether he should like to paint it if he was quite sure that no one except himself, and the few of whom he was very fond, would ever see it' (p. 158).

17–Interlaken, 24 June [1854], quoted in *The Works of John Ruskin*, V, xxxiii. The effect is increased by Ruskin's claim to have risen in the small hours to make the long climb to greet the dawn.

18–*Ex Voto*, p. 241. Butler is speaking of the Sanctuary at Crea; today there are electric lights, but they still must be turned on, in my case by a venerable padre who waxed eloquent about the architecture of the foundations.

19–*Letters (Butler/Savage)*, 2 Aug 1881, p. 255.

20–'Materials for a projected Sequel to *Alps and Sanctuaries*' [1889], *Notebooks*, ed. Jones, p. 279.

21–'On Knowing what gives us Pleasure' [1888] and 'Instead of an Article on the Dudley Exhibition', *Collected Essays*, I, *Works*, vol. 18.

22–Jones, I, p. 362.

23–Richard L. Stein, *The Ritual of Interpretation: The Fine Arts As Literature in Ruskin, Rossetti, and Pater* (Cambridge, Mass., and London, 1975), pp. 49–52. Turner's drawing of *The Pass of Faido* is placed next to Ruskin's of the same name (opposite p. 50). As Stein remarks, Ruskin despite his claims to describe the reality of nature actually offers 'a disguised interpretation of art'. See also Helsinger on this passage.

24–*Alps*, p. 80.

25–*Ibid.*, p. 81. The illustration appears after the words: 'Now was the time'.

26–*Ibid.*, p. 85.

27–*Life and Habit* (London, 1910), p. 39.

28–*Family Letters*, p. 190, Butler to his father, 26 Sept 1881, describing *Alps and Sanctuaries*. Of the sanctuaries only Varese was at all known to English travellers, he suggests. In 1820 J. C. Nattes had produced a series of pen drawings of *Views of Varese* which bears some resemblance to Butler's. (Victoria and Albert Museum, Print Room.)

29–*Alps*, p. 128.

30–'Editor's Literary Record', *Harper's Monthly* (June 1882), p. 151.

31–*The Magazine of Art* (1 Feb 1882), p. xvi.

32–*The Athenaeum*, No 2827 (31 Dec 1881). Miss Savage took this review as an attack in a letter written on the day the review appeared, and Butler replied 'There were sneering reviews of Alps and Sanctuaries in the St. James's Gazette and the Academy, both just like the Athenaeum one; these are all I know of: in the mean time the book does not sell, and must, I am afraid, be set down as no less as failure than its predecessors – or rather worse financially, as it has cost so much more to get up' (28 Jan 1882). In fact, his later judgement, 'I don't think Freshfield's review [in the *Academy*] of *Alps and Sanctuaries* was a bad one' was nearer the mark: *Letters (Butler/Savage)*, pp. 266–8.

34–*Correspondence (Butler/May Butler)*, 9 Sept 1885, p. 148.

35–In 1901 Butler recorded how badly he had done with the book: 'Bogue [then his publisher] had promised me £100 if I would write such a book. . . . Of course when the book was written he declined to take it, and I had to publish it at my own expense – with the usual result. I am still £110 to the bad with the book, and have only sold 344 copies in all these years;' (note in *Letters (Butler/Savage)*, p. 224).

36–*Correspondence (Butler/May Butler)*, 22 July 1878 (Giornico); 21 Aug 1879 (Mesocco); 16 July 1880 (Sant' Ambrogio); 30 Aug 1882 (Fénis). There are also a number of comments on his improvements in technique.

37–Larbaud had especially warm words for Butler's art criticism, which by avoiding the already known discovered a living Italy, instead of 'l'Italie sans les Italiens ou La terre des ruines, des musées et des morts, pays inhabitable'. In brief, 'les oeuvres' d'art d'Italie nous apparaissent sur le même plan que la vie italienne.' (Valery Larbaud, 'Le vain travail de voir divers pays', *Jaune bleu blanc* (1925), pp. 862–3. See Ortensia Ruggiero, *Valery Larbaud et l'Italie* (Paris, 1963), which credits Larbaud, through his adoption of the model of Butler and Landor, with having altered the French image of Italy.)

38–Friedrich Schlegel, *Gemäldebeschreibungen aus Paris und den Niederlanden in den Jahren 1802–1804*, republished in *Sämtliche Werke* (Vienna, 1846). The book was translated into English as *Descriptions of Paintings from Paris and the Netherlands (1802–1804)*, and published in Schlegel's *Aesthetic and Miscellaneous Works* (London, 1848).

39–Bruno Foucart, *Le renouveau de la peinture religieuse en France (1800–1860)* (Paris, 1987); M. Lecanuet, *Montalembert*, 3 vols (Paris, 1895–1902); Henri Dorra, 'The French "Nazarenes"', in *Die Nazarener* (Frankfurt a.M., 1977). [exhibition catalogue]

40–Rio was translated into English in 1854 as *The Poetry of Christian Art*.

41–Alexander William Crawford [Lord Lindsay], *Sketches of the History of Christian Art*, 2nd ed., (London, 1883), II, p. 3.

42–*Ex Voto*, p. 3. He is speaking of the Val Sesia (the region in which Varallo stands) in particular.

43–*Ibid.*, p. 173.

44–Jacob Burckhardt, *The Civilization of the Renaissance in Italy* (Phaidon, Oxford, 1981) 2nd ed., pp. 245–60, gives a vivid account of the range of intensely theatrical festivals that marked Italian public life. (The book first appeared in 1860; Middlemore's translation of 1878 is reproduced in this recent edition.)

45 – R. Renier, *Il 'Gelindo', dramma sacro piemontese della Natività di Cristo* (Turin, 1896), Introduction.

46 – *Ex Voto*, p. 52.

47 – Charles Seymour, Jr, *Sculpture in Italy: 1400–1500* (Harmondsworth, 1966), p. 7.

48 – *Ibid.*, p. 187.

49 – John Ruskin, 'The Relation between Michael Angelo and Tintoret' (1871), *Works*, XXII, p. 82.

50 – *Ibid.*, p. 83.

51 – William Holman Hunt, 'Pre-Raphaelitism and the Pre-Raphaelite Brotherhood', in *Pre-Raphaelitism: A Collection of Critical Essays*, ed. James Sambrook (Chicago and London, 1974), p. 38. Hunt goes on to say that the later Raphael sometimes lent himself to the production of conventional paintings, but for the most part 'the artists who thus servilely travestied this prince of painters at his prime were Raphaelites' (p. 39).

52 – Schlegel's encomia on Raphael's *Madonna della Sedia* and *S Cecilia* could scarcely be more eloquent. Moreover, the former represented not only his 'early manner' but 'the lofty development and rich maturity of his prime', before 'his later imitations of that dazzling meteor, Michelangelo, led him away from the path of love and devotion' (*Descriptions of Art Galleries*, Letter III, p. 94).

53 – Karlheinz Stierle, 'Renaissance – Die Entstehung eines Epochenbegriffs aus dem Geist des 19. Jahrhunderts', *Poetik und Hermeneutik*, XII (Munich, 1985), p. 472. Stierle argues persuasively that the notion of the Italian Renaissance as a closed epoch originated with the French, especially Michelet, partly as a way of assigning the French-dominated neo-classical period its full measure of importance.

54 – Lindsay, *Christian Art*, II, 266. This passage occurs in his account of 'The Primitive School of Bologna'.

55 – On the occasion in 1986 of the 500th anniversary of the founding of the Sacro Monte an exhibition on 'Samuel Butler and the Val Sesia', including his painting of the well outside the sanctuary, formed part of the celebrations, and was widely reported in the regional Italian press. A reissued book includes hitherto unpublished letters in Italian to correspondents in Varallo: Alberto Durio, *Samuele Butler e la Valle Sesia da sue lettere inedite a Giulio Arienta Federico Tonetti e a Pietro Calderini* [1940], (Varallo-Sesia, 1986).

56 – 'In the preface to "Alps and Sanctuaries" I apologised for passing over Varallo-Sesia, the most important of North Italian sanctuaries, on the ground that it required a book to itself. This book I will now endeavour to supply, though well aware that I can only imperfectly and unworthily do so.' (*Ex Voto*, p. 2.)

57 – *Correspondence* (Butler/May Butler), 22 July 1878, p. 71. Butler recalls that he too once was 'very enthusiastic' about Ruskin's *Seven Lamps of Architecture*, but now his feeling about Ruskin is 'one of decided dislike'. By the time of *Alps* Ruskin has become a figure whose predictable attitudes and opinions are to be dismissed: 'At Ispra there is a campanile which Mr. Ruskin would probably disapprove of, but which we thought lovely' (*Alps*, p. 259).

58 – *Ex Voto*, p. 34.

59 – *Correspondence* (29 June 1880), p. 88.

60 – *Ibid.*, p. 35.

61 – Giovanni Testori, *Gaudenzio alle Porte di Varallo* (Varallo-Sesia, 1960). The chapel was restored after 1958.

62 – Seymour, pp. 12–14.

63 – Pater, 'The School of Giorgione', *The Renaissance*, p. 113.

64 – Karl Brandí, quoted in Wallace K. Ferguson, *The Renaissance in Historical Thought: Five Centuries of Interpretation* (The Riverside Press: Cambridge, Mass., 1948), p. 179.

65 – Jacob Burckhardt, *Der Cicerone, eine Anleitung zum Genuss der Kunstwerke Italiens* (Basel, 1855); *The Cicerone: An Art Guide to Painting in Italy, for the use of Travellers and Students*, translated by Mrs A. H. Clough [1873]. A new edition, revised and corrected by J. A. Crowe (London, 1879), pp. 111–12.

66 – *Ibid.*, p. 123.

67 – *Ibid.*, p. 120.

68 – *Ibid.*, p. 121.

69 – *Ibid.* Burckhardt's book is, of course, devoted to an account of painting, not sculpture.

70 – John Addington Symonds, *Renaissance in Italy*, III, 'The Fine Arts' (London 1882), p. 481.

71 – *Harper's Monthly* (June, 1882), p. 151.

72 – *Ex Voto*, pp. 248–9.

73 – Enzo Caramaschi, 'Stendhal, Taine, Barrès face aux Léonards de Milan', *Arts Visuels et Littérature* (Paris, 1985), p. 36. 'C'est ainsi que les véritables habitants de Milan, pour Barrès à la recherche des lieux où souffle l'esprit, ne sont pas les Milanais: ils s'appellent Stendhal et Léonard de Vinci.'

74 – F. Kugler, *Handbook of Painting: The Italian Schools*, 4th ed. (London, 1874), p. iii.

75 – Butler, *Notebooks*, I, ed. Breuer, p. 84 [153].

76 – *Ex Voto*, pp. 4–5.

77 – Martin Kemp, '"Equal excellences": Lomazzo and the explanation of individual style in the visual arts', *Renaissance Studies*, I/i (Oxford, 1987), especially pp. 18–25.

78 – F. Kugler, *Handbuch der Geschichte der Malerei von Constantin dem Grossen bis auf die neuere Zeit*, 2 vols (Berlin, 1837); 2nd edition revised and enlarged by J. Burckhardt, (Berlin, 1847). Layard translated the section relating to Italian art in 1855. He discusses Gaudenzio Ferrari on pp. 423–8. Henry Layard, *Kugler's Handbook of Painting: Italian Schools*, chap. XV, 'The Lombard School', p. 432. Layard includes two illustrations of Gaudenzio's work, *Group of Angels; in the Cupola of the Church of Saronno*; and *Group of Women; from a fresco in a Chapel of the Sacro Monte, Varallo*. He himself had 'full size tracings from a fresco by G. Ferrari' made in 1852, probably for teaching purposes at the Royal College of Art (V & A Print Room). Ferrari's fine *Annunciation* in the National Gallery is part of the Layard Bequest.

79 – Morelli, *Italian Masters*, p. 441, cited by Layard, p. 424. The reference is to Giovanni Morelli, *Italian Painters*; translated from the German by Constance Jocelyn Ffoulkes with an introduction by the Right Hon. Sir A. H. Layard, G.C. B., D.C.L. (London, 1892). Ffoulkes later wrote (with Rodolfo Maiocchi), *Vincenzo Foppa of Brescia, founder of the Lombard School: His Life and Work* (London, 1909), a substantial scholarly study, adopting the 'historical' not the 'critical' point of view, and attempting to counteract the neglect of the Lombard School (p. xi). She referred briefly to Gaudenzio, whose S Maria delle Grazie, Varallo frescoes represent one in a major series of works from Foppa's now destroyed *Life and Passion of Christ* in S Giacomo, Pavia (p. 112). Foppa's altarpiece in the Brera probably formed the prototype for Gaudenzio's *Flight into Egypt* in the same fresco cycle (p. 125).

80 – Layard, p. 427.

81 – The Revd S. W. King, *The Italian Valleys of The Pennine Alps: A Tour through all the Romantic and Less-Frequented 'Vals' of Northern Piedmont, from the Tarentaise to the Gries*; With illustrations from the Author's Sketches, Maps, & c. (London, 1858). King's account of Varallo (on a second visit) is the culmination of his tour, and appears in Chapter XX, 'Val Sesia – Lago d'Orta – Lago Maggiore – Val d'Ossola', pp. 496–535. He devotes considerable space to Gaudenzio Ferrari (though none, as Butler notes, to Tabachetti) and it is his 'factual' (though inaccurate) account of the artist that Butler quotes and corrects.

82 – *Ex Voto*, pp. 14–15.

83 – Morelli, p. 179. He also pointed out that there were no works by Gaudenzio in Florence, Naples, or Palermo.

Butler reviews the matter in more detail, consulting both Colombo and a local informant; the contention of a direct link between Gaudenzio and Raphael rests not only on the legend of a journey to Rome, but on the resemblance of the architectural background of Gaudenzio's *Disputation in the Temple* in the Chapel of S Margherita in S Maria delle Grazie, Varallo, to Raphael's *Disputation in the Academy*, in Rome. Butler concludes that 'If Gaudenzio was for the moment influenced by Raphael, he soon shook off the influence and formed a style of his own, from which he did not depart, except as enriching and enlarging his manner with advancing experience' (*Ex Voto*, p. 93). Colombo, moreover, points out that Raphael's work was not finished until 1511, after the completion of Gaudenzio's.

84—Layard, p. 427.

85—*Ibid.* Layard draws attention to Varallo as Gaudenzio's birthplace, residence during most of his life, and the location of his best works: the frescoes in S Maria delle Grazie, and the *ancona* or great altarpiece in six compartments, in the church of S Gaudenzio, 'one of the most perfect of his early works, and perhaps his *chef-d'oeuvre*'.

86—*Ex Voto*, p. 219. He goes on to say that one perhaps feels the presence of 'an autumnal tint over all the luxuriance of development'.

87—*Ibid.*, p. 20.

88—*Ibid.*, p. 91. He gives Lomazzo as a source for this.

89—Butler owned Matthew Pilkington, *A General Dictionary of Painters: from Cimabue to the Present Time*, 2 vols (London, 1829), a reference work first written in the eighteenth century, but much revised for this new edition. It accords brief praise to Gaudenzio Ferrari, but again sees him as a pupil of Da Vinci (I, 334—5). (Butler's copy is in the Butler Collection, St John's College.)

90—King, *Italian Valleys*, pp. 504—5.

91—Layard, p. 426. 'The other chapels [of the Crucifixion Chapel] were decorated by his followers and imitators, such as *Tabacchetti, Miel, Testa*, and other local painters, whose works only show how rapidly Gaudenzio's influence declined and his school degenerated.'

92—G. Bordiga, *Notizie intorno alle opere di Gaudenzio Ferrari pittore e plasticatore* (Milan, 1821). Butler also consulted the edition illustrated with a large number of engravings of outline drawings of his works by S. Pianazzi (Milan, 1835). Bordiga also wrote a guide to the Sacro Monte, *Storia e guida del S. Monte di Varallo* (Varallo, 1830).

93—*Ex Voto*, p. 98. For these he refers to Colombo.

94—*Ibid.*, pp. 98—9. The argument from 'true feeling' derives ultimately from Schlegel, who saw it as essential to the revival of 'primitive' art (*Descriptions*, pp. 141—8).

95—*The Times* chided him for showing his independence by 'unsparing severity in his criticism of Raphael's school'. *The Athenaeum* held that he 'criticized Raphael's school with a boldness which was not then fashionable'. Ten obituaries were collected for his friends by R. A. Streatfeild in *Samuel Butler: Records and Memorials* (Cambridge, Printed for Private Circulation, 1903).

96—*Ex Voto*, p. 99. He cites Morelli in support of this.

97—Ethel Halsey, *Gaudenzio Ferrari: Great master in painting and sculpture* (London, 1904). She cites Butler respectfully, though not always in agreement with him; the lengthiest quotation is of his praise of the Chapel of the Crucifixion, pp. 78—9.

98—*Ibid.*, p. 33.

99—*Ibid.*, p. 9; p. 66.

100—*Ibid.*, p. 12. Current Italian criticism gives her short shrift, probably on account of her 'Pre-Raphaelite' downgrading of Gaudenzio's later career. Gaudenzio Ferrari has not received the kind of scholarly treatment in English that Botticelli achieved with Horne.

101—Ruskin, *Modern Painters*, Pt IV, chap. III, p. 57.

102—Burckhardt, *Cicerone*, pp. 177—83.

103—Bernard Berenson, *Italian Painters of the Renaissance* (London, 1952), p. 186. The four essays making up this book were originally published 1894–1907, concluding with *The North Italian Painters*. The last chapter is 'The Decline of Art'. The later edition includes an illustration of Gaudenzio's *Flight from Egypt* from the screen at S Maria delle Grazie, Varallo.

104–*National Gallery Illustrated Catalogue*, 2nd rev. ed. (London, 1986), p. 223.

105–The best available guide to it today is the Bibliography and the Register of Works (including a large selection of plates) in L. Mallé, *Incontri con Gaudenzio* (1968); together with the lavishly illustrated volume by Vittorio Viale, *Gaudenzio Ferrari* (Eri. Edizioni RAI. Radiotelevisione Italiana, 1969).

106–*Correspondence (Butler/May Butler)*, 23 Aug 1885, p. 146.

107–Lomazzo, trans. by Richard Haydocke, quoted by Butler, *Ex Voto*, p. 20.

108–Emmanuel Winternitz, *Gaudenzio Ferrari: His School and the Early History of the Violin* (Varallo-Sesia, 1967), p. 19.

109–A colour reproduction of the *Crucifixion* may be seen in Carlo Pirovano, *La Pittura in Lombardia* (Milan, 1973), p. 120. The colour values are quite false, however. A somewhat better one appears in *Arte di Piemonte e Val d'Aosta*, eds. Giovanni Arpino, *et al.* (Milan, 1986), plate 207. Compare this work with the fresco of the same subject in the centre of the screen at S Maria delle Grazie, Varallo, with the fresco at Vercelli, and with the Crucifixion Chapel, Varallo.

110–*Ex Voto*, pp. 57–8.

111–*Ibid.*, p. 70.

112–Giovanni Testori, 'Gaudenzio e il Sacro Monte', *Mostra di Gaudenzio Ferrari* (1956), p. 29. The contract was to Il Morazzone for the frescoes of the 'Ecce Homo' Chapel (1609), and instructs him: 'Si adoperi con quella perfettione che sarà possibile, imitando la mano del pittore Gaudentio e delle qualità di alcuni personaggi che sono nel Monte Calvario.'

113–*Correspondence (Butler/May Butler)*, 13 Dec 1887, p. 195.

114–The Italian edition of *Ex Voto* (Novara, 1894) includes a slightly different selection of photographs, in which the three views each of the Crucifixion Chapel (Gaudenzio) and the 'Journey to Calvary' Chapel (attributed to Tabachetti) are reduced to one each, to make room for a map of the region and a modern plan of the Sacro Monte, and two new items, the 'Portrait' and the 'Seal' of Tabachetti. This selection was preserved in the Shrewsbury Edition *Ex Voto*, and in the 1928 edition (prepared by Jones and Bartholomew) which incorporated Butler's extended and corrected copy of the revised (Italian) edition. His list of illustrations coincided 'for the most part' with the Italian edition.

115–L. Mallé, 'Fortuna di Gaudenzio', *Mostra di Gaudenzio Ferrari* (April–June 1956), Museo Borgogna, Vercelli (Milan, 1956), pp. 43–61, gives an account of criticism up to the time of the exhibition. This article was reprinted, together with a much longer and more detailed account of the work done since the exhibition, 'Fortuna di Gaudenzio, IIª. In margine alla critica gaudenziana 1956–1968' in Mallé's *Incontri con Gaudenzio* (1968), pp. 127–82.

116–Pirovano, pp. 111–12. 'Dunque, per non pochi anni, dire Sacro Monte sarà dire Gaudenzio Ferrari: e ciò non solo per il livello dalla sua fantasia pittorica, ma, più intimamente, per un radicale intervento del pittore nell'ideazione stessa, architettonica e scenografica, della sacra rapprasentazione, come ha giustamente messo in luce la critica recente; si aggiunga che anche molti gruppi plastici sono di diretta ispirazione gaudenziana, quando non assolutamente di mano sua, e si avrà l'idea di quale fosse l'intensità di participazione del nostro artista a questa grande apoteosi della clamante spiritualità di sua gente.'

117–N. Gabrielli, 'Una predella di Gaudenzio Ferrari a Borgosesia', *Bollettino della Società Piemontese degli Belli Arti* (1947), describes the restoration in the previous year and the discovery of the 'lively and brilliant colours' of Gaudenzio himself. Plates 26–7 show the fine *Calling of St Peter* and *The Fall of Simon Magus*.

118–Giovanni Testori, 'Gaudenzio e il Sacro Monte', in *Mostra di Gaudenzio* (1956), p. 25. Reprinted in Testori, *Il gran teatro montano; Saggi su Gaudenzio Ferrari* (Milan, 1965), with

'Gaudenzio alle porte di Varallo', published separately (see note 61 above), and three other essays, two of which relate to the Sacro Monte.

119 – This is dated to 1513–15. Now in Turin, Museo Civico d'Arte Antica. Colour reproduction in Viale, plate XIV.

120 – *Gaudenzio Ferrari e la sua scuola: I cartoni cinqueteschi dell'Accademia Albertina* (Turin, 1982).

121 – Gaudenzio's altarpiece at Arona (1511) is seen in this light. G. Testori writes: 'With this masterpiece he perhaps intends to reply not to Leonardo so much as to Leonardo's imitators, whose exaggerated and esoteric alchemies must above all have bored him; for it seems to say that to render a landscape stupendous it is not necessary to imagine some forest of stalagmites and stalactites, but it is enough to draw the warm, calm line of the countryside, caught in the moment in which the light of the morning trembles above and half dies; and that to render youth enchanting and as if transcendent, it is not necessary to swathe it in ambiguities, rather it is sufficient to suggest it with one stroke, with the naturalness of a breath, the antique light breeze of beauty which is in every innocent life' (*Mostra*, p. 27).

122 – Testori, *Mostra*, p. 26.

123 – Mallé, 'Fortuna di Gaudenzio', *Mostra di Gaudenzio*, p. 53; reprinted in *Incontri*, p. 20. 'Nel 1894 Butler dedica al Sacro Monte un volume e se non acume critico si attenderebbe dal grande scrittore almeno adesione poetica. Ma non accade. Egli s'inserisce nei pregiudizi del preraffaellismo che condizionano l'accostamento ma gli permettono d'amar, del Ferrari, le qualità affettive. Simpatia naturale, ma giudizi al massimo sviati. Perfino i commenti alla "teatralità" delle cappelle si spengono senza frutto.'

124 – G. Testori, *Manieristi piemontesi e lombardi del '600* (Eri. Edizioni RAI, 1966). Based on an exhibition of works by Tanzio da Varallo (Antonio d'Errico: even the spelling of d'Enrico has been italianized), Moncalvo, Cerano, Morazzone, Procaccini, Crespi, Nuvoloni, and del Cairo, held in Turin in 1955. The reassessment of Tanzio da Varallo began in 1922 when a fine *St Sebastian tended by angels*, previously attributed to Rubens, was given to Tanzio by Roberto Longhi. He is here given a leading role (with his brother) in the Varallo Chapels of 'Christ brought before Pilate'; 'Pilate washes his hands'; 'Christ brought before Herod'. Moreover, specific links to Gaudenzio are drawn attention to in the text: the first plate is an *Angel of the Annunciation* by Moncalvo, who 'knew how to incorporate Gaudenzio's models in mannerist interpretations and so to interest a new generation of painters'. In Morazzone's dramatic *Pentecost* [Plate XI], seen from above through an inrush of angels, Gaudenzio's characteristic flight of angels is placed in a deliberately archaic space, but by more precise graduation. Butler, of course, also drew attention to the probable presence at the Sacro Monte of works by Morazzoni, Procaccini, and Moncalvo.

125 – *Ex Voto*, p. 99.

126 – *The Athenaeum* (28 June 1902). *The Times* (20 June 1902), similarly credited Butler with 'rescuing from oblivion the artistic fame of Tabachetti, the sculptor of the images in the chapels of Varallo'. Reprinted in *Samuel Butler, Records and Memorials* (Cambridge, 1903). This contains ten obituaries gathered by R. A. Streatfeild, for presentation to Butler's friends.

127 – Mallé, *Incontri*, plate 130 gives the attribution to G. D'Enrico.

128 – *Ibid*. Plate 146 shows the figures of the *The Bad Thieves* (Chapel XXXV). See plate 147 for Gaudenzio's *Good Thief*.

129 – For the Italian edition (1894) he somewhat altered the list of illustrations, adding a 'Portrait' and a 'Seal' of Tabachetti, while dropping two of the photographs of the 'Calvary Chapel', and two of the 'Crucifixion Chapel'; and this arrangement was adhered to in the Shrewsbury Edition and in the 1928 reprint of *Ex Voto*.

130 – 'Il Morazzone' was Pier Mazzucchelli (1571–1626), born in the little town of Morazzone near Varese. His early works were in Rome; he worked also in S Vittore, Varese, and lived for most of his life in Milan. He decorated a large number of churches with frescoes characterized

by a dramatic realism said to be 'derived from the mystical style of Gaudenzio Ferrari'. See C. Baroni, 'Ancora sul Morazzone', *L'Arte*, XII (Oct 1941); E. K. Waterhouse, *Italian Baroque Painting* (London, 1962); and Gian Alberto dell'Acqua, in the exhibition catalogue *Le Caravage et la peinture italienne du XVIIe siècle* (Louvre, 1965).

131–*Arte di Piemonte*, p. 196. Giovanni d'Enrico is seen as working in the 'still vital Gaudenzian atmosphere, but open to the awareness of the best Lombard mannerism and the influences of a Cerano and a Morazzone'.

132–Thieme–Becker, *Künstler-Lexikon*, pp. 434–5. E. Bénézit, *Dictionnaire critique et documentaire des Peintres, Sculpteurs, Dessinateurs* (Librairie Gründ: Paris, 1976), attributes only Crea to Wespin.

133–A. Martindale, *The Rise of the Artist in the Middle Ages and early Renaissance* (London, 1972).

134–Lindsay, Letter VIII, 'Sculpture and Painting North of the Alps', Section 6, *Christian Art*, II, 380–7, p. 381.

135–*Ibid.*

136–Stephen Spender, 'The Pre-Raphaelite Literary Painters', *Pre-Raphaelitism*, ed. Sambrook, p. 118. As Spender says, 'The Pre-Raphaelites eschewed the Continent.'

137–*Ex Voto*, p. 239.

138–*Ibid.*, p. 241.

139–Lindsay, p. 303.

140–*Ibid.*, p. 294.

141–*Ibid.*, p. 295.

142–*Ibid.*, p. 304.

143–*Ibid.*, p. 305.

144–*Ibid.*, p. 307n.

145–Ruskin, *Modern Painters*, Pt IV, chap. III, p. 56.

146–*Ibid.*, p. 49.

147–*Ibid.*, p. 64. The extended comparison is even more belittling in effect: 'What with difference of subject, and what with difference of treatment, historical painting falls or rises in changeful eminence, from Dutch trivialities to a Velasquez portrait, just as historical talking or writing varies in eminence, from an old woman's story-telling up to Herodotus.'

148–Helsinger, pp. 126–7: 'His grotesque is the attempt of the limited imagination to come to grips with sin and death, but if it is true grotesque it reveals not moral corruption but moral aspiration in the perceiver. In this sense too Ruskin's grotesque is a version of the sublime.'

Ruskin's view may be read as a dilute version of Schlegel's argument in favour of the theme of martyrdom, which insists on the element of pain as the link between Jesus and human suffering (Schlegel, *Descriptions*, pp. 80–88).

149–In Rembrandt's painting, the flayed forearm of the corpse is stressed by being 'grossly overlarge', contrary to the rules of perspective, and 'anatomically inaccurate'. (Francis Barker, *The Tremulous Private Body: Essays on Subjection* (London, 1984), p. 79.)

150–Lamb, 'On the Genius and Character of Hogarth', in Hogarth, *Works*, p. 11.

151–Ruskin, *Modern Painters*, Pt. IV, chap. VIII, p. 131. For Hugo on the grotesque in Shakespeare see his *Préface* to his play *Cromwell* (1827), an important manifesto of French Romanticism, which affected the form taken by realism in French fiction.

152–Ruskin, *ibid.*, p. 138.

153–The self-contradictions may be seen on the pictorial level too, as in Holman Hunt's attempts to create 'a sublime Hogarth' which in, for example, *The Miracle of the Holy Fire* (1896–9) result in inadvertent grotesque. On Hunt's use of Hogarth see George P. Landow, *William Holman Hunt and Typological Symbolism* (New Haven, 1979), pp. 47–59.

154 – For Schlegel, Holbein was the representative of 'Upper German' art in its greatest purity, as Dürer was of 'Lower German' art (*Descriptions*, p. 124).

155 – A recent critic writes that this sophisticated 'web of painted architecture' was 'inhabited by a curious, and typically German, mixture of dancing peasant, weird animals and scenes from ancient history, including a great horseman apparently leaping from the façade at second-floor level.' (R. Boureanu, *Holbein* (London, 1979), p. 8.)

156 – Butler, 'L'Affaire Holbein–Rippel', *Works*, vol. 18. Basel still holds the drawing to be a copy, perhaps from the building itself, by the 'Monogrammatist' (MM). The illustrations we use are new photographs from Basel; for Butler's see the original *Universal Review* article or the Shrewsbury Edition.

157 – Emil Maurer, 'Holbein jenseits der Renaissance: Bemerkungen zur Fassadenmalerei am Haus zum Tanz in Basel', in *15 Aufsätze zur Geschichte der Malerei* (Basel, 1982), pp. 123–33.

158 – Recent work on Gaudenzio has suggested that the combination of sculpture and fresco at the Sacro Monte may have derived from painted perspectival bas-reliefs, used by him at Morbegno, and first used in Italy by Donatello, and by Gaudenzio at Morbegno. The Morbegno altar also uses a motif from Dürer's *Marienleben*. (A. M. Brizio, 'L'Arte di Gaudenzio Ferrari', *Mostra*, p. 12.)

159 – Ruskin, *Modern Painters*, p. 62.

160 – Frederick Burwick, 'Grotesque Bilderwitz: Friedrich Schlegel', *The Haunted Eye: Perception and the Grotesque in English and German Romanticism* (Carl Winter Universitäts-verlag, Heidelberg, 1987), p. 83. Burwick's careful comparison between Schlegel's conception and that outlined in Wolfgang Kayser's standard book *Das Groteske* (Oldenburg, 1957) is particularly helpful.

161 – *Ex Voto*, p. 120. See Butler's Plate No. 11, *The Old Adam and Eve*, facing p. 121. This illustration was removed from subsequent editions.

162 – *Ibid.*, p. 121.

163 – *Ibid.*, p. 122.

164 – The second half of Ruskin's chapter on the grotesque in *Modern Painters* is devoted to a detailed comparison of the 'true grotesque' griffin of the 'Lombard-Gothic (medieval) crafts-man' versus the 'false grotesque' griffin of the Roman (classical) sculptor. (*Ibid.*, pp. 140–48. 'The Lombard workman did really see a griffin in his imagination, and carved it from the life. . . .' (p. 141).)

It is remarkable that the reviewers of *Alps and Sanctuaries*, indignant at his appreciation of 'the griffin at Temple Bar' (p. 20), failed to recognize the witty allusion to Ruskin, and the comedy of the entire passage on the 'beauties of London', and instead took him to task for 'aesthetic impertinencies'.

165 – Naomi Schor, *Reading in Detail* (London, 1987), in an essay on the 'sharp-focus realism' of Duane Hanson, the modern American sculptor, points out that Freud's source, Ernst Jentsch's essay on '*Das Unheimliche*' (1906), pays special attention to sculptural forms of realism. She concludes that the effect is owing not to 'anatomical verisimilitude but to vestimentary realism' (p. 138). The joke in Hanson is the unveiling of art's means to deceive.

166 – Schlegel dismissed them as 'rude Italian naturalisti'.

167 – Lindsay, while according them theoretical importance, avoids describing the phenomena.

168 – Burckhardt's distaste was strongly expressed. In commenting on the representation of the Passion during the plague of 1448 at Perugia, during which the people wept aloud, he remarks on its similarity to certain pictures and statues, including Mazzoni, of the Bologna school: 'It is true that on such occasions emotional stimulants were resorted to which were borrowed from the crudest realism. We are reminded of the pictures of Matteo da Siena, or of the groups of clay-figures by Guido Mazzoni, when we read that the actor who took the part of Christ

appeared covered with weals and apparently sweating blood, and even bleeding from a wound in the side.'

169–Butler reports to his sister in a letter of 20 March 1870 on revisiting the Uffizi that he hated Guercino and the Bolognese school 'pretty heartily already, but I hate them worse now.' (*Letters (Butler/May Butler)*, p. 50).

170–Seymour, *Sculpture in Italy: 1400–1500*, pp. 184–7. Life-size votive effigies in coloured wax and real clothes were immensely popular even in Florence; in S Annunziata in Florence up to 1630 no fewer than four hundred of these life-size effigies were to be seen (*Ibid.,* p. 6 and n. 9).

In the sanctuaries Butler visited, to this day the greatest attraction is the shrines of the Black Madonna, where the figurine of the Virgin is sumptuously clothed and bejewelled. He discussed this phenomenon in 'The Medieval Girl School'.

171–Butler's photograph of *The Virgin's Grandmother* appears opposite p. 162 in *Works*, vol. 19.

172–*Ex Voto*, p. 255.

173–*Ibid.*, pp. 255–6.

174–Only one corner of the bath can be seen in this photograph, on the right.

175–'The Medieval Girl School', *Essays on Life, Art and Science*, ed. R. A. Streatfeild (London, 1908), p. 114.

176–The suggestion that Shakespeare's Life could be constructed from the sonnets was first made by A. W. Schlegel, and was carried out by Keats's friend Charles Armitage Brown in *Shakespeare's Autobiographical Poem* (1838).

177–This is inserted in a footnote in the later editions of *Ex Voto*; see p. 250 in the 1928 edition.

178–*Alps and Sanctuaries*, p. 142.

179–Francis Haskell, *Rediscoveries in Art: Some Aspects of Taste, Fashion and Collecting in England and France* (London, 1976), pp. 52–3.

180–*Ibid.*, p. 143.

181–*Ibid.*, p. 136 and p. 137.

182–*Ibid.*, p. 138.

183–*The Funeral of Tom Moody* appears on p. 159 of *Alps*.

184–*Ibid.*, p. 147.

185–*Ex Voto*, p. 249.

CHAPTER THREE

1–Samuel Butler, *The Authoress of the Odyssey*, 'where and when she wrote, who she was, the use she made of the Iliad, & how the poem grew under her hands'. With a New Introduction by David Grene (Chicago, 1967), vii. The book was first published in London in 1897; this reprint is based on the second edition of 1922. Butler had earlier published several articles and letters, in English and Italian, on his views, especially *The Humour of Homer*, a Lecture delivered at the Working Men's College, Great Ormond Street, London, January 30, 1892, and reprinted in the same year from 'The Eagle', with preface and additional matter, in pamphlet form.

His translations, first published as *The Iliad* (1898) and *The Odyssey* (1900) were also reprinted (with notes and illustrations omitted) as *The Iliad of Homer and The Odyssey* rendered into English Prose by Samuel Butler (Chicago, 1952), the title reflecting the view that the *Odyssey* is by another hand.

2–B. Farrington, *Samuel Butler and the Odyssey* (London, 1929), p. 43. Farrington had been a Classical Scholar of Trinity College, Dublin, and was Senior Lecturer in Classics at the University of Capetown when he wrote his book.

3 – Larbaud, 'Samuel Butler', *Erewhon*, p. 25.

4 – As he put it in an article for an Italian audience, 'un giro intorno la Sicilia, da Trapani a Trapani'. (Samuel Butler, 'L'Origine Siciliana dell'Odissea', Estratto dalla *Rassegna della Letteratura Siciliana*, anno I, 3–4 (Acireale, 1893), p. 4). This was translated as 'On the Trapanese Origin of the Odyssey' and reprinted from 'The Eagle' as a pamphlet (1893).

5 – Butler, *Authoress*, p. 3.

6 – Butler's main sources for the Homeric question were W. E. Gladstone, *Prolegomena: Studies on Homer and the Homeric Age*, 3 vols (London, 1858), and William Mure, *A Critical History of the Language and Literature of Ancient Greece*, 5 vols (London, 1854–9) – both defenders of the unity of Homer – and R. C. Jebb, *Homer: An Introduction to the Iliad and the Odyssey* (Glasgow, 1887), a lucid and judicious proponent of the moderate wing of the German school representing what became the mainstream of classical scholarship. Butler had two copies of Jebb in his library, one much marked, and with some annotations. On Jebb's account (p. 157) of the 'conservative' view whereby the epics were the result of a composite process yet were held to achieve a unity of tone he writes: 'self-contradictory'. The same compromise is adopted by the current generation of commentators, which holds to the composite theory yet grants to the process the honorific title of 'the great Composer' or even on occasion 'Homer'.

7 – W. E. Gladstone, *Prolegomena: Studies on Homer and the Homeric Age* (Oxford, 1858), I, 20. Hugh Lloyd-Jones, 'Gladstone on Homer', *Times Literary Supplement* (3 Jan 1975), pp. 15–17 gives an excellent brief account of Gladstone's engagement with Homer. John Myres, *Homer and his Critics* (London, 1958), devotes a chapter to Gladstone. He makes no mention of Butler.

8 – Farrington, pp. 63–74, extends Butler's mockery of this view.

9 – Gladstone, I, p. 78.

10 – *Ibid.*, pp. 45–6.

11 – Butler, *Authoress*, p. 9.

12 – See G. M. A. Richter, *The Portraits of the Greeks* (London, 1965), vol. I, for well-produced examples of the four types of ancient portrait of Homer: the Epimenides type, the Modena type, the Apollonius of Tyana type, and the Hellenistic blind type.

13 – Haskell, *Rediscoveries*, pp. 9–12; and, for Ingres's *Apotheosis of Homer*, see plate 3.

14 – Christopher Wood, *Olympian Dreamers: Victorian Classical Painters 1860–1940* (London, 1983). p. 19.

15 – *Ibid.*, pp. 140–2.

16 – Boime, pp. 80–1, and fig. 45.

17 – Butler was familiar with the traditions of representation of Nausicaa; he owned R. Engelmann and W. C. F. Anderson, *Pictorial Atlas to Homer's Iliad and Odyssey* (London, 1892), a translation of Engelmann's *Bilder-Atlas zum Homer* (1889), containing 'all known classical representations' of the poems, in clear outline, if not in reproductions that would meet modern standards. Some at least of these, as well as of the later representations, he saw at first hand. The most convenient modern collection of pictorial representations of the *Odyssey* is W. B. Stanford and J. V. Luce, *The Quest for Ulysses* (London, 1974), with an excellent accompanying text; Margaret B. Scherer, *The Legends of Troy in Art and Literature* (New York, 1963), includes the *Iliad*.

18 – Matthew Arnold, *On Translating Homer*, with Introduction and Notes by W. H. D. Rouse (London, 1905), p. 79.

19 – *Ibid.*, p. 75.

20 – *Ibid.*, p. 88.

21 – *Ibid.*, p. 86.

22 – Butler, *Authoress*, p. 145.

23 – *Ibid.*, p. 9–10. Butler cunningly finds contradictions and lapses in the text, and makes use

313

of his audience's belief in women's technical ineptitude to expose the falsity of the claim to Homer's infallibility, just as in his 'Resurrection' pamphlet (1865) he had gleefully pointed out that the testimony that Jesus had risen from the grave depended on the thoroughly unreliable Mary Magdalen, an hysterical, emotional woman of a kind more likely to be found in Italy than in sober northern lands.

24–*Ibid.*, p. 151.

25–G. S. Kirk, *Homer and the Oral Tradition* (Cambridge, 1976), p. 110.

26–*Ibid.*, p. 142.

27–Gladstone, III, 593.

28–W. B. Stanford, *The Ulysses Theme: A Study in the Adaptability of a Traditional Hero*, 2nd rev. ed. (Oxford, 1963), p. 16.

29–It is worthy of remark that Stanford, despite his range and catholicity, ignores Butler's innovation, making just two brief parenthetical mentions of him, and none whatever in *The Quest for Ulysses*. One reads as follows: 'Nausicaa plays her minor part in advancing that purpose [the return and restoration of the prince of Ithaca], and is then firmly bowed out both by Homer and Odysseus. Even if the composer of the *Odyssey* had been a woman (as Samuel Butler and an ancient critic believed), she would hardly have made it otherwise. The classical style demands strict subordination of the parts to the whole, of the episodes to the final purpose' (p. 54). He is also mentioned in two footnotes, pointing to Charles Lamb's *Adventures of Odysseus* (1807) as an influence on both Butler and Joyce.

30–Butler, *Authoress*, p. 130.

31–*Ibid.*, p. 125.

32–*Ibid.*, p. 129.

33–Again we find that modern commentators hold to the 'solidly patriarchal society' with less finesse than their predecessors, whether supporters or debunkers of Penelope as the type of the faithful wife. Thus M. I. Finley asserts: '[The suitors] placed the decision in the strangest place imaginable, in the hands of a woman. There was nothing about the woman Penelope, either in beauty or wisdom or spirit, that could have won her this unprecedented and unwanted right of decision as a purely personal triumph.' (*The World of Odysseus* [1956], Harmondsworth, 1962, p. 101.)

34–Butler, *Authoress*, p. 4.

35–Lady Mary Wortley Montagu, quoted in *English Romantic Hellenism, 1700–1824*, ed. Timothy Webb (Manchester, 1982), pp. 56–7.

36–Joseph Warton, 'On the odyssey', quoted in *English Romantic Hellenism*, pp. 104–5.

37–Johann Wolfgang von Goethe, *Italienische Reise*, trans. as *Italian Journey [1786–1788]* by W. H. Auden and Elizabeth Mayer (Harmondsworth, 1970), p. 310.

38–*Ibid.*, p. 236.

39–*Ibid.*, p. 288.

40–*Ibid.*, p. 289.

41–*Ibid.*, pp. 289–90.

42–Butler, *Notebooks*, ed. Jones, p. 193.

43–Hans-Helmut and Armin Wolf, *Der Weg des Odysseus: Tunis-Malta-Italien in den Augen Homers* (Tübingen, 1968), p. 134. This gives a clear account of the attempts to localize the *Odyssey* ('Forschungsbericht: Geschichte und Kritik der Versuche zur Lokalisierung der Odyssee', pp. 115–50).

44–Michel Gall, in *The Voyages of Ulysses*: A photographic interpretation of Homer's classic by Erich Lessing. With commentaries by C. Kerényi, Michel Gall, Hellmut Sichtermann (London, 1966), p. 18. This is a translation of *Die Odyssee* (Freiburg, 1965).

45–L. G. Pocock, *The Landfalls of Ulysses* (Christchurch, New Zealand, 1955); *The Sicilian Origins of the Odyssey* (Wellington, New Zealand, 1957); and *Odyssean Essays*.

46–A useful brief summary of his reconstruction of the route appears as 'Le Périple de Ulysse', in Jean Bérard's edition of his father's translation of the *Iliad* and the *Odyssey* (*Homère, Iliade Odyssée*, Paris, 1961, pp. 548–56).

47–'Dans cette Méditerranée où rien ne change, il put retrouver intacts les sites et les paysages qui rendaient tout leur sens aux descriptions du Poète: tels qu'ils avaient dû apparaître au fils de Laerte, lorsqu'il explorait les passes de la Mer du couchant, tels, trois mille ans plus tard, on pouvait encore les voir au début de ce siècle.' (Jean Bérard, *Dans le sillage d'Ulysse*, pp. 5–6.) For Braudel's conjuring up of Ulysses in the old fishermen of the present see *The Mediterranean and the Mediterranean World in the Age of Philip II* [1949], 2nd rev. ed., vol. II (London, 1973), p. 1239.

48–Ernle Bradford, *Ulysses Found* (London, 1963), pp. 66–7.

49–Tim Severin, *The Ulysses Voyage: Sea Search for the Odyssey* (London, 1987), p. 24.

50–*Ibid.*, p. 235. This refers to Bérard's study, *Les Phéniciens et l'Odyssée*.

51–*Ibid.*, p. 36 for Spratt's map and the Royal Navy.

52–*Ibid.*, p. 74. In discussing Telemachus' improbably rapid journeys to visit Nestor and Menelaus, he remarks, 'as so often the Odyssey contradicts itself in times and distances' (pp. 142–3). Finally, he is forced to abandon all pretence at following Homer's directions: 'After all Homer was not writing a pilot book or a gazetteer but an epic' (p. 155).

53–For Severin's map see *The Ulysses Voyage*, pp. 89, 194, and 227. On the Royal Navy maps, see p. 36.

54–Mauricio Obregon, *Ulysses Airborne*. With an Introduction by Samuel Eliot Morison. Photographs by Cristina Martinez-Irujo de Obregon (New York, 1971). This piece of 'experimental history' is by the Colombian author of *The Caribbean as Columbus Saw It* (Boston, 1964), flying his plane 'Oh Papa'.

55–The Wolfs write: 'That Butler did not see these contradictions between his theories and Homer's directions is all the more to be wondered at, since he was the first to employ a normal map on which to chart his version of Odysseus' voyage' (p. 134).

56–Howard Clarke, *Homer's Readers: An Historical Introduction to the Iliad and the Odyssey* (London and Toronto, 1981), includes a section on 'The Geographical Homer' as the third (pp. 249–63) of six sections on twentieth-century Homer criticism, under the chapter heading 'Homer Anatomized'. Making no distinction between Butler and the others, he concludes: 'The difficulties of reconciling Homer's descriptions with geographical data in the real world should give all of Homer's locators qualms about trying to do the same in the unreal world' (p. 263).

J. V. Luce, 'The Wanderings of Ulysses', in W. B. Stanford and J. V. Luce, *The Quest for Ulysses*, chap. 6, pp. 118–38, gives a sensible account – 'My aim will be to steer a middle course between the Skylla of scepticism and the Charybdis of credulity' – using recent archaeological evidence to throw light on ancient trading contacts and colonization routes. He does not, however, give a clear account of other views, and his illustrations confuse the issue; for example, he gives two full-page colour photographs, of Stromboli and of Corfu, while rejecting their identification with Odyssean places. He mentions Butler once, at the end of a long list of writers on Ulysses from Virgil to Hauptmann whom Joyce had read, 'besides works by Bérard and Samuel Butler on the authorship and geography of the *Odyssey*' (p. 220). This has the unfortunate effect of separating Butler from the literary influences on Joyce's *Ulysses*, and lumping him with the localizers.

57–*An Atlas of Antient Geography* by Samuel Butler, DD. A new edition, re-engraved with corrections. Edited by the author's son (London, 1851).

58–Svetlana Alpers, *The Art of Describing*, pp. 119–68.

59–See E. S. Shaffer, 'Samuel Butler's Fantastic Maps: Erewhon, the 'New Jerusalem', and the periplus of Odysseus', *Word & Image*, iv, 2 (1988). [special issue on maps and mapping]

60–W. E. Gladstone, *Landmarks of Homeric Study* (London, 1890), p. 114.

61–Henry Schliemann, *Troy and its Remains*, ed. Philip Smith. With map, plans, views, and cuts (London, 1875). See especially 'View of Hissarlik from the North' (frontispiece), 'Trojan Buildings on the North Side, and in the Great Trench cut through the Whole Hill' (opposite p. 143), and the confident identifications 'The Scaean Gate and Paved Road, the Tower of Ilium, City Wall, Palace of Priam' (opposite p. 321). The artist has imagined a Helen-like lady to wear the superb 'Golden Diadem'. This volume contains only a selection of the plates in the original publication, *Trojanische Alterthümer* (1874).

62–For a recent summary of the evidence for this view see Finley, *The World of Odysseus*. In 1954 there was still strong support for the opposing view that Homer describes the Mycenaean world, and that it was contemporary with him; but support for it has now virtually disappeared. Butler's source was Chrestos Tsountas and J. Irving Manatt, *The Mycenaean Age* (London, 1897), 'the latest work on the subject'.

63–Butler, *Authoress*, p. 216.

64–*Ibid.*, pp. 210–18.

65–Butler discovered the 'portrait of the Authoress' in the museum at Cortona; the circumstances surrounding it were bound to interest him: 'It is on slate and burnt, is a little more than half life size, and is believed to be Greek, presumably of about the Christian era, but no more precise date can be assigned to it. I was assured it was found by a man who was ploughing his field, and who happened to be a baker. The size being suitable he used it for some time as a door for his oven, whence it was happily rescued and placed in the museum where it now rests' (*Authoress*, xviii). The photograph he published was not his own but was supplied by Alinari.

According to Richter, the Western Greek type of the Kore was somewhat different from the Athenian; see her illustration of 'Kore, Reggio da Calabria' for a more round-faced and realistic version of the noble Athenian type (G. M. A. Richter, *Korai: Archaic Greek Maidens* (New York, 1968), fig. 556).

66–Butler took many more photographs with Odyssean allusions than he published, as the collection at St John's College reveals.

67–Photograph album, '1892', Butler Collection, St John's College.

68–Boime, *The Academy and French Painting in the Nineteenth Century*, p. 147 and fig. 123.

69–Butler, *Authoress*, p. 12. Butler names not only Sappho, but also a number of women named by her (who were not necessarily poets), as well as Corinna and Myrto, citing Smith's *Dictionary of Classical Biography* (pp. 11–12). Mure (see note 4 above) discusses the women poets of Greece at considerable length. Farrington cites Anyte, known in her own day as 'a female Homer', for her (lost) epics, a popular form with women poets (pp. 87–95). For recent views see Mary Lefkowitz, *The Lives of the Greek Poets* (London, 1981).

70–Pater, Preface to *The Renaissance*, p. xxiii.

71–Butler, *Authoress*, pp. 208–9.

72–See Harry Mathews and Georges Perec, 'Roussel and Venice: Outline of a Melancholy Geography', *Atlas Anthology*, III (London, 1985), pp. 69–94, for a brilliant and witty deciphering of the secret map of Roussel's experience.

73–Butler, *Authoress*, p. 112.

74–Butler, *Authoress*, p. 6. Butler owned *Homeri Ilias, Graece et Latine*, with annotations by S. Clarke; his copy is interleaved with comments on linguistic points, draft translations of knotty passages, and notes on mythology, geography, and manners, such as the roasting of meat; and two other nineteenth-century editions of both the *Iliad* and the *Odyssey*, also profusely annotated. Of existing prose translations apart from Butcher and Lang, he owned and consulted the Bohn Classical Library edition, translated by Theodore Alois Buckley (London, 1872–3). Butler Collection, St John's College.

75–Butler, *Notebooks*, ed. Jones, pp. 197–8.

76–*Ibid.*, p. 197.

77–M. I. Finley, *The World of Odysseus* [1954], (Harmondsworth, 1962), p. 172. Finley quotes Butler's preface to his *Iliad*: 'I very readily admit that Dr Leaf has in the main kept more closely to the words of Homer.'

78–*The Odyssey of Homer*. Done into English Prose by S. H. Butcher and A. Lang. 3rd ed. (London, 1881), p. 96.

79–*Ibid.*, p. 97.

80–*Ibid.*, p. 98.

81–*The Odyssey*, rendered into English prose for the use of those who cannot read the original. By Samuel Butler (London, 1900), p. 78.

82–*Sample Passages from a New Prose Translation of 'The Odyssey'* by Mr Samuel Butler (Edinburgh, 1894). The earlier version is a pamphlet containing about a hundred lines from each of the first and the last books.

83–A few slammed him outright, as producing a version for 'the street and the servants' hall', a 'book to cut'. As one remarked, 'Mr Butler . . . has already won some fame in this connection by his theory that the Odyssey was written by a woman, but we did not grasp until we read this book that it was written by a charwoman' (*The Speaker*, 19 Jan 1901).

Perhaps the most interesting review is 'Homer and Humour', in *The Educational Times* (1 Dec 1900), which registers the 'weird effect' of Butler's style on a variety of passages: the death of Elpenor becomes comic; the pathos of the meeting of Heracles and Odysseus in Hades becomes burlesque; the heroic slaughter of the suitors becomes 'far more horrible here than we have ever found it before'. The same reviewer points out his 'real service to all who cannot read Greek and are likely to find the fashionable Wardour Street style a bore': 'A little girl of ten peeped over the reviewer's shoulder as he was smiling at Mr. Butler's amusing version of *Circe and the pigs*. "How jolly it looks!" she exclaimed; "I should like to read that book." ' Thus the *Authoress* created a new audience for the *Odyssey*: the rising generation of modern young girls.

84–*The Spectator Supplement* (2 Nov 1901).

85–'The Aunts, the Nieces and the Dog', *Essays in Life, Art and Science*, p. 65.

86–*Correspondence (Butler/May Butler)*, p. 214.

87–J. E. Harrison, *Myths of the Odyssey in Art and Literature* (London, 1882), offered illustrations (in autotype) to the major myths: Cyclopes, Lestrygones, Circe, Descent into Hades (a particularly fine chapter), Sirens, Scylla and Charybdis. Nausicaa does not appear. Butler may have been indebted to her account of the alternative tales of Odysseus' death, as he too stresses Odysseus' death at the hands of Telegonus (his son); but for Butler the choice of this variant follows from the unfaithfulness of both spouses.

88–*Spectator* (23 April 1892).

89–*Correspondence (Butler/May Butler)*, p. 217.

90–*The Daily Chronicle* (15 Nov 1900).

91–*Notebooks*, ed. Jones, p. 198.

92–*Ibid.*

93–Frank M. Turner, *The Greek Heritage in Victorian Britain* (New Haven and London, 1981), perceives the link to Joyce, although equating Butler with Gladstone's 'Victorian domesticity' (pp. 184–5).

CHAPTER FOUR

1–*Unprofessional Sermons*, Prayer iii, in *Notebooks*, ed. Jones, pp. 213–14.

2–*Ibid.*, p. 214.

3–*Notebooks*, ed. Jones, p. 254.

4–A modern critic writing of photography that 'it creates value' is not stating a fact but a new cultural and academic presupposition of an age that has promoted photography to 'art'; Susan Sontag, *On Photography* (Harmondsworth, 1977), p. 21 and *passim*.

5–Roland Barthes, *La chambre claire, Note sur la photographie* (Paris, 1980), p. 56.

6 – If we suppose, as most commentators on photography do, that Alberti's perspectival view dominates the very machinery of the camera, the Sacro Monte and the camera are closely related 'machines for visions'. If we suppose, as Svetlana Alpers has proposed in a pregnant footnote in *The Art of Describing*, that the camera has its origins not in the Albertian perspectival painting but in the Dutch descriptive mode of 'picturing' in the way the eye receives the retinal image (as discovered by Kepler), the intriguing possibility opens that in the camera as in the Sacro Monte Butler found a combination of the art of the South and the North, and the illusion opens the way to 'mapping', which Alpers also presents as a characteristically Dutch mode. Alpers' suggestion needs more discussion. (Alpers, n. 37, pp. 243–4).

7 – Quoted in Scharf, *Art and Photography*, p. 53.

8 – *Alps and Sanctuaries*, p. 60.

9 – *Letters (Butler/Savage)*, 9 Oct 1882, pp. 278–9.

10 – The largest collection of Butler's photographs is at St John's College, Cambridge. Five albums contain many of those photographs printed at the time. The glass plates are still extant, with a number of plates not represented by a print; they are in varying stages of deterioration. Where feasible we have printed from the original plate.

11 – Ruskin, *Modern Painters*, Pt. IV, chap. VIII, pp. 137–9.

12 – *Correspondence (Butler/May Butler)*, 27 Sept 1859, p. 39.

13 – D. W. Wynfield, *Portraits of Royal Academicians in Fancy Dress* (Victoria and Albert Museum, Print Room).

14 – Forbes-Robertson, *A Player under Three Reigns*, pp. 54–5.

15 – The photograph appears in Forbes-Robertson's memoirs opposite p. 54.

16 – For the titles of unpublished photographs I am relying on Butler's inscriptions on the envelopes of the original plates, and Alfred Cathie's captions in the albums of printed snapshots. These do not always agree; Butler's are often more pungent, and longer, as the album captions had to be brief. I have used Butler's wherever they differed, or, in a few cases, amalgamated them to give further information.

17 – Margaret Harker, *The Linked Ring: The Secession Movement in Photography in Britain 1892–1910* (London, 1979), fig. 7. 9.

18 – *The Golden Age of British Photography 1839–1900*, edited and introduced by Mark Haworth-Booth (Aperture: New York, 1984), pp. 142–3. As Thomson's co-author remarked, the success of the pictures depended 'more on manners than on the skill of the photographer'.

19 – Harker, p. 162. Sutcliffe described his technique in 'Outdoor Photography and Printing', *The Yearbook of Photography and Photographic News Almanac*, 1875.

20 – Harker, *Linked Ring*, p. 68.

21 – *Life and Landscape: P. H. Emerson. Art and Photography in East Anglia 1885–1900* (exhibition catalogue from the Sainsbury Centre for Visual Arts, University of East Anglia, Norwich, 1986, edited by Neil McWilliam and Veronica Sekules). 'Ricking the Reed' appears as XXVII on p. 108, originally published in *Life and Landscape on the Norfolk Broads* (1886); 'The Sedge Harvest' as VII, p. 110, originally published in *Idyls of the Norfolk Broads* (1887).

22 – Alpers, *The Art of Describing*, pp. 175–7. See chap. 5, 'Looking at Words: The Representation of Texts in Dutch Art'.

23 – Sontag, *Photography*, p. 98. 'Thus, one of the perennial successes of photography has been its strategy of turning living beings into things, things into living beings.'

24 – John Thomson, *Street Life in London* (275–1984–255, Victoria and Albert Museum, Print Room).

25 – *Ibid.*, (275–1984–262).

26 – Eugène Atget, 'Joueur d'Orgue', plate 142, *Photographs from the Collection of the Gilman Paper Company* (White Oak Press, 1985).

27 – Harker, Fig. 7. 10.

28 – 'Paul Martin and the Modern Era', *Golden Age of British Photography*, p. 184. With these rather dull photographs the golden age ends.

29 – *Correspondence (Butler/May Butler)*, 16 Jan 1884, p. 113.

30 – *Notebooks*, ed. Jones, p. 262.

31 – Butler Collection, St John's College. A note by Jones on the first photograph reads: 'The Wife of Bath. I do not say that they are all the same woman photoed the same day; but this is what he was thinking of in the Note Books.'

32 – *Essays on Life, Art and Science*, p. 25.

33 – *Ibid.*, pp. 26–7.

34 – Maas, *Victorian Art World*, pp. 11–13.

35 – The film is Jean-Luc Godard's *Les Carabiniers*. Susan Sontag, *On Photography*, p. 3.

36 – Mike Weaver, *Julia Margaret Cameron 1815–1879* (John Hansard Gallery, 1984), handles the technique of 'soft focus' with due caution (pp. 138–40).

37 – Anne Kelsey Hammond, 'Frederick H. Evans, 1843–1943: The Interior Vision', *Creative Camera*, No. 243 (March, 1985), pp. 12–26.

38 – King, *Italian Valleys*, p. 519.

39 – *Staging the Self: Self-Portrait Photography 1840s–1980s*, ed. James Lingwood (catalogue of an exhibition held at the National Portrait Gallery, London, 3 Oct 1986–11 Jan 1987), contains reproductions of the above-mentioned photographs. All were taken between 1854 and 1892. See also the larger exhibition catalogue, *L'Autoportrait à l'âge de la Photographie*, at the Musée Cantonal des Beaux-Arts, Lausanne.

40 – Jean-François Chevrier, 'The Image of the Other', in *Staging the Self*, p. 13. Chevrier, seeing this as the tail-end of Romanticism, misses the humour.

41 – *La Fidélité des Images: René Magritte. Le cinématographe et la photographie*. Textes et Titres de Louis Scutenaire (Brussels, n. d.).

42 – *Zola photographe*, eds Françoise-Emile Zola and Massin (Paris, 1979), pp. 100–109.

43 – 'Material for a Projected Sequel to *Alps and Sanctuaries*', *Notebooks*, ed. Jones, p. 260.

44 – George Hersey, *High Victorian Gothic: A Study in Associationism* (Baltimore, 1972), p. 178.

45 – Gary Wihl, *Ruskin and the Rhetoric of Infallibility*, Appendix 2, 'Neither a palace nor of crystal: Ruskin and the Architecture of the Great Exhibition', pp. 171–2.

46 – *Alps and Sanctuaries*, p. 268.

47 – *Ibid.*, p. 270.

48 – *Ibid.*, p. 272.

49 – *Ibid.*, p. 273.

50 – *Ibid.*, pp. 273–4.

51 – *Ibid.*, p. 274.

52 – 'The Aunt, the Nieces, and the Dog', *Essays on Life, Art and Science*, p. 45.

53 – 'How to Make the Best of Life', *Essays on Life, Art and Science*, p. 83.

Select Bibliography

————

SELECTED WORKS BY SAMUEL BUTLER

The Collected Works, eds. Henry Festing Jones and A. T. Bartholomew. The Shrewsbury Edition, 20 volumes, London, 1924.

A First Year in Canterbury Settlement, eds. A. C. Brassington and P. B. Maling, Blackwood and Janet Paul: Auckland and Hamilton, 1964.

Alps and Sanctuaries, David Bogue: London, 1881; 2nd ed., with an introduction by R. A. Streatfeild, London, 1913; Alan Sutton: Gloucester, 1986.

The Authoress of the Odyssey, London, 1897, 2nd ed.: London, 1922. Reprinted with a New Introduction by David Grene, Univ. of Chicago: Chicago and London, 1967.

Erewhon [1872], The Penguin English Library, Harmondsworth, 1970.

Erewhon: or Over the Range, eds. Hans-Peter Breuer and Daniel F. Howard, University of Delaware Press: Newark, Delaware, 1981.

Erewhon Revisited, London, 1901.

Ernest Pontifex, or The Way of All Flesh, ed. with an Introduction and Notes from the original manuscript [1886] by Daniel F. Howard, London, 1965.

Essays on Life, Art and Science, ed. with an Introduction by R. A. Streatfeild, London, 1904.

Ex Voto: an account of the Sacro Monte or New Jerusalem at Varallo-Sesia, London, 1888; New York and London, 1890; translated into Italian by Angelo Rizzetti, Novara, 1894; reprint of Shrewsbury Edition *Ex Voto*, eds Henry Festing Jones and A. T. Bartholomew, London, 1928.

The Fair Haven, London, 1873.

Life and Habit [1878], A. C. Fifield, London, 1910.

Life and Letters of Samuel Butler, D.D, 2 vols, London, 1896.

Marginalia on a bound exhibition catalogue of Rembrandt's *Schilderijen*, 8–31 October 1898, Stedelijk Museum, Amsterdam.

Shakespeare's Sonnets Reconsidered, London, 1899.

Unconscious Memory, London, 1880.

The Way of All Flesh, ed. and rev. by R. A. Streatfeild. London, 1903. Reissued by James Cochrane, with an introduction by Richard Hoggart, Harmondsworth, 1966.

SHORTER WORKS

The Humour of Homer, Cambridge, 1892 [pamphlet].

The Humour of Homer and Other Essays, ed. R. A. Streatfeild. London, 1913.

'L'Origine Siciliana dell'Odissea', *Rassegna della Letteratura Siciliana*, anno I, 3–4, Acireale, 1893.

'On the Trapanese Origin of the Odyssey', Cambridge, 1893 [pamphlet].

'Ancora sull'origine dell'Odissea', *Rassegna della Letteratura Siciliana*, anno II. Acireale, 1894.

LETTERS

Letters between Samuel Butler and Miss E. M. A. Savage 1871–1885, London, 1935.
The Family Letters of Samuel Butler 1841–1886, ed. Arnold Silver, London, 1962.
The Correspondence of Samuel Butler with his Sister May, Berkeley and Los Angeles, 1962.

NOTEBOOKS

Butleriana, ed. A. C. Bartholomew, London, 1932.
The Notebooks, ed. Henry Festing Jones, A. C. Fifield: London, 1912. Reprinted with a New
  Introduction by P. N. Furbank, Chatto & Windus, London, 1985.
Further Extracts from the Note-Books of Samuel Butler, ed. A. T. Bartholomew, London,
  1934.
Samuel Butler's Notebooks: Selections, eds. Geoffrey Keynes and Brian Hill, London, 1951.
The Note-books, Vol. I (1874–1883), ed. Hans-Peter Breuer, University Press of America,
  1984.

TRANSLATIONS

Sample Passages from a New Prose Translation of 'The Odyssey', Edinburgh, 1894.
The Iliad, London, 1898.
The Odyssey, London, 1900.
The Iliad of Homer and The Odyssey, rendered into English Prose by Samuel Butler, Chicago,
  1952.
Hesiod, *Works and Days*, Central School of Arts and Crafts: London, 1923–4.

COLLECTIONS AND EXHIBITION CATALOGUES

The Samuel Butler Collection at St John's College, Cambridge, a Catalogue and a Commentary
  by H. F. Jones and A. T. Bartholomew, Heffer: Cambridge, 1921.
Samuel Butler, Catalogue of the Collection in the Chapin Library, Williams College,
  Williamstown, Mass.; The Southworth-Anthoensen Press: Portland, Maine, 1945.
British Empire Loan Collection, catalogue of a travelling exhibition shown at the National Art
  Gallery and Dominion Museum, New Zealand; Tate Gallery, Millbank, 1935.
Hill and Mountain Landscapes, Handlist of the Sixth Exhibition of the Cambridge University
  Pictorial Arts Society, held at the Fitzwilliam Museum, 24 February – 6 March 1923.
Victorian Painting, Introduction and Notes by John Woodward. Catalogue of an exhibition
  held at the Nottingham University Art Gallery, 20 January – 15 February, 1959.
The Life and Career of Samuel Butler, handlist of an exhibition held at the Chapin Library,
  Williams College, Williamstown, Mass., 20 February – 25 March, 1967.
Samuel Butler: A 150th Birthday Celebration, handlist of an exhibition held at the Chapin
  Library, Williams College, Williamstown, Mass., 4 December 1985–21 March 1986.
Samuel Butler and His Contemporaries, catalogue of an exhibition held at the Robert
  McDougall Art Gallery, Christchurch, 15–26 May 1972.
Samuele Butler e la Valle Sesia, handlist of an exhibition held at the Biblioteca Civica
  'Farinone-Centa', Varallo-Sesia, 1986.

WORKS ON SAMUEL BUTLER

Durio, Alberto, *Samuele Butler e la Valle Sesia* [1940], Varallo-Sesia, 1986.
Farrington, B, *Samuel Butler and the Odyssey*, London, 1929.

Fort, J. B., *Samuel Butler: 1835–1902: l étude d'un caractère et d'une intelligence*, Bordeaux, 1935.

—— *Samuel Butler l'Ecrivain: Etude d'un Style*, Bordeaux, 1935.

Furbank, P. N., *Samuel Butler (1835–1902)*, Cambridge, 1948.

Harris, John F., *Samuel Butler, Author of Erewhon: The Man and his Work*, London, 1916.

Holt, Lee E., 'The Note-books of Samuel Butler', *PMLA*, lx/4 (1945), pp. 1165–79.

—— *Samuel Butler*, New York, 1964.

Jones, Henry Festing, *Samuel Butler: A Memoir*, 2 vols, London, 1919.

Jones, Joseph Jay, *The Cradle of Erewhon: Samuel Butler in New Zealand*, Austin, Texas, 1959.

Knoepflmacher, U. C., *The Victorian Novel and Religious Humanism*, Princeton, N. J., 1965.

Larbaud, Valery, Préface, *Erewhon* [1920], Gallimard: Paris, 1961. [French translation]

—— *Samuel Butler*, Conférence faite le 3 novembre 1920, Maison des Amis des Livres, Paris.

McCarthy, Patrick, 'Samuel Butler', in 'Valery Larbaud and English Literature', unpublished D. Phil. thesis, Oxford, 1968.

Shaffer, E. S. 'The Ironic Mode in Biblical Criticism: Samuel Butler's *The Fair Haven*', in *Victorian Studies Newsletter*, Autumn, 1979. [abstract]

—— 'Samuel Butler's Fantastic Maps: Erewhon, the 'New Jerusalem', and the periplus of Odysseus', *Word and Image*, IV/2, 1988. [special issue on maps and mapping]

Stillman, Clara, *Samuel Butler: a Mid-Victorian Modern*, London, 1932.

Streatfeild, R. A., ed., *Samuel Butler: Records and Memorials*, Cambridge, 1903. [obituaries]

Vita-Finzi, Claudio. 'Samuel Butler in Italy', *Italian Studies*, XVIII (1963).

Willey, Basil, *Darwin and Butler: two versions of evolution*, London, 1960.

Yeats, John Butler, 'Recollections of Samuel Butler', in *Essays Irish and American*, Dublin, 1918.

BIBLIOGRAPHY

The Career of Samuel Butler: A Bibliography, Stanley B. Harkness, London, 1955.

OTHER WORKS CONSULTED

Adams, Henry, *Mont Saint Michel and Chartres* [1904], New York and Harmondsworth, 1986.

Alpers, Svetlana, *The Art of Describing: Dutch Art in the Seventeenth Century*, London, 1983.

Andrews, Keith, *The Nazarenes – A Brotherhood of German Painters in Rome*, Oxford, 1964.

Arnold, Matthew, *On Translating Homer* [1861], Introduction and Notes by W. H. D. Rouse, London, 1905.

Arpino, Giovanni, *et al.*, *Arte di Piemonte e Val d'Aosta*, Milan, 1986.

Ayres, James, *English Naive Painting 1750–1900*, London, 1980.

Ball, Patricia, *The Science of Aspects: The Changing Role of Fact in the Work of Coleridge, Ruskin and Hopkins*, London, 1971.

Bann, Stephen, *The Clothing of Clio*, Cambridge, 1984.

Barker, Francis, *The Tremulous Private Body: Essays on Subjection*, London, 1984.

Barthes, Roland, *La chambre claire: Note sur la photographie*, Paris, 1980.

Beerbohm, Max, *Rossetti and his Circle*, [1922], New Haven and London, 1987.

Benjamin, Walter, 'A Short History of Photography' [1931], trans. by Phil Patton; *Art forum*, XV (February, 1977).

Bérard, Victor, *Dans le sillage d'Ulysse*, with photographs by F. Boissonas, Paris, 1935.

Bérard, Jean, ed., *Homère, Iliade Odyssée*, translated by Victor Bérard, Paris, 1961.

Berenson, Bernard, *Italian Painters of the Renaissance* [1894–1907], London, 1952.

Boime, Albert, *The Academy and French Painting in the Nineteenth Century*, London, 1971.

Bordiga, G., *Notizie intorno alle opere de Gaudenzio Ferrari pittore e plasticatore*, Milan, 1821.

—— *Le Opere del pittore e plasticatore Gaudenzio Ferrari, desegnate ed incise da S. Pianazzi*, Milan, 1835.

Bossi, Alberto, *La Chiesa di Santa Maria delle Grazie e la grande Parete Gaudenziana di Varallo*, Varallo, n.d.

Bradford, Ernle, *Ulysses Found*, London, 1963.

Bryson, Norman, *Word and Image*, Cambridge, 1981.

—— *Tradition and Desire: from David to Delacroix*. Cambridge, 1984.

—— *Vision and Painting*, Cambridge, 1983.

Burckhardt, Jacob, *Der Cicerone; eine Anleitung zum Genuss der Kunstwerke Italiens*, Basel, 1855. Translated by Mrs A. H. Clough [1873] as *The Cicerone: An Art Guide to Painting in Italy*, 2nd rev. ed., London, 1879.

—— *The Civilization of the Renaissance in Italy* [1860], Oxford, 1981.

Burwick, Frederick, 'Grotesque Bilderwitz: Friedrich Schlegel', *The Haunted Eye: Perception and the Grotesque in English and German Romanticism*, Heidelberg, 1987.

Butler, Samuel, D. D., *An Atlas of Ancient Geography*, ed. Thomas Butler, London, 1851.

Caramaschi, Enzo, *Arts Visuels et Littérature*, Schena-Nizet: Paris, 1985.

Cardinal, Roger, *Outsider Art*, London, 1972.

Caresi, Franco, *Il Sacro Monte di Varallo*. Editurist: Varallo, n.d.

Clarke, Howard, *Homer's Readers: An Historical Introduction to the Iliad and the Odyssey*, London and Toronto, 1981.

Colombo, Giuseppe, *Vita ed opere di Gaudenzio Ferrari*, Turin, 1881.

Crawford, Alexander William [Lord Lindsay], *Sketches of the History of Christian Art*, 2nd ed., London, 1883.

Crowe, Joseph Archer and Giovanni Battista Cavalcaselle, *History of Painting in Northern Italy*, London, 1871.

Ferguson, Wallace K., *The Renaissance in Historical Thought: Five Centuries of Interpretation*, The Riverside Press: Cambridge, Mass., 1948.

Finley, M. I., *The World of Odysseus* [1954], Harmondsworth, 1962, 2nd rev. ed. 1978.

Fried, Michael, *Absorption and Theatricality: Painting and Beholder in the Age of Diderot*, Berkeley, 1980.

Forbes-Robertson, Johnston, *A Player under Three Reigns*, London, 1925.

Gabrielli, N., 'Una predella di Gaudenzio Ferrari a Borgosesia', *Bolletino della Società Piemontese degli Belli Arti*, 1947.

Gaggini, Anna Maria Bianchi, *La Via Sacra del Rosario a Santa Maria del Monte sopra Varese*, Milan, 1984.

Gaudenzio Ferrari e la sua scuola: I cartoni cinqueteschi dell'Accademia Albertina, catalogue of an exhibition held at the Accademia Albertina, Turin, March–May 1982.

Gladstone, W. E., *Landmarks of Homeric Study*, London, 1890.

—— *Prolegomena: Studies on Homer and the Homeric Age*, 3 vols, London, 1858.

Gombrich, E. H., *Art and Illusion*, 4th ed., London, 1962.

—— *Meditations on a Hobby-Horse and other Essays on the Theory of Art*, London, 1963.

Graves, Algernon, The *Royal Academy of Arts: A Complete Dictionary of Contributors and their work from its foundation in 1769 to 1904*, London, 1905–6.

Halsey, Ethel, *Gaudenzio Ferrari: Great master in painting and sculpture*, London, 1904.

Hammond, Anne Kelsey, 'Frederick H. Evans, 1843–1943: The Interior Vision', *Creative Camera*, No. 243 (March, 1985), pp. 12–26.

Harker, Margaret, *The Linked Ring: The Secession Movement in Photography in Britain 1892–1910*, London, 1979.

Harrison, J. E., *Myths of the Odyssey in Art and Literature*, London, 1882.

Haskell, Francis, *Rediscoveries in Art*, London, 1976.

——'Compromises of a connoisseur' [on Bernard Berenson], *Times Literary Supplement* (5 June 1987), pp. 595–6.

Haskell, Francis and Nicholas Penny, *'The Most Beautiful Statues': The Taste for Antique Sculpture 1500–1900*, an exhibition held at the Ashmolean Museum 26 March–10 May 1981. Oxford, 1981.

Haworth-Booth, Mark, ed., *The Golden Age of British Photography: 1839–1900*, Aperture: New York, 1971.

Hazlitt, William, *Essays on the Fine Arts*, 2nd ed., London, 1873.

——*Lectures on the English Comic Writers*, London, 1819.

——*Table-talk, or Original Essays*, London, 1821.

Hilton, Tim, *John Ruskin: The Early Years 1819–1815*, New Haven and London, 1985.

Hindley, Diana and Geoffrey Hindley, *Advertising in Victorian England 1837–1901*, London, 1972.

Holman Hunt, William, *Pre-Raphaelitism and the Pre-Raphaelite Brotherhood*, 2 vols, London, 1905.

Hunt, John Dixon, *The Pre-Raphaelite Imagination*, London, 1968.

Iconografia del Sacro Monte di Varallo. Disegni, dipinti e incisioni dal XVI al XX secolo, Michela Cometti Valle, Paolo Bellini, Vera Comoli Mandracci, eds., Varallo: Biblioteca Civica 'M. Farinone-Centa', 1984. [exhibition catalogue]

Iser, Wolfgang, *Walter Pater: The Aesthetic Moment* [1960], translated by David Henry Wilson, Cambridge, 1987.

Jebb, R. C., *Homer: An Introduction to the Iliad and the Odyssey*, Glasgow, 1887.

Kemp, Martin. '"Equal Excellences": Lomazzo and the explanation of individual style in the visual arts', *Renaissance Studies*, I/1 (1987), pp. 1–26.

Kermode, Frank, *Forms of Attention*, Chicago, 1985.

Kerényi, C., Michel Gall, and Hellmut Sichtermann, *Die Odyssee*, Freiburg, 1965. Translated as *The Voyages of Ulysses*. A photographic interpretation of Homer's classic by Erich Lessing, London, 1966.

King, S. W., *The Italian Valleys of the Pennine Alps: A Tour through all the Romantic and Less-Frequented 'Vals' of Northern Piedmont, from the Tarentaise to the Gries*, London, 1858.

Kirk, G. S., *Homer and the Oral Tradition*, Cambridge, 1976.

Kugler, Franz, *Handbuch der Geschichte der Malerei von Constantin dem Grossen bis auf die neuere Zeit*, 2 vols, Berlin, 1837; 2nd ed. revised and enlarged by J. Burckhardt, Berlin, 1847. Translated into English by Henry Layard as *Kugler's Handbook of Painting: Italian Schools*, London, 1855.

Lamb, Charles, *Adventures of Odysseus*, London, 1807.

——'On the Genius and Character of Hogarth', introduction to *The Works of William Hogarth*, 2 vols, London, 1872.

Landow, George P., *William Holman Hunt and Typological Symbolism*, New Haven, 1979.

Larbaud, Valery, *Jaune bleu blanc*, Paris, 1925.

Lawrence, D. H., *Twilight in Italy* [1913], London, 1956.

Lingwood, James, ed., *Staging the Self: Self-Portrait Photography 1840s–1980s*, catalogue of an exhibition held at the National Portrait Gallery, London 3 October 1986 – 11 January 1987.

Lloyd-Jones, Hugh, 'Gladstone on Homer', *Times Literary Supplement* (3 January 1975), pp. 15–17. Reprinted in *Blood for the Ghosts*, London, 1982.

Lubbock, Jules, 'Walter Pater's *Marius the Epicurean* – The Imaginary Portrait as Cultural History', *Journal of the Warburg and Courtauld Institutes*, 46 (1983), pp. 166–89.

Maas, Jeremy, *The Victorian Art World in Photographs*, London, 1984.

—— *Victorian Painting*, London, 1969.

Mallé, L., *Incontri con Gaudenzio*, Turin, 1969.

Mathews, Harry and Georges Perec, 'Roussel and Venice: Outline of a Melancholy Geography', *Atlas Anthology III*, London, 1985, pp. 69–94.

Maurer, Emil, 'Holbein jenseits der Renaissance. Bemerkungen zur Fassadenmalerei am Haus zum Tanz in Basel'. In: *15 Aufsätze zur Geschichte der Malerei* (Basel, 1982), pp. 123–33.

McWilliam, Neil and Veronica Sekules, *Life and Landscape: P. H. Emerson. Art and Photography in East Anglia 1885–1900*. An exhibition catalogue from the Sainsbury Centre for Visual Arts, University of East Anglia, Norwich, 1986.

Mendelssohn–Bartholdy, Felix, *Letters from Italy and Switzerland*. Translated by Lady Wallace, London, 1862.

Morelli, Giovanni, *Italian Painters*. Translated from the German by Constance Jocelyn Ffoulkes. London, 1892.

Mure, William, *A Critical History of the Language and Literature of Ancient Greece*, 5 vols, London, 1854–9.

Neve, Christopher, 'London Art School in Search of a Home – Heatherley's I', *Country Life* (17 Aug 1978); 'A Question of Survival – Heatherley's School of Art II', *Country Life* (31 Aug 1978).

Obregon, Mauricio, *Ulysses Airborne*. With an Introduction by Samuel Eliot Morison. Photographs by Cristina Martinez-Irujo de Obregon. New York, 1971.

Pater, Walter, *The Renaissance: Studies in Art and Poetry*. The 1893 text ed. Donald L. Hill, University of California Press: Berkeley, Los Angeles and London, 1980.

—— *The Renaissance*, with an Introduction and notes by Kenneth Clark, New York, 1976.

Paulson, Ronald, *Book and Painting: Shakespeare, Milton and the Bible; Literary texts and the Emergence of English Painting*, Knoxville, Tennessee, 1986.

Pilkington, Matthew, *A General Dictionary of Painters . . . from Cimabue to the Present Time*, 2 vols, London, 1829.

Pinacoteca di Varallo: recuperi e indagini storiche, Marco Rosci and Stefania Stefani Perrone, eds. Catalogue of an exhibition held at the Palazzo dei Musei, Varallo, September–October 1981, Borgosesia, n.d.

Pirovano, Carlo, *La Pittura in Lombardia*, Milan, 1973.

Pocock, L. G., *The Landfalls of Ulysses*, Christchurch, New Zealand, 1955.

Proust, Marcel, *On Reading Ruskin*. Prefaces to *La Bible d'Amiens* and *Sésame et les Lys*, translated and edited by Jean Autret and William Burford, New Haven and London, 1987.

Ray, Gordon N., *The Illustrator and the Book in England 1790–1914*, Oxford, 1976.

Rees, A. L. and F. Borzello, eds., *The New Art History*, London, 1986.

Renier, R., *Il 'Gelindo', dramma sacro piemontese della Natività di Cristo*, Turin, 1896.

Reynolds, Graham, *Painters of the Victorian Scene*, London, 1953.

Richter, G. M. A., *Korai: Archaic Greek Maidens*, New York, 1968.

—— *The Portraits of the Greeks*, 3 vols, London, 1967.

Rio, Alexis-François, *De la poésie chrétienne, dans son principe, dans sa matière et dans ses formes*, Paris, 1836.

—— *De l'art chrétien*, Paris, 1851. Translated as *The Poetry of Christian Art*, London, 1854.

Rosenberg, John, *The Darkening Glass: A Portrait of Ruskin's Genius*, New York, 1961.

Rosenblum, Robert, *Modern Painting and the Northern Romantic Tradition: Friedrich to Rothko*, London, 1975.

Ruggiero, Ortensia, *Valery Larbaud et l'Italie*, Paris, 1963.

Ruskin, John, *The Complete Works*, eds. E. T. Cook and A. Wedderburn, London, 1904.

——*The Seven Lamps of Architecture*, rev. ed., London, 1882.

—— *The Stones of Venice*, London, 1851–3.

Sambrook, James, ed., *Pre-Raphaelitism: A Collection of Critical Essays,* Chicago and London, 1974.

Scharf, Aaron, *Art and Photography*, London, 1968.

Schlegel, Friedrich, *Gemäldebeschreibungen aus Paris und den Niederlanden in den Jahren 1802–1804*. Translated as *Descriptions of Paintings from Paris and the Netherlands (1802–1804)*, in *Aesthetic and Miscellaneous Works*, London, 1848.

Schliemann, Heinrich, *Trojanische Alterthümer*, Leipzig, 1874. Translated by Philip Smith as Henry Schliemann, *Troy and its Remains*, London, 1875.

Scherer, Margaret B., *The Legends of Troy in Art and Literature*, New York, 1963.

Schor, Naomi, *Reading in Detail*, London, 1987.

Severin, Tim, *The Ulysses Voyage: Sea Search for the Odyssey*, London, 1987.

Seymour, Charles, Jr., *Sculpture in Italy: 1400–1500*, Harmondsworth, 1966.

Sontag, Susan, *On Photography* [1973], Harmondsworth, 1977.

Stanford, W. B., *The Ulysses Theme: A Study in the Adaptability of the Traditional Hero*, 2nd rev. ed., Oxford, 1963.

—— and J. V. Luce, *The Quest for Ulysses*, London, 1974.

Stein, Richard, L., *The Ritual of Interpretation: The Fine Arts As Literature in Ruskin, Rossetti, and Pater*, Cambridge, Mass., and London, 1975.

Stevenson, Lionel, ed., *Victorian Fiction: A Guide to Research*, Cambridge, Mass., 1964.

Stierle, Karlheinz, 'Renaissance – Die Entstehung eines Epochenbegriffs aus dem Geist des 19 Jahrhunderts', *Poetik und Hermeneutik*, Vol. 12, Munich, 1985.

Symonds, John Addington, *The Renaissance in Italy*, 2nd ed., Parts 1–3, London, 1880–82.

Testori, Giovanni, *Gaudenzio alle Porte di Varallo*, Varallo-Sesia, 1960.

—— *Il gran teatro montano: Saggi su Gaudenzio Ferrari*, Milan, 1965.

—— *Manieristi piemontesi e lombardi del '600*, Eri. Edizioni RAI, 1966. [exhibition catalogue]

Tsountas, Chrestos and J. Irving Manatt, *The Mycenaean Age*, London, 1897.

Trachtenberg, Alan, ed., *Classic Essays on Photography*, Leete's Island Books: New Haven, Conn., 1980.

Turner, Frank M., *The Greek Heritage in Victorian Britain*, New Haven and London, 1981.

Viale, Vittorio, *Gaudenzio Ferrari*, Eri. Edizioni RAI. Radiotelevisione Italiana, 1969.

—— ed., *Mostra di Gaudenzio Ferrari*, catalogue of an exhibition, April–June 1956, Museo Borgogna, Vercelli, Milan, 1956.

Weaver, Mike, *Julia Margaret Cameron 1815–1879*, John Hansard Gallery, 1984.

Webb, Timothy, *English Romantic Hellenism 1700–1824*, Manchester, 1982.

Wihl, Gary, *Ruskin and the Rhetoric of Infallibility*, New Haven and London, 1985.

Wolf, Hans-Helmut, and Armin Wolf, *Der Weg des Odysseus: Tunis-Malta-Italien in den Augen Homers*, Tübingen, 1968.

Wood, Christopher, *Dictionary of Victorian Painters*, Woodbridge, Suffolk, 1971.

—— *Olympian Dreamers: Victorian Classical Painters 1860–1940*, London, 1983.

Zola, François-Emile et Massin, eds., *Zola photographe*, Editions Denoël: Paris, 1979.

List of Illustrations

All works are by Samuel Butler unless otherwise indicated. Measurements are given in centimetres, followed by inches.

1. *Church Porch at Rossura*, 1879, etching, 136 x 110 (5⅜ x 4⅜). St John's College, Cambridge, Butler Collection.
2. *Soazza Church*, pen and ink. St John's.
3. *Portrait of Samuel Butler* (photograph by Alfred Cathie, 1890). St John's.
4. *Butler Family* (photographer unknown). St John's.
5. *An Interior, c.* 1854, watercolour, 12.7 x 16.2 (5 x 6⁴/₁₀). Shrewsbury School.
6. *An Interior, c.* 1854, watercolour, 12.7 x 17 (5 x 6⁷/₁₀). Shrewsbury School.
7. *Smite Bridge, Langar, c.* 1854, watercolour, 11.9 x 16.5 (4⁷/₁₀ x 6⁵/₁₀). Shrewsbury School.
8. *Gateway and Tree, c.* 1854, watercolour, 12.1 x 17.2 (4⁸/₁₀ x 6⁸/₁₀). Shrewsbury School.
9. *Shrewsbury from above the bathing-place, c.* 1854, watercolour, 12.1 x 17.2 (4⁸/₁₀ x 6⁸/₁₀). Shrewsbury School.
10. *Belvoir Castle, nr Langar, c.* 1854, watercolour, 11.9 x 16.7 (4⁷/₁₀ x 6⁶/₁₀). Shrewsbury School.
11. *Langar Rectory*, 1854, watercolour, 19 x 26.5 (7⁴/₁₀ x 10⁴/₁₀). Canterbury Museum, Christchurch, New Zealand.
12. *Beach Scene, England, c.* 1866, watercolour, 28 x 37 (11 x 14⁴/₈). Canterbury Museum, Christchurch.
13. *Boulogne*, 1868, pen, ink and wash, 15.2 x 20.3 (6 x 8). British Museum.
14. *The Old George Inn, Edgeware*, 1880, pencil and wash, 16.7 x 26 (6⅝ x 10¼). St John's.
15. *Dinant on the Meuse, c.* 1866, watercolour, 24.8 x 16.5 (9⅞ x 6½). St John's.
16. *Houses, c.* 1881, etching, 8.2 x 4.4 (3¼ x 1¾). St John's.
17. *Rakaia River Valley, Headwaters*, 1960 (photograph by John Pascoe). Alexander Turnbull Library, Wellington, New Zealand. John Pascoe Collection
18. *Map of Erewhon and Erewhon Revisited*, Anon. St John's.
19. *Hand and Foot*, 1868, pencil, 33 x 48.2 (13 x 19). St John's.
20. *Antinous as Hermes*, 1868, pencil, 67.9 x 40.6 (26¾ x 16). St John's.
21. *Sketch of his own Head*, 1878, oil, 53.3 x 43.1 (21 x 17). St John's.
22. *Self-portrait, c.* 1873, oil, 30.4 x 25.4 (12 x 10). Alexander Turnbull Library, Wellington.
23. *Self-portrait*, 1866, oil, 36 x 31.1 (14³/₁₆ x 12¼). Chapin Library, Williams College, Williamstown, Mass., USA.
24. *Portrait of an Unidentified Woman*, 1873, oil, 30.4 x 25.4 (12 x 10). Alexander Turnbull Library, Wellington.
25. *Two Heads after Bellini*, 1866, oil, 44.4 x 55.8 (17½ x 22). St. John's.
26. *Portrait of Thomas Cass*, 1868, oil, 52 x 40.6 (20½ x 16). Canterbury Museum, Christchurch.
27. *Portrait of John Marshman*, 1866, oil, 35.5 x 25.4 (14 x 10). Canterbury Society of Arts, Christchurch.
28. *Portrait of Alfred Cathie*, 1898, oil, 44.4 x 34.2 (17½ x 13½). St John's.
29. *Family Prayers*, 1864, oil, 40.6 x 50.8 (16 x 20). St John's.

30 *The Christening at Fobello*, 1871, unfinished watercolour sketch, 17.1 x 19.6 (6¾ x 7¾). St John's.
31 *The Christening at Fobello*, 1871, oil, 71.1 x 88.9 (28 x 35). Chapin Library, Williams College.
32 *Mr Heatherley's Holiday*, 1873, oil, 91.4 x 60.9 (36 x 24). Tate Gallery, London.
33 Charles Gogin, *The Pan-Anglican Synod,* in *The Universal Review* (Sept–Dec 1888). St John's.
34 *Primadengo, near Faido, c.* 1878 (figures by Charles Gogin). St John's.
35 *The Washing-place, Varallo*, 1871, oil, 50.8 x 40.6 (20 x 16). St John's.
36 *Wassen*, 1901, 16 x 23.4 (6⅜ x 9¼). St John's.
37 *Chiavenna*, 1887, oil, 23.4 x 34.2 (9¼ x 13½). St John's.
38 *Tengia, c.* 1880, oil, 29.2 x 21.5 (11½ x 8½). St John's.
39 *Dalpe, c.* 1880, pen and ink, 19.3 x 27.9 (7⅝ x 11). St John's.
40 *Calonico Church, No 1,* 1881, pen and ink, 22.2 x 29.4 (8¾ x 11⅝). St John's.
41 *Calonico Church, No 2,* 1881, pen and ink, 22.2 x 29.4 (8¾ x 11⅝). St John's.
42 *Campo Santo at Campiognia*, 1881, pen and ink, 22.2 x 29.4 (8¾ x 11⅝). St John's.
43 *Sacro Monte, Locarno No 2, c.* 1881, pen and ink. St John's.
44 *Sacro Monte, Locarno No 1, c.* 1881, pen and ink. St John's.
45 *Sacro Monte, Varese*, 1892, photograph. St John's.
46 *S Giorio – Comba di Susa, neighbourhood of S Ambrogio,* 1880, pen and ink. St John's.
47 *S Ignatius Loyola, from a fresco near Ceres,* 1879, pen and ink, 10.16 x 8.3 (4 x 3⅓). St John's.
48 *Lazarus Bovollinus, 1534,* Mesocco, 1879, rubbing. St John's.
49 *Si Recte Tute S. M.,* Fénis, 1887, rubbing. St John's.
50 *Circumcision Chapel,* Sacro Monte, Varese, 1891, photograph. St John's.
51 *Women looking into chapel,* Sacro Monte, 1891, photograph. St John's.
52 *Inner Court of the Sanctuary of Oropa, c.* 1880, pen and ink, 17.7 x 24.7 (7 x 9¾). St John's.
53 *Chapels of the Sanctuary of Oropa, looking down towards Lombardy, c.* 1880, pen and ink, 8.2 x 12.1 (3¼ x 4⅞). St John's.
54 *Fucine, near Viù,* 1880, pen and ink (figures by Charles Gogin), 26.9 x 17.1 (10⅝ x 6¾). St John's.
55 *Plan of the Sacro Monte in 1671,* reworking (18th-century etching) of Gaudenzio Sceti, *Il vero Ritratto del Sacro Monte di Varallo.* Museo Sacro Monte, Varallo.
56 *Sacro Monte, Varese, c.* 1882, pen and ink, 27.9 x 40.6 (11 x 16). St John's.
57 *Stefano Scotto with Mr S Butler,* Ecce Homo Chapel, Sacro Monte, Varallo, photograph. St John's.
58 Gaudenzio Ferrari, *The Madonna of the Orange Tree,* 1529, S Cristoforo, Vercelli.
59 Gaudenzio Ferrari, *The Annunciation,* before 1511. National Gallery, London.
60 Tabachetti, or Giovanni D'Enrico, *Il Vecchietto,* Chapel of the Descent from the Cross, Sacro Monte, Varallo, photographer unknown.
61 *Jones and Professor Voglino in the Presentation Chapel,* Crea, 1891, photograph. St John's.
62 Hans Holbein the Younger, or copyist, *The Peasants' Dance* (detail), drawing of the façade of the *Haus zum Tanz,* Basel, c. 1525. Öffentliche Kunstsammlung, Kupferstich-kabinett, Basel.
63 Model of Hans Holbein's designs for the *Haus zum Tanz,* Basel, 1878. Öffentliche Kunstsammlung, Kupferstichkabinett, Basel.
64 *The Old Adam and Eve,* Sacro Monte, Varallo, photograph by Samuel Butler. Chapin Library, Williams College.
65 *The Virgin's Grandmother,* Chapel of the Birth of the Virgin, Montrigone, photograph by Samuel Butler, 1889. Cambridge University Library.
66 Henry Festing Jones, *Fresco at Mesocco – 'March',* 1879, pen and ink, 19.8 x 19.8 (4⅞ x 4⅞). St John's.
67 'Natural artist', *The Windmill,* 19.8 x 18 (4⅞ x 7⅛). St John's.
68 'Natural artist', *Blowing up a mine,* 19.8 x 18 (4⅞ x 7⅛). St John's.

69 Tabachetti, *Chapel of the Journey to Calvary, c.* 1599, Sacro Monte, Varallo, photograph by Samuel Butler, 1888. St John's.

70 Tabachetti, *Chapel of the Journey to Calvary*, Sacro Monte, Varallo. Detail: *St Veronica and Christ with the goitred Man and Flagellator*, photograph by Samuel Butler, 1888. St John's.

71 *Chapel of the Birth of the Virgin*, Crea, photograph by Samuel Butler, 1891. St John's.

72 Tabachetti, *Chapel of the Marriage at Cana, c.* 1605, Crea, photograph by Samuel Butler, 1891. St John's.

73 Tabachetti (attrib.), *The goitred Man*, Chapel of the Journey to Calvary, Sacro Monte, Varallo, photograph by Samuel Butler. St John's.

74 *Chapel of the Birth of the Virgin*, Crea, photograph by Samuel Butler, 1891. St John's.

75 Tabachetti, *Chapel of the Martyrdom of St Eusebius, c.* 1598, Crea, photograph by Samuel Butler, 1891. St John's.

76 Tabachetti, *Chapel of the Martyrdom of St Eusebius, c.* 1598, Crea, photograph by Samuel Butler, 1891. St John's.

77 Tabachetti, *Chapel of the Journey to Calvary*, Sacro Monte, Varallo. Detail: *St Veronica*, photograph by Samuel Butler, 1888. St John's.

78 Giovanni D'Enrico (attrib.), *Ecce Homo Chapel, c.* 1608, Sacro Monte, Varallo. Detail: *Man with two children*, photograph by Samuel Butler, 1888. St John's.

79 Giovanni D'Enrico (attrib.), *Ecce Homo Chapel, c.* 1608, Sacro Monte, Varallo. Detail: *Man with staff*, photograph by Samuel Butler, 1888. St John's.

80 Giovanni D'Enrico (attrib.), *Ecce Homo Chapel, c.* 1608, Sacro Monte, Varallo. Detail: *Stooping man*, photograph by Samuel Butler, 1888. St John's.

81 Gaudenzio Ferrari, *St John the Baptist in the Wilderness*, Montrigone, photograph by Samuel Butler, 1890. St John's.

82 Gaudenzio Ferrari, *Crucifixion Chapel*, 1518, Sacro Monte, Varallo, photograph by Samuel Butler, 1889. St John's.

83 Gaudenzio Ferrari, *Crucifixion Chapel*, 1518, Sacro Monte, Varallo, photograph by Samuel Butler, 1889. St John's.

84 Gaudenzio Ferrari, *Chapel of the Adoration of the Magi*, 1528, Sacro Monte, Varallo, photograph by Samuel Butler. St John's.

85 Gaudenzio Ferrari, *The Marriage of the Virgin, c.* 1528, S Cristoforo, Vercelli.

86 Gaudenzio Ferrari, *St Joachim expelled from the Temple*, before 1510. Galleria Sabauda, Turin.

87 Gaudenzio Ferrari, *Two Nurses preparing the Bath*, detail of *The Birth of the Virgin*, 1546, S Maria della Pace, Milan.

88 Gaudenzio Ferrari, *King*, 1528, Chapel of the Adoration of the Magi, Sacro Monte, Varallo.

89 Gaudenzio Ferrari, *Cupola of S Maria dei Miracoli, Saronno*, 1534–7. Photograph by Alfredo Fusetti.

90 Gaudenzio Ferrari, *Three Angels with musical instruments*, 1534–7, detail of Cupola, S Maria dei Miracoli, Saronno. Photograph by Alfredo Fusetti.

91 *La Musa Polinnia* ('Authoress of the Odyssey'), reproduction owned by Butler (St John's) of oil on wood panel, 1st century AD. Museo dell' Accademia Etrusca, Cortona.

92 *Head of Kore* (Greek maiden; type of Nausicaa), 6th century BC. Acropolis Museum, Athens.

93 *Odysseus making his appearance to Nausicaa and her companions*, Attic red-figure pyxis and lid attributed to Aison, late 5th century BC. Museum of Fine Arts, Boston.

94 Pieter Lastman, *Ulysses and Nausicaa*, 1609, oil. Bayerische Staatsgemäldesammlungen, Munich.

95 John Flaxman, *Ulysses following the car of Nausicaa*, from *The Odyssey of Homer engraved from the Compositions of John Flaxman* (1805). Cambridge University Library.

96 Frederic Leighton, *Nausicaa*, 1878, oil. Private collection.

97 Camille Corot, *Homer and the Shepherds*, 1846, oil. Musée des Beaux-Arts, Saint-Lô.

145 *Shylock, Smyrnah*, 1895, photograph. St John's.
146 *An old Turk smoking his hookah, Smyrnah*, 1895, photograph. St John's.
147 *Girl at fountain, Trapani*, 1893, photograph. St John's.
148 *Professor Romano at Cefalu*, 1892, photograph. St John's.
149 *Mr and Mrs Marchini*, 1891, photograph. St John's.
150 *The Lame Boy, Sacro Monte*, 1891, photograph. St John's.
151 *Old Beggar at S Eusebio Chapel, Crea*, 1892, photograph. St John's.
152 *Boy and Basket, Chiavenna*, 1895, photograph. St John's.
153 *Sleeping pigs in piazza Gaudenzio Ferrari, Varallo*, 1889, photograph. St John's.
154 *Sleeping men, Trapani*, 1894, photograph. St John's.
155 *Men sleeping*, 1892, photograph. St John's.
156 *Man sleeping, Paris*, 1891, photograph. St John's.
157 *Man sleeping, Trapani*, 1894, photograph. St John's.
158 *Boy sleeping, Trapani*, 1893, photograph. St John's.
159 *Padre Grazie, Catalafimi (Sicily)*, 1895, photograph. St John's.
160 *Nuns on Steamer*, 1895, photograph. St John's.
161 *Carrying the Madonna, Civiasco*, 1889, photograph. St John's.
162 *Old priest*, 1894, photograph. St John's.
163 *Mycenae, Tomb of Atreus with Ladies*, 1895, photograph. St John's.
164 *Priest and group looking up, the Gobelins*, 1892, photograph. St John's.
165 *Steps of S Gaudenzio, Varallo*, 1892, photograph. St John's.
166 *Chiavenna, c.* 1895, photograph. St John's.
167 *Dionysus' Ear, Syracuse*, 1893, photograph. St John's.
168 *The Washing-place, Varallo*, 1892, photograph. St John's.
169 *Monastery on Mt Lycabettus, Athens*, 1895, photograph. St John's.
170 *Church at Bormio through an opening*, 1891, photograph. St John's.
171 *Church of Madonna di Trapani*, 1891, photograph. St John's.
172 *Dinant*, 1891, photograph. St John's.
173 *Wayside Oratory at Dinant*, 1893, photograph. St John's.
174 *'St Christopher', Castiglione d'Olona*, 1892, photograph. St John's.
175 *Church Porch at Meien*, 1895, photograph. St John's.
176 *The Count, Erice*, 1893, photograph. St John's.

Index

(Figures in italics refer to illustrations)

332